DISCARDED

REGULATED INDUSTRIES

IN A NUTSHELL

FOURTH EDITION

By

RICHARD J. PIERCE, JR.
Lyle T. Alverson Professor of Law
George Washington University

and

ERNEST GELLHORN
Professor of Law,
George Mason University

**WEST
GROUP**

ST. PAUL, MINN.
1999

PREFACE

This text is designed for the student, lawyer, judge or regulator whose exposure to economics and the law relating to economic regulation has been limited. It seeks to provide an introduction from which agency regulation of business, including cases and rules imposing such constraints as well as sophisticated articles and texts discussing them, can be considered more carefully. As such, we have deliberately focused on central ideas and concepts and adopted simpler rather than more complex explanations. Occasionally—especially in discussing economic theories not familiar to lawyers and other non-economists who are the primary audience—such simplifications mask real problems. We acknowledge this cost and have sought to minimize it by identifying additional sources or limitations in the footnotes where appropriate. In any case, the reader is alerted to the fact that this text is only an introduction to the basic law and economic issues in regulated industries.

The past decade has been a period of revolutionary change in regulated industries law and policy. In many industries, the federal government has initiated a transition from traditional cost-of-service regulation to methods of regulation that allow market forces to play a greater role. We have in-

cluded in this third edition updated discussions of
the issues that have long dominated the practice of
regulated industries law, e.g., calculating rate base
and rate of return, cost allocation, and rate design.
We have also added discussions of the many new
market-oriented forms of regulation, e.g., service
unbundling, equal access to bottleneck facilities,
competitive contracting, managed competition in
healthcare, and incentive regulation.

E.G.
R.J.P.

Arlington, VA
Washington, D.C.

OUTLINE

TABLE OF CASES

References are to Pages

TABLE OF CASES

TABLE OF CASES

TABLE OF CASES

TABLE OF CASES

*

TABLE OF ACTS

References are to Pages

TABLE OF ACTS

TABLE OF STATUTES AND REGULATIONS

UNITED STATES

UNITED STATES CONSTITUTION

UNITED STATES CODE ANNOTATED
5 U.S.C.A.—Government Organization and Employees

7 U.S.C.A.—Agriculture

15 U.S.C.A.—Commerce and Trade

TABLE OF STATUTES AND REGULATIONS

UNITED STATES CODE ANNOTATED
42 U.S.C.A.—The Public Health and Welfare

49 U.S.C.A.—Transportation

STATUTES AT LARGE

CODE OF FEDERAL REGULATIONS

TABLE OF STATUTES AND REGULATIONS

FEDERAL REGISTER

EXECUTIVE ORDERS

REGULATED INDUSTRIES

IN A NUTSHELL

FOURTH EDITION

*

CHAPTER I

INTRODUCTION[1]

The regulation of business and its activities by government is as varied as it is often pervasive. Controls may limit entry into or exit from the business, regulate the type or amount of a product or service offered, set the price and quality provided, and determine the sale terms and level of profits allowed. Even though the economy's organizing premise remains one of *laissez faire*, virtually no business is immune from some form of government regulation.[2]

While government business regulation may at times be so intense as to be indistinguishable from government ownership, in most instances the degree of oversight is less rigorous and the regulated business is allowed considerable freedom to make basic investment and operating decisions. In gen-

1. See generally, 1 & 2 A. Kahn, *The Economics of Regulation* (1970–71); ABA Commission on Law and the Economy, *Federal Regulation: Roads to Reform* chs. 3–4 (1979); Baker, *Competition and Regulation: Charles River Bridge Recrossed*, 60 Corn.L.Rev. 159 (1975); Jones, *Government Price Controls and Inflation—A Prognosis Based on the Impact of Controls in the Regulated Industries*, 65 Corn.L.Rev. 303 (1980).

2. This paradox reminds us of Will Rogers' comment about his home state of Oklahoma, that its citizens "will vote dry as long as they can stagger to the polls."

eral, the degree of oversight varies depending on why the regulation is imposed. For example, if it is thought that the market favors natural monopoly, comprehensive cost-of-service ratemaking by regulatory commission is imposed as a substitute for the constraints competitors otherwise generate as a matter of marketplace discipline. Alternatively, if the reason for the regulation is the need to control spillovers such as air pollution not otherwise constrained by market forces, then government intervention will be limited to setting air quality standards requiring the reduction of the harmful pollutants. To be sure, even this regulatory scheme may be comprehensive, relying on command-and-control rules. Yet it is often recognized that such regulation need not be all-encompassing and thus reliance may be placed on competitive forces operating within the constraints of government developed performance standards. Even less intrusive are regulatory programs such as those applied to product advertising which seek to assure and improve the dissemination of information about product characteristics and performance; here the proper identification of the product or service as against verifiable claims may satisfy regulatory demands.

Whatever the approach or scope of the regulatory mandate, its application to private businesses involves persons outside the business relationship—i.e., neither the owner nor managers of the business nor its customers—in making the decisions that will rule business operations. This deviation from the principle of private control of economic decision making is generally justified on the ground that the public interest requires public control. The theory is that the market has failed either to protect or to represent consumers or other public interests adequately. Government regulation, in other words, supplies the elements of responsibility missing from these markets. Keeping regulation within a legal mold—the assignment of the law of regulated industries—also assures that both private and public interests are properly protected.

This text outlines in brief compass the major types of administrative regulation and the regulatory tools used by government agencies, the bureaus assigned the task of administering business regulation, to satisfy public demands and protect private interests. Our aim is to develop an understanding of the several approaches taken by business regulation and to raise questions about these methods as well as about the substantive rules and procedures they rely upon to accomplish their ends. Although generally beyond our coverage, it should be noted that the actions and decisions of regulatory agencies are subject to a specialized body of procedural requirements outlined in administrative law, and in particular (in federal law) of the Administrative Procedure Act (APA). 5 U.S.C.A. §§ 501–706. Administrative law is an intricate and often convoluted body of doctrine whose understanding is necessary for anyone seeking to master the field of government business regulation.[3] Of particular importance is the fact that regulatory decisions are often announced as procedural rulings, although in fact substantive policy is at stake. Compare Citizens Comm. to Save WEFM v. FCC, 506 F.2d 246 (D.C.Cir.1973) (en banc) (grant of radio station format change over listener protest must be preceded by a hearing), with WNCN Listeners Guild v. FCC, 610 F.2d 838 (D.C.Cir.1979) (en banc) (FCC required by statute to regulate radio formats in accordance with the "public interest" standard).

In general, the APA requires that agencies develop and announce important policies only after giving advance notice, thereby allowing those affected by the proposed rule an opportunity to present arguments and evidence for or against the policy, and also providing a public record of the reasons for the rule. In addition, agency policy is frequently developed in adjudicative, trial-type hearings or through informal actions not confined by any schedule of procedural requirements. Whatever procedure is used, regulatory rules and policies cannot be applied against a person without an opportunity for an individualized hearing, and if the adjudicative decision is adverse and objection is raised it must be supported by substantial evidence and written findings and reasons. However developed or applied,

3. Nor has the APA simplified its understanding. Professor Louis Jaffe best summarized this elliptical statute, when he observed that it is "inexpressibly complex, a Chinese puzzle compounded of particular circumstances and special cases." *The American Administrative Procedure Act*, 1956 Public Law 218, 219.

agency decisions must be rational and reached through fair procedures, and they must also be able generally to withstand scrutiny on judicial review.

This legal framework means that regulatory programs operate under several constraints. First, actions by regulatory agencies must be authorized by statute, adhere to prescribed procedures, meet tests of reasonableness, and not contravene constitutional commands. That is to say, the regulatory commissions must meet the "rule of law." Second, following American legal tradition, the regulated industry is likely to have a formal adversary relationship with the regulating agency. The underlying assumption is that without the regulatory agency's oversight, the regulated business would act in accordance with its private interests and that this would not be consistent with the public interest. On the other hand, appearances may be deceiving, for in practice regulatory agencies have been among the staunchest defenders of the businesses they regulate. Nonetheless, it is also true that regulatory agencies are institutional bureaucracies that operate through rules and regulations. This practice of relying on formal processes often limits the flexibility essential to most business operations and frequently means that decisions of regulated businesses can only be explained because they must conform to easily administered rules. This does not mean that the rule of profit maximization has been repealed for regulated businesses; but it may explain behavior that otherwise seems to be guided by contradictory or unusual goals. Finally, new regulatory programs invariably copy many if not most of their distinguishing features from old ones. Until recent times, this has meant that U. S. regulatory commissions, whether federal or state, have been modeled after the Interstate Commerce Commission first established in 1887.[4] In copying each other's methods and procedures, reliance has often been placed on judicial-type procedures and on protecting regulated enterprises from outside competition— even though the commissions were frequently created to avoid the formality and cost of oral (judicial) hearings bound by cumbersome rules of hearsay evidence. This also means that the history of a regulatory program may be as important as its governing statute, required rules of procedures, or theoretical justifications in understanding particular policies and their application.

A. SCOPE, RANGE AND TYPES OF REGULATION

Government regulation of industry is but one of many types of legal control on the uses of private economic power. Others also range broadly and include criminal laws prohibiting business espionage and arson[5] as well as white-collar crimes, laws

4. For an analogue to the ICC statute see the British Regulations of Railways Act of 1873. Although soon determined to be a failure by a Parliamentary committee, casual American observers viewed it favorably and its organizational premise and approach was applied in the ICC Act. See R. Cushman, *The Independent Regulatory Commissions* 511–512 (1941).

5. For evidence that these activities were once part of the business arsenal, at least when engaged in monopolistic actions,

regulating direct political campaigning and indirect assistance such as money contributions by business, or antitrust laws designed to encourage rivalry, keep competition within legitimate bounds and assure consumers the benefits of lower prices and increased innovation. These other legal restrictions are different from economic regulation in that they operate indirectly, generally *proscribing* particular conduct and only implicitly specifying what can or should be done.

Economic regulation, on the other hand, is more direct and specific. Whether partial or pervasive, to the extent government regulation is applied it explicitly substitutes the judgment of regulators for that of either the business or the market place. The explicit goal of regulatory decisions is to assure fair prices, reasonable service, adequate quality or whatever particular policy the regulatory scheme is designed to serve. In reaching these judgments, government regulators balance assigned public needs with the need to assure an investment climate that will permit the regulated entity to attract capital at reasonable rates—or the consumer will quickly bear this burden. While also relying on rules that spell out prohibited conduct, economic regulation cannot be limited to negative commands if it is to accomplish its more extensive responsibility. Thus, many if not most rules of regulatory commissions are *prescriptive* and identify specifically what the regu-

see Standard Oil Co. of N. J. v. United States, 221 U.S. 1 (1911). But see McGee, *Predatory Price Cutting: The Standard Oil (N.J.) Case*, 1 J. of Law & Econ. 137 (1958).

lated business can and must do. In connection with public utility regulation, for example, the ruling agency will specify who can enter the business, what service they must provide, what prices they may lawfully charge (albeit, usually at the private firm's initiative), and what investments they can include in their rate base. Even when the regulation is less comprehensive, as with radio/tv broadcast licensing, environmental regulation or false advertising controls, the responsible regulatory agency will frequently set forth particular requirements that businesses subject to its oversight must meet or face civil and criminal charges.

Despite common complaints about unnecessary government regulation, economic regulation is widespread and affects virtually every business or individual in some way. Some regulations are specifically directed at business operations, as with licensing authorities that have total control over whether one can enter an occupation (e.g., as a lawyer) or serve a particular route (e.g., as a common carrier). Others are less obvious, as with the Federal Reserve System's decisions affecting the money supply, although each of us is substantially affected by the inflation or deflation that may result. Another striking characteristic is that economic regulation is imposed by both state and federal authorities. There is no central plan, although some fields such as communications and transportation require federal coordination for effective regulation. It is a fragmented system of divided responsibility, and as with the example of occupational licensure, often obviously designed to protect market incumbents against the inroads of new competition.

Although numerous categories can be developed and artful distinctions drawn, the underlying framework of government business regulation is readily seen by separating the various regulatory schemes into two basic types of situations. The first involves a reliance on regulation where competition cannot work in theory or practice because only one firm can exist and there is, as a consequence, no rival competing with it. Called a "natural monopoly," regulation is required in this situation as an alternative to competition in order to control the misuse of private economic power. The technical explanation is that economies of scale are so pervasive that one firm can offer the product or service (often even at monopoly prices) cheaper than two; fixed costs are so large that duplicating services are uneconomic. Classic examples of natural monopoly where competition would be an idle gesture are thought to include the local distribution of natural gas, water and sewer, electricity, and basic telephone communications. In other words, even if several firms sought to compete in providing local electric service, one firm would quickly win out as it was able to reduce unit costs and serve its customers at a lower price. With competition no longer protecting consumers, economic regulation is imposed to achieve the same market place goals of allocative and productive efficiency. That is to say, the goal of regulation here is to keep costs and prices low and service and quality high.

The second type of regulation is a broader, all-inclusive category involving those situations where the unregulated market does not secure specifically defined social goals. Regulation of airlines, trucks and ships, for example, was initially justified because of the need to control "excessive competition." Similarly, profit and rent controls are installed where sudden supply failures allow those owning the scarce goods to earn a windfall profit or to impose a hardship on users of the goods considered to be too great. This is the justification offered for control on landlord rents, regulation of oil company supply allocations and prices, or "excess" profit taxes. Widespread bank failure during the depression of the 1930's resulted in bank regulation to avoid further disruption to the economy or the placement of these losses on innocent depositors. Similar reasoning has justified a complex regulatory scheme for investment securities. Whatever the purpose, and this listing canvasses only a few, this second type of regulation is quite different from the first. It is limited in scope and purpose. It does not displace competition as a major method of control. Here regulation is a supplement to the market place and is designed to achieve specific purposes.

B. GOALS AND TOOLS OF REGULATION

We have already noted that economic regulation generally relies for its enforcement on administrative agencies whose processes and procedures are governed by principles of administrative law. These procedures are influenced by statutory goals and vice versa. While numerous particular goals have been identified, they generally can be classified under three headings.

The most important goal of almost every regulatory scheme is economic efficiency. That is, scarce goods are allocated to their most highly valued use and are used most efficiently in production. The goal, in other words, is to have prices set at a low level based on costs which are prudently incurred. A related and historically important goal of economic regulation of common carriers is the requirement that all users be served on an equal and nondiscriminatory basis. Contrary to the usual rule in the private market, a regulated business cannot refuse to deal without an accepted justification. The final set of regulatory goals—minimum service reliability, honesty and fair dealing, informed choice and full disclosure of relevant information, and health, safety and environmental protection—are more recent in origin and do not require full-scale intervention in the business. Thus they need not involve displacement of market forces or of traditional controls over the exercise of private economic power, such as antitrust laws.

Four different methods or regulatory weapons are used to accomplish these objectives. The most common and pervasive is "cost-of-service" ratemaking whereby the regulator seeks to determine the regulated firm's costs, including the cost of raising capital, as a prelude to determining the revenues needed to cover its costs. From this revenue calculation the commission figures the price that can be charged by the firm for its product or service. Since capital costs are included, these prices will include an opportunity to recover a competitive return on investment (popularly known as "profit"). Where the regulated firm serves several classes of customers or provides different services, the regulator must also determine the rate structure or price charged for each class or service. This is the usual approach taken to regulate electric, telephone and other common carrier transportation. As will be explored later, it is easier to state this goal for administratively established prices identical to those that would exist in a properly functioning competitive market than it is to achieve it.

A second, less precise way of regulating the allocation of scarce resources—especially where the scarcity is due to government regulation, as with liquor licenses, hospital certificates of need or airline routes—is to assign the task to the regulatory agency under a "public interest" standard. Instead of concentrating on the price at which the regulated firm sells its product or service, the focus here tends to be on the applicant itself. This regulatory approach is taken where a valuable license is to be awarded without the use of a market price (i.e., auction) or other simple objective measure (e.g., lottery, chronological listing). Since the license is in effect being awarded below the market price, there are invariably more qualified applicants than allocations. Thus, the regulator is required to choose which among the competing applicants is "best" qualified. Despite years of trying and intense debate, the development of criteria and their application under the public interest standard is necessarily vague and undefined. As Justice Breyer has observed,the "problem is the tension between a desire to find standards that will 'objectively' select the winner ... and a belief that the exercise of subjective judgment is inevitable because no set of standards exists that will work uniformly to select the 'best' applicants in terms of the objective of the regulatory program." *Analyzing Regulatory Failure: Mismatches, Less Restrictive Alternatives, and Reform*, 92 Harv.L.Rev. 547, 567 (1979).

Partly because of the difficulties of applying either the cost of service or public interest methods, prices and allocations are often set on an historical basis. Where price or wage controls are imposed on an economy-wide basis, the only practical method is an historically based system. Any other approach seems administratively impossible. Similarly, historic data are often likely to be more objective and reliable than the public interest approach in allocating scarce goods. As the experience with price and allocation controls for petroleum products during the 1970s illustrated, historically based systems work only temporarily, are unstable as conditions change and exceptions demanded, and evolve toward either a cost of service or public interest standard.

The fourth approach is one of standard setting, whereby minimum or other requirements are established by the regulatory commission for businesses

and individuals to follow. Health and safety requirements are a common example. As with the public
interest allocation method, the primary question
here is where to set the standard—for example, at
the level of current technology for air pollution or
one that forces technology to improve (and at what
cost). Increasingly, regulators are focusing on a
comparison of costs and benefits, least costly alternatives, most cost-effective requirements or similar
concerns. Where precise standards cannot be formulated, individualized screening is often relied upon
to supplement reliance on agency standard setting
as a tool of regulatory compliance.

We focus primarily on economic regulation: that
is, regulation of prices and terms and conditions of
service. The most powerful justification for economic regulation is the existence of a natural monopoly,
although the U.S. has often imposed price controls
in markets that are not natural monopolies. Economic regulation has a rich history in the Anglo–
American legal system. Until the 1970s, economic
regulation was a relatively stable field. The dominant approach was cost-of-service regulation: that
is, a firm was required to sell at prices based on a
regulator's calculation of the costs the firm incurred
to provide a good or service. There were important
legal and methodological debates, changes in applicable law, and changes in dominant methodologies
that took place throughout the nineteenth and
twentieth centuries. We describe those debates and
changes in chapters 3 through 14 of this book. The
changes in law and methodology that took place

between the mid-nineteenth century and the 1970s were incremental, however. The debates focused primarily on how to implement a system of cost-of-service regulation.

The nature and scope of the debate changed dramatically in the 1970s. Relying primarily on studies of regulated industries by economists, many members of Congress, and even some members of regulatory agencies, came to believe that economic regulation often harmed consumers. Congress and some regulatory agencies began to experiment with changes in legal regimes that placed greater reliance on unregulated competition and less reliance on government regulation as the primary means of providing consumers access to high quality goods and services at low prices. The results of those experiments were so encouraging that Congress deregulated several important markets, e.g., air transport, trucking, financial services, and to a lesser extent, railroads.

Deregulation of those markets produced dramatic socially-beneficial results. In each case, consumers are now saving many billions of dollars per year as a result of deregulation. See R. Crandall & J. Ellig, *Economic Deregulation and Customer Choice: Lessons for the Electric Industry* (1997). Congress was careful in choosing which markets to deregulate, however. Each of the markets it deregulated was not characterized by natural monopoly conditions. In some cases, the market was never a natural monopoly. In other cases, changes in technology and economic conditions had transformed the market from a natural monopoly to a market that could support effective competition.

In the 1980s and 1990s, proponents of regulatory reform turned their attention to the "network industries"—natural gas, electricity, and telecommunications. The goal of regulatory reform is the same in each context—to increase the role of unregulated competition and to decrease the role of regulated monopoly in providing goods and services. That goal is much more difficult to attain in the context of the network industries than it was in the contexts of transportation and financial services, however.

Provision of natural gas, electricity, and telecommunications services requires firms to perform many different functions. Thus, for instance, provision of natural gas service requires production, gathering, transportation, storage, sale, and distribution of gas. Some of these functions, e.g., production and sale, clearly are susceptible to governance by an unregulated competitive market. Other functions, e.g., physical distribution, are classic natural monopolies. The status of still other functions, e.g., gathering, transportation, and storage, is subject to fair debate. The electricity and telecommunications industries are analogous to the natural gas industry in this respect: that is, provision of electricity and telecommunications services requires firms to perform some functions that are susceptible to unregulated competition, some functions that are natural monopolies, and some functions that are subject to fair debate.

Until the 1980s, the U.S. approached each of the network industries in about the same manner. Each of the services was provided on a "bundled" basis, primarily by firms that performed all of the functions required to provide service to consumers. Each of those firms operated as a regulated monopolist. The reform efforts that were initiated in the 1980s began by "unbundling" the many functions that must be performed to provide service to consumers. Unbundling requires firms to separate their natural monopoly functions from their functions that are susceptible to unregulated competition. That separation can take the form of corporate divestiture, establishment of independent operating subsidiaries, or establishment of independent divisions of a firm. The nature and degree of the separation necessary to unbundle functions is one of the hotly debated issues in the efforts to reform regulation of each of the network industries.

Once the functions have been unbundled, they are subjected to completely different legal regimes depending on their economic characteristics. The functions that are susceptible to governance by unregulated competition are deregulated. Thus, for instance, the U.S. has deregulated natural gas production, sales of natural gas at the wellhead, wholesales of natural gas, some retail sales of natural gas, most electricity generation, most wholesales of electricity, some retail sales of electricity, and provision of long distance telephone service. The functions that remain natural monopolies continue to be regulated, however. Thus, for instance, the U.S. continues to regulate transportation and distribution of natural gas, transmission and distribution of electricity, and provision of local telephone service.

The U.S. is not alone in the process of reforming regulation of the network industries. Every industrialized nation in the world is undertaking similar reforms. This process is not yet complete in any context or in any nation. It is complicated, exciting, and uncertain, in terms of the ultimate industry structure and combination of legal regimes it will produce.

We discuss this ongoing process of regulatory reform and industry restructuring in chapter 15. The reader should be aware, however, that the traditional issues we discuss in the chapters 3 through 14 remain important in the ongoing debates about reforming regulation of the network industries. Most of those issues are now arising in the new context of unbundled network industries. In fact, many of those traditional issues have become even more important in this new context.

Ironically, unbundling a network industry and subjecting many of its functions to unregulated competition has the effect of increasing the importance of subjecting the residual monopoly functions in each industry to effective and efficient regulation. As a result, legislatures, agencies, and courts are now returning to many of the debates that took place over the last two centuries with a renewed interest in trying to identify the best resolution.

This point is illustrated well by the Supreme Court's most recent foray into the field of regulated industries. In AT & T v. Iowa Utilities Board, 119 S.Ct. 721 (1999), the issue before the Court was the propriety of the FCC's rules governing the rates at which a provider of local telephone service must provide access to its facilities to firms that want to compete with it to provide local service. That is a new issue raised by the enactment of the Telecommunications Act of 1996. Yet, the Court recognized that this seemingly new issue actually required agencies and courts to revisit issues that the Supreme Court addressed in its 1898 decision in Smyth v. Ames, 171 U.S. 361 and in its 1944 decision in FPC v. Hope Natural Gas, 320 U.S. 591. The lesson is clear. Any lawyer who wants to participate effectively in the great regulatory reform and industry restructuring debates of the twenty-first century must first understand the great regulatory debates that took place in other contexts during the nineteenth and twentieth centuries.

C. UNREGULATED AND OTHER MARKETS: ANTITRUST AND PUBLIC GOODS

There are at least two alternative approaches to the scheme of economic regulation that are also relied upon to control private economic power. One such system, and the predominant approach taken in the U. S. economy, is to rely on competition to prevent excessive use of private economic power. Where competition exists, purchasers will have a range of choices, companies will have an incentive to become more efficient, and individual firm power will be constrained by their rivals' power. On the other hand, it is also recognized that competition may fail. All firms in a particular product or geographic market may decide that it is more profitable if they do not compete and instead band together and limit output, thereby also raising prices. Alternatively, a firm (or group of firms) with market power may act to exclude others from a particular market with the same effects. In either case, competition will not have the effect of coercing economic efficiency and consumers will not be well served by competitive rivalry for their purchases. Recognizing that private constraints may be imposed to defeat market place competition, Congress passed the Sherman and Clayton Acts, 15 U.S.C.A. §§ 1–7, 12–27, and similar antitrust laws. They make cartels, mergers, monopolization and similar collusive or exclusionary practices illegal. Their aim is to assure market competition by limiting the use of private economic power. Individual efforts at rivalry are encouraged; joint efforts at cooperation may be approved if they tend to increase output and their benefits outweigh their dangers. However, when individual or joint efforts are likely to create overwhelming market power or block new entry, the rules of antitrust generally prohibit such practices.

Where a competitive market can adequately perform its "regulatory" function of coercing economic efficiency from firms in the market, antitrust enforcement is designed to prevent the development of market imperfections relied upon to justify government regulation. Similarly, where classical comprehensive economic regulation is present, antitrust rules are often superceded. The latter policy is explored more fully in Chapter 13 since economic regulation is often incomplete and reliance is placed on antitrust to police aspects of the market. The interaction of the two systems has created its own set of principles and applications. On the other hand, antitrust is not considered capable of dealing with all problems thought to require the replacement of competitive markets. Its enforcement is cumbersome and often sporadic; government regulation has the capacity to be systematic and efficient. Antitrust is aimed at achieving the *conditions* of a competitive market; in contrast to regulation, it is not designed to replicate the *results* of competition or to correct inherent structural defects such as natural monopoly. On the other hand, antitrust relies on private ownership and the principle of profit maximization to serve the public through rivalry for their purchases. It therefore does not require constant supervision, oversight, command or control.

There is a third, alternative regime at the other end of the spectrum from antitrust and more closely related to government regulation of industry. It usually involves government ownership of the means of production, a form of economic organization common throughout much of the world. It is also relied upon in the U. S. economy to provide "public goods"—those products or services which are indivisible and nonexcludable. National defense, the provision of police and fire protection for the community, mosquito abatement, public radio and television, weather forecasts, and clean air are examples of public goods exhibiting these characteristics. They are indivisible in that consumption by one person of the protection offered by the armed forces does not diminish the possibility of its consumption by another. Indeed simultaneous consumption is possible. Similarly, once the product or service is provided, it is not possible effectively to exclude others from enjoying it. At least, it is not economical to prevent others who did not pay for it from using the service. Because public goods are indivisible and nonexcludable, individuals who wish to have these goods provided have an incentive to behave strategically—namely, to hide their preferences in the hope that others will pay for these services. In that circumstance, those who have not displayed their desire for the service and have not paid for it will be able to ride free on the efforts of others who did. This free ride seems unfair; also, without some government intervention, the market will not assure that an optimal amount of the good will be provided. That is, if everyone waits for others to pay for police or fire protection, no one will be protected.[6] Thus, government is called upon to intervene and decide (through the political in contrast to the private market place) how much will be produced and who will pay for it. On the other

6. This analysis has an ancient lineage. Aristotle, for example, observed: "that which is common to the greatest number has the least care bestowed upon it."

hand, even under this system the production of the public goods may be by either public or private enterprise. Often we rely on both. The distinguishing feature is that the decision of what and how much should be produced is not made in the private market place.

As this illustrates, government regulation of business is an intermediate approach to the provision of goods and services in a complex economy.

CHAPTER II

REASONS FOR REGULATING

A. THE MARKET ECONOMY

Economic regulation is imposed because of perceived flaws in the operation of competition in a particular market. To understand the types of flaws that can create a need for regulation, it is necessary first to examine the way in which competitive markets function.

The market economy is based upon the belief that through competition consumer wants will be satisfied at the lowest price with the sacrifice of the fewest resources. To express this in economic terms, competition maximizes consumer welfare by increasing both allocative efficiency (making what the consumer wants) and productive efficiency (using the least amount of resources), and by encouraging progressiveness (invention). Competition maximizes aggregate consumer wealth but it does not necessarily produce an ideal distribution of wealth among consumers. Thus, market competition maximizes the size of the consumers' economic pie; that pie can be redistributed through legislation.

The "market" system (free enterprise) decides what shall be produced, how resources shall be allocated in the production process, and, most importantly, to whom the various products will be distributed. The market system relies on the consumer to decide (by his willingness or refusal to buy) what and how much shall be produced and on competition among producers to determine (through the production of the appropriate quality product at the lowest price) who will manufacture it.

Decisions to regulate and, if so, how to regulate, involve basic economic issues. Microeconomics—the study of the behavior of individual economic units (the consumer, firm, and industry)—therefore falls within the regulatory lawyer's province. The hiring of an expert economic consultant or witness will not discharge the responsibility; the specialist in regulatory law must possess an understanding of basic price theory. To understand regulation thoroughly, it is essential to have a working knowledge of the economic theory of competition, and the range of factors that can cause competition to produce undesirable results. An understanding of basic economic theories helps clarify thought, aids in understanding efficient resource allocation, and brings a conceptual basis to an untidy area of the law. This chapter focuses on basic principles of economic theory which bear directly on regulatory decisions. It is not intended as a substitute for the study of economics. Rather, the emphasis here is on the central core.

1. SOME BASIC EXPLANATIONS AND BEHAVIORAL ASSUMPTIONS

a. The Demand Schedule

When economists refer to "demand" or "the demand function," they are identifying a *demand schedule*—a statement of the different quantities of a particular good or service that a consumer would purchase at each of several different (alternative) price levels. Because the amount of an item that a person will purchase cannot be determined without also considering its price, demand cannot be identified as a set, specific quantity. Rather, it is a *range* of alternative quantities which constitutes the demand for a particular product. It is this relationship between the prices and the quantities demanded at these prices that constitutes the demand schedule.

The demand schedule or demand curve for any good can also be illustrated on a simple, two-dimensional price/quantity graph as shown in Figure 1.

Notice that the demand curve slopes downward, reflecting the law of diminishing value. Simply stated, this rule holds that the more one has of any good, the lower the (personal substitution) value it possesses for him. The value which a consumer will attach to successive units of a particular commodity diminishes as his total consumption of that commodity increases (the consumption of all other commodities being held constant). For example, even the most ice cream-addicted child will begin to experience diminishing marginal utility after his fifth chocolate soda in the same afternoon.

FIGURE 1: DEMAND CURVE

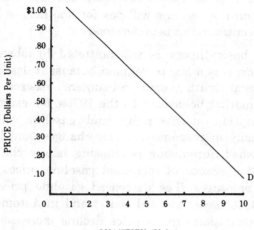

QUANTITY (Units)

Notice as well that the reverse is also true, namely, the higher the relative price for the good, the lower its rate of consumption. This simple statement, which applies to all economic goods, that one will seek to buy less as the price is raised (or more as the price is lowered), is a key economic theory central to an understanding of basic price theory and to our analysis of economic regulation. It can be stated many ways: technically—the quantity demanded varies inversely with price; graphically—the demand curve is negatively or downwardly sloped; popularly—the more you have the less you want. It matters not whether one remembers this fundamental law of demand on the basis that the demand curve for all commodities is negatively sloped, that the rate of consumption will increase as price falls, or that the more sodas one drinks in an afternoon the less one will pay for another, as long as the central point is understood.

The basic theory is substantiated by observed behavior; it is a law of demand because it describes a general truth about consumers' desires and about market behavior.[1] In the 1970s, for example, consumption of electricity and gasoline shifted drastically in response to price changes, and long-established automobile purchasing habits changed radically because of increased gasoline prices and other pressures. The decreased gasoline prices of the 1990s have reversed that trend in automobile purchasing patterns. A price decline increases the rate of consumption because more of the item will be consumed in current uses, because new uses will develop (which were valued at too low a level to have justified paying the former, higher rate), and because new users will appear from among consumers whose marginal utilities or incomes were too low. The reverse, of course, holds true for the case of higher prices. All of these factors explain why a change in the price of a commodity causes a change in the amount demanded.

1. Sometimes it is argued that consumer behavior defies this proposition, that consumers in fact occasionally buy more of some goods where the price rises. Three examples are usually offered: where the good is sought for speculative purposes; where the demand is for prestige goods; and where price is an index of quality. For a cogent explanation of why these examples further support or at least do not detract from the theory, see A. Alchian & W. Allen, *Exchange and Production* 67–68 (2d ed. 1977).

b. Profit–Maximizing Behavior by Firms

The economic theory of the business firm assumes that each firm has but one primary goal, namely, to make as much money as possible. That is, every firm seeks to maximize its profits. It follows, then, that a firm's ultimate objectives will not be influenced by who in the firm manages it (makes decisions) or the type of firm involved; the motive of generating profits is pervasive in all firms, whether they be corporate giants or individual proprietorships.[2] Businessmen sometimes may not consciously maximize their profits, but positive analysis demonstrates that economic forces will drive them to act as if they were. Firms fail or prosper depending on how successful they are in approximating this result.

On this theory are based further predictions about the firm's behavior. For example, in making production decisions, the firm will adhere to the principle of substitution—that for a given set of technical possibilities, efficient (profit-maximizing) production will substitute cheaper factors (of labor, land, or capital) for more expensive ones. It also follows that a firm's method of production will tend to change with shifts in the relative prices of factors involved. Therefore, if labor costs increase relatively (or if material costs decline), a firm will become capital intensive, and vice versa. The theory of the

2. Of course, taxes, legal restraints on corporate control, etc., may distort the methods by which this objective is achieved by the firm. But in making policy choices governing firm conduct, it is necessary first to understand the basic aim and operation of the firm where such conditions are not controlling.

firm *suggests* that in order to achieve its goal of profit maximization the firm will seek to organize its factors of production efficiently and put its resources to their most valuable (highest valued) use. It only suggests this result, however; whether this result is likely to be attained (or perhaps, is even inevitable) depends on the skill of management and on the operation of the market in which the firm operates.

Efficient production generally means lower costs and, if prices remain stable, increased profits. A profit maximizing firm will continue to produce a product or will increase production of it as long as the last unit (i.e., the "marginal" unit) of production increases the firm's profits. And this occurs if the marginal, or last, unit adds more to revenues than it does to costs—namely, as long as the marginal revenue exceeds or equals marginal cost.[3] If the firm finds that greater production increases profit, it will expand output; if greater production decreases profit, output will be reduced. This rule of profit-maximizing behavior is readily illustrated as shown in Figure 2.

3. "Cost" as used here (and by economists), is viewed on a long-run basis and therefore must include a normal, competitive return on investment necessary to attract capital into the industry. See note 4, p. 31 infra.

FIGURE 2: PROFIT MAXIMIZATION BY A FIRM *

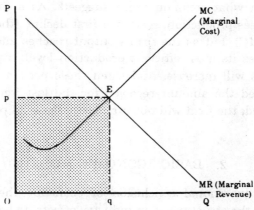

* In this and subsequent figures, "*P*" on the vertical line stands for "price (per unit)," and "*Q*" on the horizontal line stands for "quantity (units)."

Thus, if it is profitable for a firm to produce at all, it will expand output whenever marginal revenue (*MR*) is greater than marginal cost (*MC*) and keep expanding output until marginal revenue equals marginal cost (or the intersection of *MC* and *MR* at equilibrium point *E*).[4] The profit-maximizing price for the hypothetical firm, then, is *p* which equates with output *q* (and generates total revenues reflected by the shaded square bounded by the lines drawn between points *p–E–q–O*, assuming a single

4. This analysis stops short of exploring long-run versus short-run factors which would require consideration of fixed and variable costs, average and total costs, and long-and short-run variations. Obviously these distinctions and concepts are important, but they are not explored here because examination of these additional factors would merely confirm the basic principles and their introduction now is likely to confuse rather than clarify.

price). Again, this technical explanation merely sets forth what common sense suggests. As a firm increases production, costs will first decline (the hook on *MC*), but as the firm's output reaches and then passes its most efficient production level, marginal costs will increase. And when these per unit costs exceed the amount received for the last item produced, the firm will not further increase its production.

2. BASIC ECONOMIC MODELS

A traditional conclusion of economic theory is that the structure of an industry affects its behavior and, ultimately, its performance. To clarify thought, it is helpful to examine two economic models— perfect competition and monopoly. These structural models, though merely theoretical constructs, yield predictions about likely firm and market behavior.

They are presented as analytic models, however, not as complete explanations of the real world. Actual markets are in fact located somewhere between the polar extremes of perfect competition and monopoly and are affected by many forces. Nevertheless, an understanding of these models is vital because they assist in understanding how markets operate, in deciding whether to regulate a market, and in evaluating the effects of regulation. Court opinions, with increasing frequency, also rely on these economic concepts.

a. Perfect Competition

The following conditions, which define the existence of perfect competition, are useful in suggesting whether competitive behavior is likely in a market:

(1) There are large numbers of buyers and sellers.

(2) The quantity of the market's products bought by any buyer or sold by any seller is so small relative to the total quantity traded that changes in these quantities leave market price unaffected.

(3) The product is homogeneous; there is no reason for any buyer to prefer a particular seller and vice versa.

(4) All buyers and sellers have perfect information about the prices in the market and the nature of the goods sold.

(5) There is complete freedom of entry into the market.

In reality such conditions are useful only in suggesting whether rivalrous behavior is likely, since markets having substantially different conditions also exhibit competitive behavior. In other words, these conditions neither define perfect competition nor are a priori present where competitive rivalry is inevitable or likely.

An example illustrates the workings of a perfectly competitive market.[5] In a mythical industry produc-

5. For a similar description, see R. Bork, *The Antitrust Paradox* 91–98 (1978).

ing a standardized product known as a widget, there are 100 well-informed sellers and 500 well-informed buyers. No individual seller (or buyer) can affect the price of a widget, as each has a trivial portion of the market. Graphically, the situation confronting any particular seller may be represented as shown in Figure 3.

The *individual* seller is confronted with a level, or *horizontal demand curve* since 99 other firms sell widgets that are perfect substitutes for his widget.[6] The seller takes whatever price is set by the market and is therefore often called a price-taker. Regardless of the amount of his output that he offers in the market, the price will be p. Thus, if he raises his price above p, his sales will drop to zero. Nor does he have an incentive to charge less than the market price because all that he can produce can be sold at the prevailing price. Here the seller is providing a product that is, in technical terms, highly price elastic. Price elasticity refers to the responsiveness of the quantity demanded to a change in price. That is, when a small change in price leads to a large shift in the quantity demanded, as in the present case, demand is characterized as highly price elastic.[7]

6. The widget *industry* faces a *downwardly sloping demand curve* similar to that shown in Figure 1; however, because each firm sells such a small fraction of the amount demanded, the demand curve facing each seller appears to be horizontal.

7. Correlatively, when a change in price has little effect on the quantity purchased (e.g., as in the case of emergency medical care), the product is considered less price elastic, and in the limiting case, price inelastic.

FIGURE 3: OUTPUT OF A COMPETITIVE FIRM

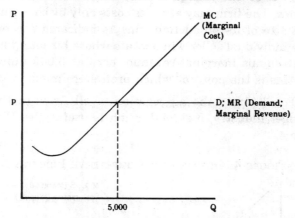

The output of a seller who is a price-taker is determined by his costs. Since a price-taker can sell all, or as little as he wants at the market price, his marginal revenue curve—the revenue he receives from the last unit sold—is identical to the demand curve; with a horizontal individual demand curve, each unit sold by the seller adds the same amount of revenue because there is no reduction in receipts from other (previous) sales. But as the seller increases his sales the costs of production will rise, as he tries to squeeze extra production from a limited facility, pays overtime, buys raw materials from a greater distance, etc.[8] This is reflected in the rising

8. The theory of perfect competition also requires that each firm's costs eventually rise as output is increased. Continually decreasing costs would lead a firm to increase output until it produced the entire industry output, in violation of the premise of many firms. This is the situation described as natural monopoly. See F. Scherer, *Industrial Market Structure and Economic Performance* 482 (2d ed. 1980). See section 2 B1.

nature of the marginal cost curve in Figure 3, supra. The firm may alter its costs only by changing the size of its production run. As indicated earlier, the individual seller will operate where his marginal cost equals marginal revenue, here at 5,000 units, as this is the point at which profits are maximized.

To illustrate the aggregation of all firms in the widget industry, a second graph is useful. See Figure 4.

FIGURE 4: OUTPUT OF A COMPETITIVE INDUSTRY

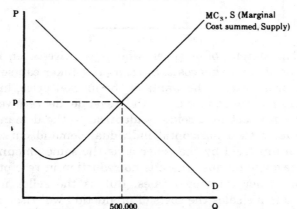

The *industry* marginal cost curve represents the sum of individual cost functions; it is also the industry supply schedule. The industry demand curve is *downwardly sloping* as there is no close substitute for widgets. The individual firm's demand curves were flatter, indicating greater price elasticity of demand (greater responsiveness of the amount demanded to a change in price), because the widgets of the other 99 firms were a perfect substitute. However, as there is no perfect substitute for widgets, the industry demand curve will reflect some inelasticity. Thus, a decrease in the price of widgets (e.g., due to new cost-cutting technology) will increase the quantity demanded; an increase in the industry price (e.g., due to a cartel controlling a factor of production) will cause a decrease in the quantity demanded.

The result of competition is favorable to consumers because resources are used and distributed efficiently. The demand curve facing the industry represents a social ranking of wants, that is, the amount consumers are willing to pay for a widget as compared to an alternative expenditure. The marginal cost curve expresses the cost in resources to society of producing another widget. Under such a system, products are produced until the value of the next unit would not be justified in the eyes of any available consumer. The economy is productively efficient as factors of production are employed where their value is the greatest. And the economy is allocatively efficient as products are produced in the quantity consumers want.

The essential points bear repetition so that they are not missed. In a perfectly competitive market the individual firm is merely a quantity adjuster. All firms sell at marginal cost and earn only a normal return on investment. Each firm takes price as given to it by the market; no firm can affect the price by adjusting output or affect output by raising of lowering price. Each firm pursues the goal of maximizing profits by adjusting its output (either increasing or decreasing the quantity sold) until its marginal cost equals the prevailing market price. In this circumstance the consumer is sovereign. The firms in a competitive market respond to rather than dictate changes in the market prices. Finally, the free-market system coerces efficiency from individual firms, and no firm realizes monopoly profits.

b. Monopoly

In general terms, private monopoly presents the other side of the theoretical coin of perfect competition. Monopoly markets are also often described by four structural and functional factors, namely:

(1) A single seller occupies the entire market.

(2) The product it sells is unique.

(3) Substantial barriers bar entry by other firms into the industry.

(4) Knowledge (of price, quality, sale terms, etc.) in the industry is imperfect.

Again, however, such conditions are useful only in suggesting where monopoly pricing (and output) is likely since markets with substantially different conditions also exhibit monopoly practices. In other words, despite suggestions to the contrary, these conditions do not define or determine whether monopoly effects will exist.[9]

9. As a practical matter, both economists and lawyers often define monopoly simply in terms of effects. That is, they suspect a market is monopolized if its firms consistently make supranormal profits, if their costs are greater than costs at the most

By definition, monopoly describes the situation where one seller produces the output of an entire industry or market—and the *downwardly sloping* industry demand curve is ipso facto identical with that seller's demand curve. If all widget manufacturers in our discussion of perfect competition had merged into one firm, it would be in such a monopoly position.

As a consequence of being faced by the downwardly sloping market demand curve rather than the competitive firm's flat demand curve, the monopolist does not maximize his profits at the competitive output of 500,000 units. The reason is simple. For the competitive seller marginal revenue is the same at all output levels, and always equal to market price. His output decision has no impact on price and is determined by the shape of his marginal cost curve. The monopolist, on the other hand, finds marginal revenue always less than price because his demand curve is downwardly sloping. If only a single price is charged, every expansion of output reduces average revenue and, therefore, the last unit sold produces less revenue than the preceding sale. The central point is that a monopolist who expands output will have to accept a lower price, not just on the additional units, but on all units sold. Additional sales may be obtained only by lowering the price charged on the monopolist's entire output. The choice for the monopolist is between a higher selling price (with fewer sales) and a

efficient scale of production, or if selling expenditures are excessive or technological progress is inadequate.

lower price (with greater sales). In making this choice, the monopolist will maximize profits at less than the competitive output level—namely, where marginal revenue equals marginal cost. Thus, contrary to the competitive result, the monopolist will maximize profits by restricting output and setting price above marginal cost.

This description of the monopoly market can also be understood by reference to the demand curve which was plotted in Figure 1, supra. Viewing that as the market demand for widgets, the monopolist has the same curve for his firm's demand. Knowing this demand, he can determine the price which would maximize his profits by determining his marginal revenue (i.e., the revenue earned from the last widget sold). Assuming that he could manufacture widgets at a cost of ten cents each, the seller can determine his total revenue from each price, then the marginal revenue from each additional unit sold, and finally, the profit from each additional unit sold:

TABLE 1—DEMAND SCHEDULE, MARGINAL REVENUE AND ECONOMIC PROFIT

Price	Amount Demanded	Total Revenue	Marginal Revenue	Marginal Cost	Total Cost	Economic Profit
$1.00	1	$1.00	$1.00	$.10	$ .10	$ .90
.90	2	1.80	+ .80	.10	.20	1.60
.80	3	2.40	+ .60	.10	.30	2.10
.70	4	2.80	+ .40	.10	.40	2.40
.60	5	3.00	+ .20	.10	.50	2.50
.50	6	3.00	0	.10	.60	2.40
.40	7	2.80	− .20	.10	.70	2.10
.30	8	2.40	− .40	.10	.80	1.60
.20	9	1.80	− .60	.10	.90	.90
.10	10	1.00	− .80	.10	1.00	0

As is evident from this table, the seller's most profitable position is to sell five units at $.60. At this point his economic profit is $2.50, a return on investment that he cannot improve upon. That is, the seller maximizes his profits at a price of $.60 because there would be no additional profit from selling an additional unit.

Another way of seeing why the monopolist exercises his pricing/output option in this way is to graph the monopolist's demand (or average revenue) and marginal revenue curves. See Figure 5.

FIGURE 5: PRICING BY A MONOPOLIST *

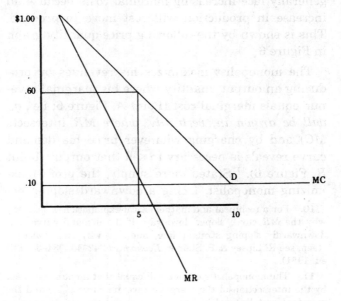

* Actually, the monopolist would like to increase output slightly since his profit-maximizing position is where marginal revenue and marginal cost intersect. See Figure 6, p. 38 infra. This could be achieved if widgets were sold in partial units (and price were set at less than 10 cent intervals). The illustration rounds these figures for sake of simplicity.

As stated earlier, the marginal revenue line is always less than price because the monopolist has to lower his price on *all* units in order to sell an extra (last, or marginal) unit.[10]

To describe a more realistic monopolist, then, one need only alter Figure 5 to show an increasing marginal cost curve. Both the competitive industry (as shown in Figure 4, supra) and the monopolist generally face increasing marginal costs because an increase in production will cost more to produce. This is shown by the following price/quantity graph in Figure 6.

The monopolist maximizes his revenues by producing an output quantity where his marginal revenue equals marginal cost (Point *A*, Figure 6; i.e., q_m *will be drawn in, vertically, where MR intersects MC*) and by charging whatever price his demand curve reveals is necessary to sell that output (Point *B*, Figure 6).[11] Stated more simply, the profit-maximizing monopolist, facing a downward sloping de-

10. For a technical and mathematical explanation of not only why the *MR* curve slopes downward if the demand curve is a downwardly sloping straight line, but also why it is twice as steep, see R. Lipsey & P. Steiner, *Economics* 242–43, 934–35 (6th ed. 1981).

11. The monopolist's output will equal that amount revealed by the intersection of the marginal revenue curve (*MR*) and the marginal cost line (*MC*). The output *q* will be sold at price *p*.

mand curve, will increase his output only as long as his profitability increases.[12] The monopolist's total net revenue no longer increases when marginal cost (MC) exceeds marginal revenue (MR) for a unit because, by definition, the cost of producing and selling this last unit of sales then exceeds the revenue garnered by that sale. That is, it is sold at a loss. And in order to maximize his profit the monopolist sets the price (p) at which the market demand curve intersects this quantity (q_m). If, for example, he sets price above this level, at say p_x, consumers would buy only quantity q_x. While unit price (p_x) and profit per unit would be higher, total profits would be reduced. Similarly, if prices were set below this level and quantity were unchanged, he would not be charging "all the market could bear." Remember, profits are *always* maximized by selling the quantity indicated where marginal costs equal marginal revenue.

12. For purposes of exposition, it is assumed that the monopolist's profit is his total revenue less his marginal cost. In fact, the monopolist's profit is determined by his average total cost curve. All that is in fact known when marginal cost equals marginal revenue is that the monopolist does better at this output level than at any other output, not whether his operation is particularly profitable.

FIGURE 6: PROFIT-MAXIMIZING MONOPOLIST

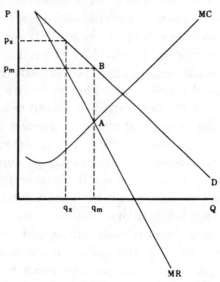

Before closing this section, it is appropriate to note that the theory of monopoly describes a seller who is insulated from the loss of customers by sellers of other identical or substitute products. However, all products face some substitutes for the services they provide, so that total monopoly power never exists. Monopoly power is, in other words, a variable or a matter of degree not an absolute; it is not the complete counterpart to perfect competition.

c. Competition and Monopoly Compared

The primary effects of monopoly, when compared to perfect competition, are reduced output, higher prices, and transfer of income from consumers to producers.[13] In short, should a perfectly competitive industry become monopolized, and all cost curves remain unaffected, price will rise (from p_c to p_m, Figure 7) and quantity produced will decline (from q_c to q_m, Figure 7). This is readily seen when the price/quantity graphs for the two industries are overlaid on one another. See Figure 7.

FIGURE 7: MONOPOLIZING A COMPETITIVE INDUSTRY *

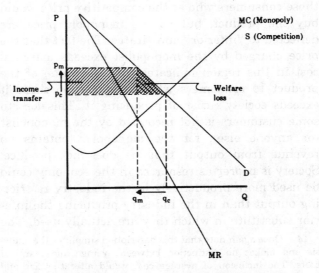

* This figure merely duplicates onto one graph Figure 4 and 6 supra.

For example, when the industry is competitive, price will be at p_c and output at q_c. Should the

13. The magnitude of the transfer of income is shown in Figure 7.

industry become monopolized, output would be reduced to q_m and price raised to p_m. A transfer of income from consumers to producers would also occur which, if costs remain unchanged, will be reflected in increased profits for the monopolist as generally illustrated by the diagonally-lined rectangle.[14]

In addition, monopoly pricing leads to a dead-weight welfare loss, illustrated by the cross-hatched triangular area. It represents the loss in value to those consumers who at the competitive price would buy the product, but at the monopoly price are deflected to "inferior" substitutes. The fact that the price charged by the monopolist exceeds marginal cost in this region indicates that the value of the product to consumers who no longer purchase it exceeds society's cost of producing it. This loss to some customers is not recouped by the monopolist (or anyone else), for the monopolist obtains no revenue from output that he does not produce. Society is poorer as resources in the economy could be used more productively in the industry restricting output than in the industry producing the inferior substitute in which they are actually used. The

14. Once again note that this description simplifies the analysis and makes no distinction between average and marginal costs. The inclusion of average cost would alter the size and shape of the rectangle, but it would not dispute the basic point that income is being transferred from consumers to producers.

According to one commentator, the diagonally-lined rectangle is a rough approximation of the cost resulting from competition among firms to become a monopolist. Thus, the area of this rectangle may also represent a resource cost to society. See R. Posner, *Antitrust Law* at 11–13 (1976).

area of this deadweight loss is an indicator of society's welfare loss due to monopolistic resource misallocation.[15]

While most emphasis is placed on the undesirable features of monopoly in comparison with competition, especially with respect to allocative and productive efficiency, it should be noted that monopoly is not universally condemned. Monopoly may, according to some theories, generate profits which support innovation; it may be inevitable and result in a reduction of price and an increase of output where it alone would bring economies of large scale production. It may also provide the product variety which consumers desire and which perfect competition might preclude.[16]

B. MARKET FAILURE

When a market fails to produce the efficiency predicted by the theory of competition, society has several options. It can choose to tolerate the suboptimal results of the market. It can attempt to restore an environment conducive to competition through application of the antitrust laws. It can replace private ownership of firms in the market

15. For a more complete examination of this effect, see F. Scherer, supra at 17–18, 459–64. On the other hand, according to the theory of "second best" the dead-weight loss may be overstated. See R. Posner, supra at 13–14; P. Areeda *Antitrust Analysis* 39–40 (3rd ed. 1981).

16. It should be noted, however, that by definition a monopoly profit is an unnecessary payment to a firm; it would have produced the same goods even at a competitive price.

with government ownership. Or, it can retain private ownership of firms subject to government regulation of the activities of the firms, often including direct control of the prices the firms are permitted to charge. In this section, we will describe the most common types of market failures that have been the basis of societal decisions to substitute government regulation for market competition.

1. NATURAL MONOPOLY

In many circumstances, the inefficiencies created by monopoly can be avoided or corrected through enforcement of the antitrust laws. Firms are deterred from becoming monopolists by the Sherman Act's prohibition on monopolization. Their ability to obtain monopoly power through merger or acquisition is restricted by the Clayton Act. If a firm does become a monopolist, it can be divided into several smaller firms in order to restore a competitive market. In at least one circumstance, however—natural monopoly—antitrust remedies are inappropriate and counter productive responses to monopoly.

A natural monopoly exists because of a combination of market size and industry cost characteristics. It exists when economies of scale available in the process of manufacturing a product are so large that the relevant market can be served at the least cost by a single firm.

Most industries have marginal costs that decrease over an initial range of output because of economies of scale in producing a good, and then increase with

each additional unit produced because less efficient
factors of production (labor, land, capital) must be
used to increase production above a given level.
This typical situation can be illustrated by considering a wheat farmer with a small tractor and 200
acres of fertile soil. Initially, the farmer may produce 1,000 bushels of wheat a year at a cost of $1.00
per bushel. He may discover that he can double his
production by purchasing an additional 200 acres
and hiring an employee to help him. His tractor
may have enough capacity to cover all 400 acres, so
his additional cost may consist only of the cost of
the extra 200 acres, the salary of the employee and
the extra cost of fuel for the tractor. As a result, the
second 1,000 bushels of wheat may cost him only
$.90 per bushel to produce. He may be able to
reduce his marginal cost of wheat still further by
purchasing 400 more acres of land, hiring two more
employees and replacing his small tractor with a
tractor with twice the capacity, if the large tractor
costs less than twice as much as the small tractor.
At some point, however, he will no longer be able to
lower his marginal cost of producing wheat by increasing his output. Adding another 800 acres, 4
employees, and large tractor would not decrease the
farmer's marginal cost. In fact, his marginal cost
would begin to increase with increases in output as
the farmer is forced to put into use less efficient
resources in order to expand his output (less fertile
land, less able employees, etc.). Thus, the farmer's
marginal cost curve would fall initially and then
begin to rise, as shown in Figure 2, supra.

In some industries, however, economies of scale are available up to a very large output level. Natural gas transmission is a classic example of an industry typified by substantial economies of scale. A single large pipeline can transport gas at a lower unit cost than can several smaller pipelines. Thus, the marginal cost of transporting natural gas can be shown in the graph in Figure 8.

FIGURE 8: MARGINAL COST OF A NATURAL MONOPOLY

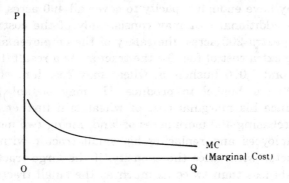

Many industries with very high capital costs have a marginal cost curve of the type shown in Figure 8, such as electricity distribution, waterworks, and local telephone systems.

At some level of output, the economies of scale are exhausted, and the need to add less efficient factors of production causes the firm's marginal cost to increase with increases in output. This level of output, however, may be above the range of outputs that can be sold in the relevant market. Thus, determining whether a natural monopoly exists requires a comparison of the demand for the product in the relevant market with the extent of the economies of scale available in the production of the product. For purposes of this comparison, the relevant market is largely a function of the cost of transporting the good from one area to another. For instance, if a kilowatt hour of electricity costs 5 cents to generate and 1 cent per mile to transport, the market relevant to determine whether natural monopoly conditions exist is a very small geographic area. If a kilowatt hour of electricity can be transported at a cost of 1 cent per one hundred miles, the relevant market would include a much larger area. It follows that changes in either the economies of scale available in the production of a product or the cost of transporting the product can cause an industry to become a natural monopoly or to cease having the characteristics of a natural monopoly.

Electricity generation illustrates the ways in which cost changes can transform the natural structure of an industry. Technological advances allowed the cost of transmitting electricity to decline consistently and significantly over the past century. Moreover, between the 1970s and the 1990s, other technological advances created a situation in which relatively small generating plants, i.e., 250 to 350 megawatts, can generate electricity at a unit cost as low as larger generating plants. As a result of this combination of changes in technology and costs, electricity generation is no longer a natural monopoly. If all generators have equal access to transmission lines, scores of independent generating companies can compete to provide electricity to any market. This transformation from a natural monopoly market to a market that can sustain effective competition has major implications for regulatory policy. It has given rise to the combination of regulatory unbundling of products and services, mandatory equal access to natural monopoly facilities, and competitive contracting for power supplies discussed in section 15C.

If a firm is a natural monopoly, its pricing and output decisions create the same problems as those of any other monopolist—reduced output, higher prices, and transfer of wealth from consumers to the firm. Yet, in the case of natural monopoly, restoration of competition through antitrust remedies cannot be a successful response to the monopoly problem.

If a natural monopolist were divided into three separate firms in order to permit competition, the result necessarily would be an increase in the total cost of manufacturing the quantity of product previously manufactured by a single firm. Assuming the market is divided among the three firms, each of the three would produce at a higher marginal cost than the single firm, because none would take full advantage of the available economies of scale.

Moreover, healthy competition among the three firms could not be sustained for very long. Each firm would have an incentive to sell at a price equal to its marginal cost. Marginal cost for each firm would always be below average cost, however, as shown in Figure 9.

FIGURE 9: MARGINAL AND AVERAGE COST OF A NATURAL MONOPOLY

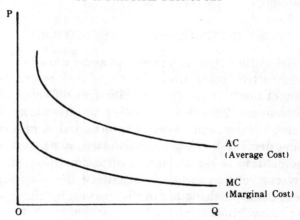

Hence, none of the firms would earn enough to cover its fixed costs. Eventually, one firm would drive the other two out of business as its marginal cost declined with increases in its quantity sold, or the firms would merge. In either event, the natural incentive to take advantage of available economies of scale would lead back to a situation in which a single firm supplies the entire market.

A common response to the natural monopoly problem is to allow the firm to continue its monopoly, but to limit through regulation the maximum price the firm can charge. Through this means, the advantages of economies of scale are retained, but price regulation limits the firm's ability to increase price, reduce output, and earn monopoly profits. The nature of the regulation typically imposed on a natural monopoly is described in Chapters 4 through 7.

2. DESTRUCTIVE COMPETITION

Regulation often is imposed to avoid the effects of "destructive competition." The term "destructive competition" is used to describe two different circumstances. Sometimes, it refers to any market in which competition causes the eventual demise of some firms. When used in this manner, destructive competition is synonymous with competition, since any competition is likely to destroy the least efficient firms participating in the market. By eliminating competition in normal competitive markets under the guise of avoiding destructive competition, regulation eliminates all of the advantages of market competition described earlier.

Sometimes destructive competition is used in a more narrow sense to describe the effects of competition in a market with the following particular characteristics. If a capital-intensive competitive industry develops substantial excess capacity, the marginal cost of the firms with excess capacity falls. A firm's marginal cost falls when it has excess capacity because it no longer considers the need for future investment in capital assets in determining its marginal cost. By definition, it already has too many capital assets. Its prior excessive (at least in retrospect) investment in capital assets is a sunk cost which the firm will not consider in calculating its marginal cost or in setting its price. They are part of the firm's fixed costs—e.g., past capital investments paid for over time whose costs do not vary by output—which must be recovered to pay bonded indebtedness. (Fixed costs also include taxes, insurance and the like which also do not vary with output changes.) However, in this circumstance, the firm's aggregate revenue from charging prices based on marginal cost will not be sufficient to permit it to recover its variable costs and its fixed costs. Minimum rate regulation sometimes is imposed in this circumstance to permit firms with high fixed costs and excess capacity to charge rates sufficient to permit recovery of fixed costs. These industry characteristics that often lead to minimum rate regulation tend to be shortlived, however. It is doubtful that the substantial inefficiencies created by minimum rate regulation can be justified as a response to the short-run problem of destructive competition. The nature of regulation typically imposed to avoid the effects of destructive competition is described in Chapters 9 and 10.

3.　SCARCITY

Almost all resources are scarce in the sense that, if a resource were made available at no cost, consumers would use more of the resource than could be supplied. Indeed, the primary function of the competitive market is to allocate scarce resources among competing uses, with price indicating the scarcity of the resource relative to the demand for the resource. Unanticipated increases in the relative scarcity of a resource, however, can create changes in the distribution of wealth that society may desire to avoid or to limit on equitable grounds.

The unanticipated scarcity basis for regulation can be illustrated through an extreme example. Assume that an unanticipated flood strikes an inland town, imperiling the lives of hundreds of residents and isolating the town from outside sources of assistance. There are only three boats in the town—each boat is owned by a different person who ordinarily rents the boat for $10 per hour for recreational uses. When the flood occurs, the owners of the boats make them available for rescue work—but at a rent of $10,000 per hour. The dramatic change in the scarcity of boats relative to the demand for boats may permit the boat owners to exact this enormous rental for a few days. Most people would agree that it is inequitable to allow the boat owners to earn such "outrageous windfall profits" or excessive rents by permitting the market alone to allocate boats in this situation. The local authorities either would impose rate regulation on boat owners or, more likely, would commandeer the boats for public use and pay the boat owners "just compensation" for taking the boats.

On a less extreme level, unanticipated increases in relative scarcity create the potential for windfall profits or excessive rents regularly throughout the economy. The primary basis for regulating the prices charged by producers of crude oil and natural gas was the desire to limit the rents that could be earned from the sale of a resource that had become unexpectedly more scarce. When the Organization of Petroleum Exporting Countries (OPEC) created a shortage of liquid and gaseous hydrocarbons in 1973 be restricting the quantity supplied by its members, the price of oil and gas rose dramatically in a short period of time. The increased relative scarcity of oil and gas meant that producers would have to incur higher costs to find, develop and produce new supplies of oil and gas. But what of the supplies of oil and gas discovered years or even decades earlier that producers could continue to extract from underground reservoirs for many more years? Producers could earn "windfall profits" from the sale of such "old" oil and gas at a price equal to the marginal cost of producing new supplies. The cost of producing the old supplies was much lower than the new industry marginal cost, and the producer's original investment to produce the old supplies probably was made in anticipation of much lower prices indicative of the relative abundance of the resource that was believed to exist when the investments were made.

In this situation, the competitive market continues to serve the goal of allocative efficiency. The much higher price of oil and gas sends accurate price signals to consumers indicating that the resource has become more scarce. Eventually, the price of oil and gas declines as the higher price induces producers to increase the quantity supplied and consumers to reduce the quantity demanded. For a few years, however, consumers are providing some producers greater revenues than are necessary to induce the producers to make the resource available for consumption. Presumably, producers of "old" oil expected to sell their oil for only two or three dollars per barrel. They would continue to do so even if increased relative scarcity had not increased the value of their oil in the ground. To some people, it seems unjust to permit the producers to sell that oil for a price many times higher than they expected to obtain based on the unanticipated increased scarcity of the resource.

It is important to remember that price regulation designed to limit excessive rents or windfalls is not imposed to enhance allocative efficiency; indeed, it interferes with allocative efficiency by creating prices that are substantially below marginal cost and that mislead consumers into believing that the resource is more abundant than it actually is. Moreover, price controls perpetuate the shortage that gave rise to the price controls. The sole justification for price regulation in this situation necessarily lies in the belief that owners of resources should not be permitted to enhance their wealth substantially when unanticipated increases in relative scarcity increase the value of their resources.

The potential for windfall profits exists from time to time in any market. Yet, only occasionally does it lead to a decision to regulate prices—urban residential rent control programs and the regulation of oil and gas producers during the 1970's are the classic examples. Why do we choose to limit windfalls in some circumstances and not in others? For instance, landowners are permitted to earn enormous windfalls from the sale of their property when increased relative scarcity causes the value of that property to increase. The increased scarcity of oil and gas permitted the owners of resources that can be used to insulate homes to make enormous windfalls. In neither case have we attempted to eliminate these windfalls through regulation. Why are some windfalls tolerated, while we attempt to limit others through complicated price regulation mechanisms? The answer must lie in the political arena; these situations cannot be distinguished in terms of their economic effects. We discuss scarcity as a basis for regulation further in Chapters 11 and 12.

4. EXTERNALITIES

The allocative efficiency produced by a competitive market is premised in part on the assumptions that (1) all costs of producing a product are incurred by the producing firm and (2) all benefits of producing a product are reflected in the producing firm's revenues. Under these assumptions, a competitive market yields socially optimal levels of output by forcing each firm to consider the marginal revenue and marginal cost of producing an additional unit of the product. With societal costs and benefits equal to the costs and benefits perceived by the firm, its decisions based on its desire to maximize profits also will maximize the net benefits to society. In fact, however, production of any good involves some costs and/or benefits that are not reflected in the costs or revenues of the individual firms that produce the product. These costs and benefits are commonly referred to as externalities.

Beneficial and detrimental externalities can be illustrated through two polar examples—a lighthouse and a liquor store. A lighthouse may produce enormous benefits to society in the value of mariners' lives, ships, and cargoes saved, but it would be difficult to devise a system that would permit the owner of the lighthouse to charge all the individuals who desire benefits from the existence of the lighthouse a price reflecting the value of those benefits. If we relied entirely upon the competitive market to determine the number of lighthouses built, we probably would have fewer lighthouses than are thought necessary to equate the marginal social costs and benefits of lighthouses, since only a fraction of the societal benefit is likely to be reflected in the revenues received by lighthouse owners.[17]

At the other extreme, a liquor store imposes upon society many costs that are not incurred by the owner of the store. These costs are in the form of increased traffic accidents, lost time on the job, costs of caring for the children of alcoholics, etc. If the market determined the amount of liquor sold and consumed without any government intervention, more liquor would be sold than a societal cost-benefit analysis would show to be optimal, since

17. But see Coase, *The Lighthouse in Economics*, 17 J. Law & Econ. 357 (1974).

only a fraction of the social costs of liquor are borne by liquor store owners.

In less extreme form, externalities exist throughout the economy. The air and water pollution created by many manufacturing operations are common examples of detrimental externalities. Firms that provide transportation and communications services may create beneficial externalities, because these services are part of the central infrastructure that permits other forms of commercial and non-commercial interaction to take place.

If a product generates detrimental externalities, and the government does nothing, the market will cause more of that product to be produced than is optimal. Government can attempt to correct the operation of the market in this situation through any of several means. It can use legal mechanisms to force firms to reduce their detrimental externalities or to internalize the social costs they create. The legal mechanisms used most commonly to achieve these ends are tort law and government safety and environmental regulation. Government can impose taxes in a magnitude roughly equivalent to the detrimental externalities produced by the firm. All of these actions have the effect of raising the cost incurred by the firm to a level closer to the total social cost of producing the product, with a resulting reduction in the quantity of the product produced. Alternatively, government can limit the quantity of the product directly through regulation. We discuss methods of integrating economic and environmental regulation in Section 15D.

If a product generates beneficial externalities, and government does nothing, the market will cause less of that product to be produced than is optimal. Again, government has several means through which it can correct the operation of the market in this situation. It can coerce those who derive benefits from a firm's products into paying the firm for the benefits they receive. (For instance, ships using specified port facilities could be required to pay fees representing the approximate value to them of the lighthouses in the vicinity of those ports, with the fees going to the owners of the lighthouses.) Government can subsidize firms that make the product. All of these are means of increasing the quantity of the product produced by increasing a firm's revenues from the product or by decreasing the firm's costs in order to approximate the quantity that would be shown to be optimal by a social cost-benefit analysis. Of course, government can simply take over the function of supplying the product entirely, and determine the quantity it will produce independent of considerations of private costs and revenues.

If a firm subject to price regulation produces a product that generates external benefits, a regulatory agency can reflect the existence of those beneficial externalities in two ways. It can force the firm to sell the product at a price below the firm's marginal cost, and it can force the firm to continue to produce an unprofitable product by restricting the firm's power to exit from a market. Through either mechanism, the agency forces the firm to subsidize the product that generates external benefits. These methods of reflecting external benefits and detriments in regulatory decisions are discussed in Chapters 6 through 8.

5. FURTHERANCE OF SOCIAL POLICIES

A substantial proportion of government regulation is designed to further social policies. The enforcement of laws prohibiting discrimination based on race, sex, and age, for instance, is designed to further the broad social policy of providing equal opportunities to individuals of all races, genders, and ages. We do not consider this type of direct regulatory control of hiring practices, etc. within the scope of this text. Occasionally, the agencies engaged in economic regulation that are the focus of our attention here become involved indirectly in furthering the goals of antidiscrimination and equal opportunity legislation. See, e.g., NAACP v. FPC, 426 U.S. 290 (1976) (FPC must disallow firm costs attributable to illegal discriminatory hiring practices). For the most part, however, the role of economic regulatory agencies in furthering social policies of this type is peripheral. But see 47 C.F.R. § 73.2080 (FCC rule requiring all broadcast licensees to adopt affirmative action programs in hiring and personnel policies).

Economic regulatory agencies can become more directly involved in furtherance of social policies, however, through the manner in which they determine permissible prices and regulate other practices of firms subject to price regulation. Through several different types of actions, agencies can use economic regulation to redistribute wealth between regulated firms and their customers and among various classes of customers of regulated firms. Indeed, much of the impetus for enacting and leaving in place regulatory statutes appears to be the desire to affect the distribution of wealth.

The most obvious way in which regulatory agencies can redistribute wealth is through their determinations of the maximum and minimum prices regulated firms can charge. By setting the maximum price below the level competition would yield, the agency can redistribute wealth from regulated firms to the customers of regulated firms. Regulation of the maximum prices charged by natural gas producers had this effect in the 1970's. Not all consumers benefit from such a price determination, however. By setting the maximum price below the level the market would produce, the agency reduces the quantity of a product the regulated firms are willing to supply. The reduced quantity of a product must then be allocated administratively among competing purchasers. Thus, customers who still can obtain the product gain, but customers who are not able to purchase the product at the lower than market price suffer a loss in consumer welfare by being forced to substitute a less desirable product for the product they would otherwise obtain from the regulated firms. Assume, for instance, that natural gas would sell for $2 per unit in a competitive market. If an agency sets the maximum price for natural gas at $1 per unit, the quantity of gas demanded will increase and the quantity of gas supplied will decrease. The resulting supply shortfall then must be allocated administratively. As a result, the regulated firms lose wealth, consumers who receive allocations of gas gain wealth, and consumers who would buy gas at a unit price of $2 but who do not receive an allocation of gas lose wealth (because they must substitute energy supplies that are less valuable or more costly to them).

By setting minimum price at a level above the price that would be produced by a competitive market, the agency can redistribute wealth from consumers to regulated firms. Minimum price regulation of trucking firms had this distributive effect for years. Assume, for instance, that a competitive market would produce a price of $.50 for a unit of truck transport. If a regulatory agency sets the minimum rate at $.75, this decision will tend to have the effect of increasing the wealth of the regulated firms and decreasing the wealth of their customers. The effect on the wealth of the regulated firms is not always favorable, however. The number of units of truck transport demanded will be less at the $.75 unit rate than at the $.50 unit rate. If demand for truck transport is highly elastic (i.e., price sensitive consumers now buy much less), the adverse effect of the reduced quantity demanded on the firm's revenues may exceed the beneficial effect of the price increase, thereby yielding a net loss in wealth to both the regulated firms and their customers. Minimum price regulation of airlines apparently reduced the wealth of both the airlines and their customers through this sequence of events before the CAB's power to set minimum prices was effectively eliminated in the Airline Deregulation Act of 1978, 49 U.S.C.A. §§ 1301–1551.

Agencies also can redistribute wealth among the customers of regulated firms through either of two different methods. First, an agency can set the maximum price for a regulated product below the level that would be set by the market, thereby increasing the quantity of product demanded and decreasing the quantity supplied, and then allocate the available product selectively among the customers who desire to purchase the product at the below market price. The customers who receive preferred access to the product through the allocation scheme at a below market price experience a gain in wealth; the customers who can not obtain the product through administrative allocation but would have purchased the product at the market price experience a reduction in wealth, since they must substitute an inferior product for the regulated product.

The second way in which an agency can redistribute wealth among the customers of a regulated firm is through its rate design decisions. Assume a regulated firm provides the same product to two groups of customers. The unit cost of serving each class of customers is $1. The agency can redistribute wealth between the two classes of customers by requiring one class to pay a unit price of $1.20 and allowing the other class to purchase the product at a unit price of $.80. This rate design decision can have the effect of decreasing the wealth of the first class of customers and increasing the wealth of the second class. It is possible, however, for this rate design decision to reduce the wealth of both classes of customers, depending on the shape of the demand curve associated with each class of customer. If, for instance, the first class of customers reduces the quantity of product it demands as a result of the price increase from $1 to $1.20 by more than the second class increases the quantity it demands as a result of the price decrease from $1 to $.80, and the firm has substantial economies of scale, the loss of sales to the second class of customer may ultimately force the firm to raise its prices to the second class of customer above the original $1 unit price.

These methods of redistributing wealth through regulation are described in greater detail in Chapters 6, 7, 9, and 11.

6. PROTECTING EXISTING REGULATION

The emergence of unregulated competition for firms that are subject to price regulation can, in some circumstances, form the basis for the extension of regulation to the new unregulated competition in order to permit the original regulatory scheme to serve some of its purposes effectively. This extension of regulation to protect existing regulation typically occurs in one of two situations— when unregulated competition threatens to undermine minimum price regulation, and when unregulated competition threatens to interfere with the pursuit of social policies through rate design.

Minimum price regulation is imposed on an industry most frequently as a means of avoiding the adverse effects of destructive competition. See sections 2 B2 and 9A. The theory underlying this type of regulation is that competition in the particular market regulated would unduly impair the revenues and financial integrity of the competing firms to the ultimate detriment of the public. Thus, unregulated competition in the market served by the regulated firms constitutes a direct threat to the ability of minimum rate regulation to protect the revenues and financial condition of the regulated firms. If the regulated firms are permitted to respond to unregulated competition by charging prices below the prior minimum price set by the agency, their revenues are likely to decline unless output increases are sufficient to make up the lost revenues. If they are not permitted to lower their prices, their revenues will decline as a result of losing customers to the unregulated competition. Extension of regulatory control to the previously unregulated competition is a typical response to this problem. The agency then can set minimum prices applicable to the previously unregulated competitors to limit their ability to take customers from the first regulated firms or to force the first regulated firms to reduce their prices.

Rate design refers to the relationship between the various prices charged by a regulated firm in different markets or to different types of customers. The emergence of unregulated competition for a market or a class of customers previously served by a regulated firm can threaten the continued viability of two different kinds of rate designs—those that have the effect of forcing one class of customer or market to subsidize another class of customer or market, and those that attempt to base all rates on the firm's fully allocated costs.

As described in sections 6C3 and 9F, regulatory agencies often establish maximum prices applicable to sales in a particular market or to a particular class of customer below the cost a regulated firm must incur to serve that market or class of customer in order to redistribute wealth or to permit the sale of a product that generates beneficial externalities. When the agency chooses to do this, the regulated firm must have some source of revenues to cover the difference between the below cost maximum price and its costs of serving the market in order for the firm to remain financially viable. Occasionally, the firm is given a direct government subsidy for this purpose, but often no direct subsidy is available. In this situation, the firm must be permitted to earn the additional revenue necessary to offset its losses on its below cost sales by charging prices above cost in some other market or to some other class of customer. Thus, in order to justify requiring the firm to provide a product at a price below cost in one market, the agency must permit the firm to charge a price above cost in another market. If, however, unregulated competition appears in the market in which the firm has been permitted to charge a price above cost, the continued existence of the cross-subsidizing rate design is jeopardized. The unregulated competition could force the regulated firm to reduce its prices to a level closer to its costs in order to avoid loss of customers. If this took place, the regulated firm no longer would have a source of revenue to subsidize the market in which it is forced to sell at a price below cost, and the agency would be forced to allow the firm to raise its prices in the previously subsidized market. Again, in this circumstance, the threat to the viability of the regulatory scheme can be avoided by extending regulation to the new, previously unregulated competition and by setting minimum prices that preclude the previously unregulated firm from forcing the previously regulated firm to lower its prices to a level approaching its costs.

For reasons discussed in Chapter 7, regulatory agencies often prefer to set the prices a firm can charge in various markets based on the firm's fully allocated cost of providing service to the market rather than its marginal cost. If, however, the regulated firm confronts competition from unregulated firms in some markets, it may be forced to reduce its prices in those markets below fully allocated costs to a level approaching marginal cost. If competition forces the firm to reduce its price in a market below the fully allocated cost of serving that market, the firm is likely to bring pressure on the agency to permit it to increase its prices to a level above fully allocated cost in another market. Yet, the result then would be an asymetrical rate design in which some prices are based on the firm's relatively low marginal cost and others are above the firm's relatively high fully allocated cost. Here again, the problem can be avoided by extending regulation to the unregulated competition and setting minimum prices applicable to the previously unregulated firms that preclude them from forcing the regulated firm to reduce its prices below fully allocated cost.

We discuss the nature of regulation imposed to protect existing regulation in greater detail in Chapters 6, 7, 9, and 10.

7.   THIRD PARTY PAYERS AND DECISION MAKERS

In most markets, the same person decides whether to buy a product, pays for the product, and derives the benefits of obtaining the product. In some markets, however, these three functions are divided among different individuals and institutions. When someone other than the consumer chooses whether to buy a product or pays for the product, market distortions are virtually inevitable. The U.S. healthcare market is characterized by serious problems attributable to the roles of third parties. Doctors, rather than patients, decide which prescription drugs are appropriate to treat a patient's illness. Since doctors do not pay the cost of the drugs they prescribe, they have little incentive to consider cost in their prescription decisionmaking. If three drugs are available to treat a given illness, the doctor is likely to choose the drug she considers most effective even if it costs $100 and an alternative drug costs only $10. If the patient were making the decision, he might choose to sacrifice some incremental therapeutic efficacy by purchasing the $10 alternative. The doctor's role in choosing prescription drugs, but not paying for those drugs, creates a situation in which drug manufacturers often can sell a product at an unusually high price either because it is slightly better than the functional alternatives or because the manufacturer has been able to convince doctors that it is slightly better even if it is not.

More broadly, most patients do not pay the full cost of their medical care. In 1991, for instance, patients paid only 20% of the national healthcare bill, government paid 44%, and private insurance companies paid 36%. When consumers can obtain the benefits of a good without having to pay for the good, excess prices and excess consumption are inevitable. Traditionally, we have attempted to blunt the distortive effects of third party payments for healthcare by charging consumers co-payments, e.g., the patient must pay 20% of the cost of a diagnostic or therapeutic procedure. A 20% co-payment is functionally indistinguishable from an 80% subsidy, however, so it has only a limited effect on price and on quantity demanded. If we provided an 80% subsidy for cars, we could predict with confidence that the average price of cars and the number of cars purchased would soar. The healthcare market has reacted in the same manner. As the proportion of healthcare costs paid by third parties increased between 1970 and 1993, the total cost of healthcare in the U.S. soared.

It is difficult to eliminate market distortions created by the roles of third parties. There are at least three responses available. First, we could eliminate third party roles entirely, but only by sacrificing other important social goals. If we gave consumers complete discretion to choose among alternative drugs, we would risk adverse health effects attributable to the predictably frequent consumer errors in choosing among thousands of powerful drugs with varying efficacy and side effects. If we eliminated private health insurance, we would deprive consumers of their ability to spread the risks of incurring the catastrophic costs of a major illness or accident over time and across groups of consumers. If we eliminated the government's role in paying for healthcare provided to elderly people and to poor people, we would sacrifice distributional and humanitarian goals. Second, we could impose price controls on healthcare, but only at considerable risk of reducing both the quantity and quality of healthcare available. See sections 2B3 and 8C. Finally, in section 15F, we discuss a third alternative that is usually referred to as managed competition.

Government guarantees and government insurance often create market distortions similar to those created by third party payments for healthcare. Government insurance was among the principal causes of the savings and loan (S & L) crisis of the 1980s. S & L's had made long-term home loans at interest rates of 3–5% during the low inflation rate 1950s and early 1960s. S & L's could obtain capital from depositors during the high inflation rate 1970's, however, only by paying interest rates of 6–8%. As a result, S & Ls lost a great deal of money during the 1970s. By 1981, a large number of S & Ls had a negative net worth, although inappropriate accounting practices disguised this fact. In 1981, Congress simultaneously increased the scope of government insurance of deposits in S & Ls and gave S & Ls discretion to make a wider range of investments. S & Ls with a negative net worth responded to their new incentives and opportunities by offering depositors high interest rates for new capital and then investing that capital in extraordinarily high risk ventures. This response was entirely rational, since the government, rather than the S & Ls or their depositors, bore all of the risk that the investments would decline in value. Each of the many government insurance and guarantee programs has analogous potential distortive effects. Again, our potential responses are limited. We can eliminate a government insurance program, reduce its scope, or engage in aggressive regulatory oversight of insured entities in an effort to keep them from responding to the unhealthy incentives created by the availability of government insurance.

CHAPTER III

LEGAL BASIS OF REGULATION

Although the legal study of industry regulation has focused primarily on the federal agencies beginning with the first great independent regulatory commission, the Interstate Commerce Commission, many state and local governments in fact created administrative agencies before the ICC was established. Most states, for example, had some sort of insurance or banking regulatory commission before 1870. L. Friedman, *A History of American Law* 384 (1973). Indeed, it was the states that first sought to regulate the railroads and this effort dominated their regulatory administration during the second half of the 19th century—just as railroads dominated tort and corporation law.

The history of state regulatory commissions can be traced back to a Rhode Island law of 1839. Nonetheless, the initial focus of state regulation was on specific requirements written by the legislatures themselves as they sought to control the railroads by detailed statutory specification of interconnecting services, rates, and other practices as well as of their related warehouse businesses. This task proved more than the legislatures could handle. They were part-time bodies without institutional expertise in railroads or warehousing; they were not in a position to measure costs, evaluate claims for exemption, or modify rates in accordance with changing conditions. Nor could they supervise quality and service, both of which were necessary if rate regulation was to be effective. The legislatures also proved highly susceptible to railroad pressure and manipulation so that it is now difficult to determine whether the legislatures were unable or simply unwilling to regulate railroads effectively.

The next stage in the development of business regulation, in particular of the railroads, was the widespread creation of state administrative commissions. The first experiments in this direction assigned agencies the limited task of investigating and making recommendations to the legislature on rate levels as well as other conditions of service. This model, used mostly in the eastern states, only further strengthened the railroads' apparent economic power as the agencies seemingly acceded in every case to railroad requests. Responding to the demands of the Granger movement, several midwestern states took a further step and created "railroad and warehouse" commissions which were delegated the task of regulating railroads, warehouses and grain elevators. These commissions, rather than the legislatures, were to control the rates and services of the regulated businesses.

Again the regulatory control system proved ineffective. One reason was that the railroads were as adept at controlling the state commissions as they were the legislatures that created them. Another was that when challenged the state regulatory programs were often held unconstitutional insofar as they interfered with shipments involving interstate commerce. The commerce power of the federal government, which the Constitution made superior to the power of the states, was read to protect shipments with interstate origins or destinations from state control. Thus in Wabash, St. L. & Pac. Ry. v. Illinois, 118 U.S. 557 (1886), the Court held that states could not regulate commerce if it came from or was destined for a point outside the state. Only the federal government had this right, which meant that state regulation of discriminatory passenger and freight rates was doomed since a significant amount of railroad traffic was now beyond state control.

These limitations on state regulation of the railroads added force to the campaign already underway in Congress for a federal railroad commission. The *Wabash* decision was the apparent catalytic event as Congress created the Interstate Commerce Commission the next year, in 1887. This commission was assigned responsibility to assure just and reasonable rates and to prohibit undue discrimination. Later chapters will examine decisions under this statute (and later amendments) for they are often foundational in understanding the legal framework of economic regulation. Important as the ICC and successor agencies are to this study, the legal foundation of public control of business was laid over a decade earlier when the Supreme Court upheld another Illinois state regulatory scheme against constitutional challenge.

A. BUSINESS "AFFECTED WITH THE PUBLIC INTEREST"

In 1871 the Illinois state legislature adopted a statute setting the maximum price that elevators in Chicago could charge for the transfer and storage of grain. Objecting to this statute, the elevator operators challenged it under the fourteenth amendment, contending that it violated their constitutionally protected right to due process. The statute had placed a ceiling on the earnings of grain elevators that not only limited operator income but also thereby reduced the market value of the elevator property. These were argued to constitute a taking of property without required legal process—namely a valuation in a legal hearing and adequate compensation for the property taken—and therefore unconstitutional.

However, in Munn v. Illinois, 94 U.S. 113 (1876),[1] over the powerful dissent of Justice Field who characterized the elevators simply as private businesses indistinguishable from tailors and shoemakers, the Supreme Court analogized grain elevators to such common carriers as ferrymen, innkeepers and hackney coachmen whose businesses were "affected with a public interest" and therefore subject to state regulation. The Court identified the elevators as a "virtual monopoly," and concluded that where the public could not rely on competition to protect

1. For an exceptional analysis of the historical setting as well as the opinions in *Munn*, see Kitch & Bowler, *The Facts of Munn v. Illinois*, 1978 Sup.Ct.Rev. 313.

itself, it was permissible for the state to regulate the business in the public interest. The legal theory was narrower than that, with the Court ruling that when one "devotes his property to a use in which the public has an interest, he, in effect, grants to the public an interest in that use, and must submit to be controlled by the public for the common good, to the extent of the interest he has thus created."

The Court did not have before it whether the statutory rate was reasonable or unreasonable since the elevator operators had argued that there was no legislative power (of any kind) to set prices. This has led to some confusion about the Court's statement that:

We know that this is a power which may be abused; but that is no argument against its existence. For protection against abuses by legislatures the people must resort to the polls, not to the courts.

It has been read as holding that "once it was determined that a business was 'clothed with a public interest,' the legislature was free to impose whatever rate regulations seemed to it desirable." E.g., D. Boies, & P. Verkuil, *Public Control of Business* 103 (1977). This reading of the Supreme Court's view of state legislative authority is then contrasted with subsequent cases (e.g., Smyth v. Ames (U.S.1898)) permitting judicial review of regulated rates and overturning them if confiscatory, the suggestion being that the two were inconsistent and possibly irreconcilable.

Careful scholarship, however, has revealed that this statement by the Court in *Munn* was only a response to the argument that rate regulatory authority could not be conceded to the state legislatures because they might abuse the power by raising the price at the behest of the regulated elevator companies. Kitch & Bowler, supra at 340 (quoting from the briefs of the plaintiff). While the elevator operators' argument was prophetic, at that time it was only implausible hyperbole (there being only a few relatively small, nonmonopolistic businesses involved). Thus the Court's comment that the public had adequate recourse through the polls seems only a common sense response that ceding such regulatory power to the state legislatures was not giving them unbridled discretionary authority they were likely to abuse.

More difficult to explain, indeed left unanswered by the Court's over-long opinion, is its unsupported conclusion that grain elevators were like common carriers affected with a public interest and thus properly subject to government regulation. What was it that distinguished them from other businesses such as tailors and shoemakers (who, it was conceded, were not common carriers subject to maximum price regulation)? A theoretical case might have been made for the Court's holding if its analysis had been based on the elevators' supposed natural monopoly or if the Court had connected their market power to the common law prohibition of unfair competition. Neither route was chosen; the facts did not justify finding the former and the common law of unfair competition (to the extent it existed) did not justify state legislative regulation. Nor did subsequent cases find any explainable path despite numerous decisions upholding some regulations and denying others. See generally, Chas. Wolff Packing Co. v. Court of Industrial Relations, 262 U.S. 522 (1923) (listing four basic rationales for validated state regulation). Ultimately, of course, the Supreme Court was led to reject the distinction first stated in *Munn* when, during the New Deal, the Court overturned its follow-on rule of substantive due process and concluded that all economic activity is subject to state regulation unless preempted by Congress. See, e.g., Nebbia v. New York, 291 U.S. 502 (1934), discussed in section 3 B1.

That the majority in *Munn* chose not to explain its rationale for finding grain elevator transfer and storage prices subject to state regulation is not exceptional, even though the absence of any logical link specially connecting this business to the "public interest" was sharply debated to it by the parties and the dissent. Several possible explanations have been offered, however, and their insights are instructive. One is the Court's narrow view then of the fourteenth amendment, as expressed two years later in the Slaughter–House Cases, 83 U.S. 36 (1873). There the Court ruled that the amendment did not guarantee the substantive fairness of laws passed by the state legislatures and that the equality it promised was only to protect newly freed black slaves from discriminatory state laws. In point of fact, it was not until nine years after *Munn* that the Court decided that a corporation was a "person" entitled to due process protection. See Santa Clara County v. Southern Pac. R. R. Co., 118 U.S. 394 (1886).

More persuasive, however, is the explanation that the Court majority was seeking a satisfactory rationale to justify other state business regulation, including the railroad rate regulation challenges in the *Granger Cases* then working their way to the Supreme Court. See, e.g., Chicago, Burlington & Quincy R. R. Co. v. Iowa, 94 U.S. 155 (1877). The railroads had been arguing that their state charters placed them in a distinctive category separate from other businesses (such as grain elevators) because these charters granted them power to establish rules and regulations governing their railroad business. These special grants of "state sovereignty" to the railroads were argued by them as denying the states any authority to regulate their prices. However, by deciding *Munn* under the "affected with a public interest" rationale, the Court could avoid the railroads' difficult and politically sensitive interpretation of their state charters. That is, after this decision the Court had only to note that the railroads were common carriers and as such "under . . . *Munn* [were] subject to legislative control as to their rates of fare and freight, unless protected by their charters." Applying the *Munn* rule, the burden of proving the railroads' special classification fell on the roads rather than the states. Not finding that they had proved that their state charters provided any special protection, it followed that the railroads were like grain elevator operators and thus were subject to state regulation.

B. SUBSTANTIVE DUE PROCESS

Paradoxically, even as the Court was outlining this "affected with a public interest" standard to justify a general policy of noninterference with legislative judgments, it was also developing a jurisprudence that would impose severe substantive limits on legislative lawmaking power.

1. FEDERAL LAW

First in dicta and then in holding the Supreme Court ruled under the fourteenth amendment that a state could not set rates so low as to "require a railroad corporation to carry persons or property without reward." Compare Railroad Commission Cases, 116 U.S. 307 (1886) (recognizing the "just compensation" principle) with Smyth v. Ames, 169 U.S. 466 (1898) (establishing the "fair value" doctrine as the basis for judging whether confiscation had occurred), discussed in section 5A. This inroad into legislative prerogatives was limited, however, to holding that if a state chooses to act in regulating business, its regulation must be reasonable and its decisions could not be imposed arbitrarily. That is, the focus was on the *application* of established standards; the role or authority of government to regulate the business once it met the "affected with a public interest" test was seemingly accepted.

This acceptance of any economic regulation proved short-lived. Building on this process-oriented concern with fairness as well as other rulings that "governmental authority has implied limits which preserve private autonomy,"[2] the Court moved to give the fourteenth amendment's due process (and equal protection) terms a more expansive and substantive reading. The initial step was taken in Mugler v. Kansas, 123 U.S. 623 (1887), where the Court gave notice that it would scrutinize the substantive reasonableness of state legislation and invalidate statutes justified under the state's police powers if in fact they had "no real or substantial relation" to public health, morals or safety, and were "palpable invasion[s] of rights secured by the fundamental law." *Mugler*, however, in fact sustained a state statute prohibiting the sale of alcoholic beverages as being within a reasonable exercise of state authority. But subsequent decisions relied upon its reasoning to strike state laws. Through a series of decisions, beginning with Allgeyer v. Louisiana, 165 U.S. 578 (1897), and culminating in Lochner v. New York, 198 U.S. 45 (1905), the Court established its now famous (or infamous) doctrine of substantive or economic due process under which it reviewed the constitutionality of state and federal legislation[3] against charges that it arbitrarily and unnecessarily interfered with the liberty of contract between an employer and his employees or otherwise served no legitimate state end. Thus in *Lo-*

2. L. Tribe, *Constitutional Law* § 8–1, (2d ed. 1988)

3. Federal legislation is subject to substantive judicial review under the fifth amendment's due process clause.

chner the Court invalidated a New York statute regulating the hours a baker could work because there was, the Court said, no legitimate government purpose in regulating labor conditions or practices where the regulation was not a true health or safety measure.

This prohibition against legislation that is arbitrary or bears no rational relation to legitimate state ends held sway in constitutional law for almost fifty years until, in the mid–1930's, the Court showed a renewed deference to legislative judgments about the permissible ends of government or the proper means for achieving them. The intervening period was a tumultuous one as almost 200 state and federal regulations were invalidated by the High Court.[4] Application of the rule was never easy or predictable. Numerous contradictions in case applications cast doubt on the entire theory, as the Court came to recognize exceptions allowing regulation on behalf of vulnerable groups in dependent positions. See, e.g., Muller v. Oregon, 208 U.S. 412 (1908) (upholding working hour limits for women); Bunting v. Oregon, 243 U.S. 426 (1917) (same for men). Other inconsistencies were revealed in the Court's treatment of tax legislation and in its decisions on the taking of private property by government.

The danger of substantive review of economic regulation had been identified from the very beginning, and in particular in Justice Holmes' historic

4. However, an even larger number of challenged regulatory laws were upheld. See L. Tribe, supra § 8–2.

dissent in *Lochner*. There his celebrated remark
that the fourteenth amendment "does not enact
Mr. Herbert Spencer's Social Statics" vividly called
attention to the Court's imposition of its own nor-
mative beliefs about proper economic policy under
the guise of constitutional interpretation. Ultimately it was this perception—that absent an explicit
constitutional mandate, it was inappropriate in a
democracy for an unelected judiciary to impose its
own set of values or beliefs on the legislature—that
led to the abandonment of the doctrine. See Ferguson v. Skrupa, 372 U.S. 726 (1963). Also persuasive
was the argument that the Constitution was not
written to place a "straight jacket" on government
either by limiting its choice of policy tools or by
foreclosing its experimentation with new (and possibly superior) policy responses. See New State Ice
Co. v. Liebmann, 285 U.S. 262 (1932) (Brandeis, J.,
dissenting). See generally, Lincoln Fed. Labor Union v. Northwestern Iron & Metal Co., 335 U.S. 525
(1949). This last point was particularly persuasive
in building pressure against the doctrine as government struggled to lead the country out of the worst
depression in its history.

The first crack in the doctrinal foundation of
substantive due process began when the Court relied upon the negative implications of *Munn* to void
a series of legislative regulations. That is, instead of
finding state regulations arbitrary and unrelated to
proper ends under economic due process, the Court
invalidated them because the regulated business
was not "affected with a public interest" and thus

did not meet the *Munn* standard. See, e.g., Chas. Wolff Packing Co. v. Court of Industrial Relations, 262 U.S. 522 (1923) (requirement of compulsory arbitration in the food industry); Tyson & Bro. v. Banton, 273 U.S. 418 (1927) (regulation of business of selling theater tickets); Ribnik v. McBride, 277 U.S. 350 (1928) (employment agency practice and rate regulation); Williams v. Standard Oil Co., 278 U.S. 235 (1929) (regulation of retail gasoline prices); New State Ice Co. v. Liebmann, 285 U.S. 262 (1932) (requirement of license to enter ice business). In each of these decisions, the ruling relied on a finding that the regulated business was not affected with a public interest rather than on a substantive due process formulation that regulation in this circumstance served no legitimate state end.

The next pillar to fall was the *Munn* doctrine itself, at least insofar as the public interest standard was read as an effective limitation on governmental authority to regulate business. Thus in Nebbia v. New York, 291 U.S. 502 (1934), the Court reviewed a New York regulatory scheme that set minimum prices for the retail sale of milk. Rejecting the contention that the business was not affected with a public interest and could not be regulated, the Court ruled that "there is no closed class or category of business affected with a public interest." While this result—upholding state regulation—differed dramatically from *Lochner* and its progeny, the Court did not go so far as to overturn the doctrine of substantive due process. Indeed, *Nebbia* stated that the judicial function was "to determine in each case whether circumstances vindicate the challenged regulation as a reasonable exertion of governmental authority or condemn it as arbitrary or discriminatory," language that followed traditional substantive due process analysis. Still, the Court's analysis seemed far removed from the narrow scope allowed government regulation in *Lochner*, especially when it also said that "a state is free to adopt whatever economic policy may reasonably be deemed to promote public welfare, and to enforce that policy by legislation adopted to its purpose."

The revolution suggested by the provocative analysis in *Nebbia* was completed only three years later when the Supreme Court dramatically reversed itself[5] and upheld state minimum wage legislation for women in West Coast Hotel v. Parrish, 300 U.S. 379 (1937). Distinguishing contrary past decisions, the Court rejected substantive due process arguments as "a departure from the true application of the principles governing regulation by the State of the relation of employer and employed." *Lochner*, it seemed, was no longer the law. Although, as Professor Tribe has noted, the Court's opinion in *West Coast Hotel* spoke more about the justice of minimum wages than it did to legislative authority to

5. The drama was heightened by President Roosevelt's effort to change the Court's direction in seeking authority to appoint additional justices and by the Court's ruling a year earlier that had invalidated an identical law of another jurisdiction on substantive due process grounds. See Morehead v. New York ex rel. Tipaldo, 298 U.S. 587 (1936). For an explanation of "this switch in time that saved nine," see L. Tribe, supra § 8–6.

enact them without judicial interference, subsequent cases made clear that this was more than a temporary policy shift limited to one case or class and that the demise of substantive due process as an active vehicle for controlling government economic regulation in federal constitutional law was permanent. One year later, in upholding federal legislation prohibiting interstate shipment of "filled" milk, the Court stated the new standard it has followed ever since: "where the legislative judgment is drawn in question, [the Court's role] must be restricted to the issue whether any state of facts either known or which could reasonably be assumed, affords support for [the legislation]." United States v. Carolene Products Co., 304 U.S. 144 (1938).

As this summary indicates, the Supreme Court has not totally repudiated any "rational relation" review of economic legislation, and technically this minimal aspect of the substantive due process requirement must still be satisfied. However, the cases also reveal an extreme judicial deference to the legislative judgment. See, e.g., Williamson v. Lee Optical of Oklahoma, Inc., 348 U.S. 483 (1955) (requirement that persons using an optician to fit or duplicate eyeglass lenses must first obtain a prescription from an opthalmologist or optometrist upheld); Ferguson v. Skrupa, 372 U.S. 726 (1963) (limitation of debt adjusting business to legal practice upheld); North Dakota State Bd. of Pharmacy v. Snyder's Drug Stores, 414 U.S. 156 (1973) (law that pharmacy must be owned by registered pharmacists upheld). Indeed, the Supreme Court has not invalidated any economic regulation on substantive due process grounds since 1936.[6]

2. STATE LAW

The picture of state law applying similar state constitutional requirements is less clear. Many have followed the federal lead and now uphold economic regulation under theories of imagined rationality that make even the most lax Supreme Court decisions appear narrow and confining. See, e.g., Roosevelt Raceway, Inc. v. County of Nassau, 271 N.Y.S.2d 662 (1966); State v. Lockey, 152 S.E. 693 (N.C.1930) (upholding certification of barbers because "[v]enereal disease and other diseases can be transmitted [apparently through barber chairs or clippers], so it was the judgment of the General Assembly to have barbers . . . subjected to reasonable sanitary regulations. . . . "); but see Dunbar v. Hoffman, 468 P.2d 742 (Colo.1970) (statute prohibiting Sunday work by barbers only in larger cities invalidated).

Other state courts have been more rigorous, however, although they have not sought to return to the *Lochner* standard. Instead they have demanded some assurance that the regulatory means chosen

6. The only exception is a Supreme Court case invalidating economic legislation under the *equal protection* clause on rational relation grounds. See Morey v. Doud, 354 U.S. 457 (1957). However, it was overruled as a "needlessly intrusive judicial infringement on the State's legislative powers" in City of New Orleans v. Dukes, 427 U.S. 297 (1976).

be sufficiently related to the selected legislative ends. See, e.g., Isakson v. Rickey, 550 P.2d 359 (Alaska 1976) (overturning state regulation limiting entry into commercial fishing business based on past participation and economic dependence); cf. Gunther, *Foreword: In Search of Evolving Doctrine on a Changing Court: A Model for a Newer Equal Protection*, 86 Harv.L.Rev. 1 (1972) (suggesting a narrower means-focused test where the Court would, except when fundamental rights and suspect classifications were involved, consider whether the legislative means have a substantial relationship to the legislative purpose). Borrowing the fundamental right/suspect classification distinction from equal protection caselaw, the California Supreme Court has developed a separate rule for occupational regulation on the ground that employment is a fundamental interest. Thus, in California regulation of the "common occupations" (but not the professions) requires strict judicial scrutiny to assure that regulation serves a legitimate state end. Why the professions deserve less protection from arbitrary regulation was not satisfactorily explained.

Many state courts go even further and continue the practice of vigorous substantive due process and equal protection scrutiny of state and local economic regulation abandoned by the federal courts for over sixty years. See Note, *State Economic Substantive Due Process: A Proposed Approach,* 88 Yale L.J. 1487–88 & n. 5 (1979) (collecting authorities). As a consequence, state regulation must still be justified by a showing of the legitimacy of the legislative end as well as of a demonstration that the means chosen are necessary and proper. Three justifications are given for this different state of affairs. First is a concern that the state or local regulation was developed in favor of a particular group at the expense of the public and the "public interest." Although supported by public choice theory that logrolling can result in "private interest" legislation, the argument founders in its reliance on an insulated judiciary to keep institutions of representative democracy operating, especially since there is no showing that the legislative process has been abused or used illegally (for if such abuse can be shown, it would constitute a separate basis for challenging the legislation). A related argument is that the regulation resulted from undue pressures on the legislature, including its narrowed time span and limited institutional resources and expertise. Judicial review, in other words, can act as a desirable check or balance, especially where the legislative choice turns out to be defective or flawed in fact. Finally, it is contended that active judicial review of the authority for economic regulation has the effect of airing and critiquing the underlying basis for the regulation, thus informing the legislature and the public of its rationale and, where deficient, of the need for revision. Although an argument can be made that state regulation is often exceedingly parochial in scope and biased in approach,[7] the authority to use state

7. For particularly effective empirical and theoretical analyses, see W. Gellhorn, *The Abuse of Occupational Licensing*, 44 U.Chi.L.Rev. 6 (1976); M. Friedman, *Capitalism and Freedom*, ch. IX (1962).

constitutional provisions to examine and overturn such legislation is not evident and the danger that this approach will lead to constitutionalizing the economic beliefs of the judiciary seems ever present. But see McCloskey, *Economic Due Process and the Supreme Court: An Exhumation and Reburial*, 1962 Sup.Ct.Rev. 34.

CHAPTER IV

RATE REGULATION: AN INTRODUCTION

A. REVENUE REQUIREMENTS AND RATES

As discussed, economic regulation has been imposed for many reasons (see Chapter 2). This introduction focuses on rate regulation designed to limit the aggregate revenue of the firms subject to rate regulation. Later (in Chapters 6, 7, 10 and 12), variations in approach and emphasis are introduced which serve other regulatory goals such as assuring fair prices to individual customers, avoiding harmful effects of destructive competition, and controlling inflation.

Rate regulation, as examined here, is designed to prevent monopoly profits and to assure fair prices and service to consumers. It is also designed to assure that a regulated firm earns that amount necessary to remain in business. In the context of firms with monopoly power, the regulatory constraint on total revenues is intended to avoid the adverse consequences of "the monopoly problem"— prices above competitive levels, output below competitive levels, and transfer of wealth from consumers to producers—and to yield a mix of price, output and profits approximating the mix that would be produced by the competitive model.

The most common method used to control aggregate revenue and to set maximum rates has evolved over more than one hundred years of regulation. It begins with calculation of a firm's revenue requirements through application of the formula: $R=O+B(r)$, where R is the firm's allowed revenue requirements, O is the firm's operating expenses, B is the firm's rate base, and r is the firm's rate of return allowed on its rate base. Agencies, courts and commentators often vary the symbols or notations used to indicate the terms in this equation, but the same equation is employed consistently to constrain aggregate revenues.

Once the firm's aggregate allowed revenue requirements are determined, the regulatory agency establishes the maximum rates the firm can charge for each of its products to each class of customers based on the agency's calculation of the rates that, when multiplied by the expected number of units of each product or service sold, will yield to the firm its aggregate allowed revenue requirements. For most regulated firms with multiple products and customers, this process of establishing maximum rates predicted to allow the firm to earn its revenue requirements is complex. (It is discussed in further detail in Chapters 6 and 7.) For now, however, a simplified view of the relationship between maximum rates and allowed revenue requirements is helpful to an understanding of the significance of the determination of revenue requirements. If a regulated firm provided only one product to one class of customers, the agency would establish the maximum rate the firm could charge for each unit of that product through use of the formula: $P = {}^R\!/\!v$ where P is the maximum unit rate—i.e., price per unit—the firm is permitted to charge, R is the firm's allowed revenue requirements, and V is the number of units or volume of the product the firm is expected to sell.

B. INVESTMENT AND RATE OF RETURN

The B term in the equation for calculating allowed revenue requirements, usually referred to as rate base, represents the firm's investments in capital assets that are used to provide the products that are subject to economic regulation. The r term represents the rate of return the firm is allowed to earn on that investment. In theory, r is the firm's cost of capital, or the amount of money it must spend to obtain the capital it uses to provide regulated products. Rate of return is the weighted average cost of the firm's various sources of capital—the interest it pays on its debt and the rate of return on its equity—that is necessary to permit the firm to continue to attract the capital required to provide the regulated product. Both B and r are sources of great controversy in economic regulation.

C. EXPENSES

The *O* term in the equation refers to the operating expenses the firm incurs to provide the regulated product. It encompasses both out-of-pocket costs, such as wages and raw materials, and depreciation of capital assets used to provide the regulated product. Determination of *O* also is the source of considerable controversy in economic regulation. Rates are determined prospectively for the future. Thus *O* should represent the firm's future operating expenses. Since the future is difficult to forecast, however, *O* traditionally has been determined based on actual expenses incurred by the firm in a recent past period, often referred to as the "test year."

D. GENERAL EFFECT OF RATE REGULATION AND ALLOWED REVENUE REQUIREMENTS

Setting the maximum rates to be charged for a product based on determination of a firm's allowed revenue requirements does not guarantee the firm that it will actually earn the allowed revenue requirements or the allowed rate of return. Rather, the methodology is designed to permit the firm the *opportunity* to earn the allowed revenue requirements and allowed rate of return. The actual revenues earned by the firm may exceed or fail to reach the allowed revenue requirements if the units actually sold by the firm differ from the projected volume of sales that formed the basis for calculating the maximum rate. Even if actual revenues equal allowed revenue requirements, the actual rate of return earned by the firm will differ from the allowed rate of return if the company's actual investment or actual operating expenses differ from the amounts included by the regulatory agency in the *O* and *B* terms of the formula for calculating allowed revenue requirements. Since the volume of sales, rate base and expenses used to calculate the firm's maximum rates are projections based on historical experience, a firm's actual revenues and rate of return often differ significantly from the revenues and rate of return allowed by the regulatory agency.

CHAPTER V

MAXIMUM PRICE REGULATION

Individuals invest in businesses and other productive assets because they expect a return on the capital they invest. Unless this return is equivalent to the amount they could earn from investments of comparable risk, they will not invest capital in a particular firm. Thus, a regulatory decision setting maximum rates at a level that will not permit investors in a firm to earn an adequate return on their investment has two undesirable consequences—it deters future investment in the firm and it takes from existing investors the expectation they had when they made their original investment.

Determining the appropriate rate of return on capital allowed to investors in regulated firms raises significant practical and theoretical problems. The theoretical question that has presented the greatest challenge is whether to determine the appropriate rate of return with reference to an accounting measure or an economic measure of the value of capital assets. From an accounting standpoint, the value of capital invested in a firm is measured by the historic level of investment. From an economic standpoint, however, the value of a firm's capital assets depends upon the amount and value of the resources society saves by having available today the productive capital assets of the firm. Thus, changes in the amount of resources required to perform a function or changes in the value of those resources can cause the economic value of the firm's capital assets to increase or decrease over time.

Proponents of the accounting measure of the value of capital assets as a basis for determining appropriate rate of return argue that it is equitable to permit investors to earn a return based on the amount of capital originally invested in those assets—no more and no less. Proponents of the economic measure of the value of capital assets contend that it provides a superior basis for determining return because (1) to attract new capital investment, a firm must offer potential investors the expectation that they can earn a return on new investments based on the current cost of those investments; and (2) it provides more accurate price signals to consumers by reflecting in the price of a regulated product the present value of the resources used to produce the product. This debate between accounting cost and economic cost is a recurrent theme in economic regulation. We will see it reflected first in the decision to use reproduction cost or original cost as the basis for determining the value of a firm's rate base, and then later in the choice of average cost or marginal cost as the basis for calculating rates charged individual consumers.

As discussed below, many controversies in economic regulation—including the accounting cost versus economic cost dispute—originally were debated on a constitutional law level because establishing a maximum rate at a level that does not permit an investor to earn an adequate rate of return has the effect of "taking without just compensation" the investor's prior expectation of earning an adequate return. The modern trend away from resolving these controversies on a constitutional level probably reflects more the Court's belief that it has little institutional expertise in analyzing economic problems than its belief that important constitutional issues are not raised by the process of establishing maximum rates.

A. CONSTITUTIONAL LIMITS

The fifth and fourteenth amendments to the Constitution prohibit the government from taking private property for a public use without just compensation. These provisions have been held applicable to government regulation of maximum rates, with the effect of establishing a constitutionally-based floor below which a rate ceiling must be reversed by the courts as confiscatory. See Georgia Railroad & Banking Co. v. Smith, 128 U.S. 174 (1888).

Initially, the courts attempted to enforce this floor on maximum rates through limits derived from the Constitution and applied to an agency's determination of a regulated firm's rate base. In Smyth v. Ames, 169 U.S. 466 (1898), the Supreme Court held that rate ceilings must be based on the "fair value" of the property used in the regulated business. That fair value was to be determined from a consideration of "the original cost of construction, the amount expended in permanent improvements, the amount and market value of its bonds and stock, the present as compared with the original cost of construction, the probable earning capacity of the property under particular rates prescribed by statute, and the sum required to meet operating expenses...."

The Court never indicated which of these considerations should control where they are in conflict. Rather, it held that each consideration was to be given "such weight as may be just and right in each case." The Court, however, reversed several agency maximum rate determinations because the agency gave insufficient weight to the reproduction cost of the firm's plant and equipment. See, e.g., McCardle v. Indianapolis Water Co., 272 U.S. 400 (1926).

At the same time the Court continued to enforce the prohibition against confiscatory rates by reviewing agency determinations of rate base, it began to review determinations of rate of return under a constitutional standard. In Bluefield Water Works & Improvement Co. v. Public Service Commission, 262 U.S. 679 (1923), the Court held:

A public utility is entitled to such rates as will permit it to earn a return on the value of the property which it employs for the convenience of the public equal to that generally being made at the same time and in the same general part of the country on investments on other business undertakings which are attended by corresponding risks and uncertainties; but it has no constitutional right to profits such as are realized or anticipated in highly profitable enterprises or speculative ventures. The return should be reasonably sufficient to assure confidence in the financial soundness of the utility and should be adequate, under efficient and economical management, to maintain and support its credit and enable it to raise the money necessary for the proper discharge of its public duties.

The Court also enforced the constitutional prohibition against confiscatory rates by reversing agency maximum rate determinations that did not permit full recovery of operating expenses. Thus, in West Ohio Gas Co. v. Public Utilities Commission of Ohio, 294 U.S. 63 (1935), the Court reversed an agency decision refusing to allow recovery of advertising expenses with the following broad statement:

Good faith is to be presumed on the part of the managers of a business. . . . In the absence of a showing of inefficiency or improvidence, a court will not substitute its judgment for theirs as to the measure of a prudent outlay.

Throughout the period from 1889 until 1944, the courts engaged in detailed review of each of the three major components of agency maximum rate decisions—rate base, rate of return, and operating expenses—to enforce the constitutional prohibition against confiscatory rates, notwithstanding increasingly sharp dissents arguing that the constitutional standards established were both unnecessary and unwise. The requirement that agencies consider reproduction cost in determining a firm's rate base came under particularly heavy attack beginning in the 1920's. See Missouri ex rel. Southwestern Bell Telephone Co. v. Public Service Commission, 262 U.S. 276 (1923) (dissenting opinion of Justices Brandeis and Holmes); McCardle v. Indianapolis Water Co., 272 U.S. 400 (1926) (dissenting opinion of Justices Brandeis and Stone). The dissenting Justices argued that reproduction cost was too speculative and difficult to determine. The "fair value" standard was even worse as a stable benchmark for determining rate base because it required agencies to consider and reconcile in some unspecified manner widely differing measures of rate base determined with reference to reproduction cost, original cost, and market value of stocks and bonds. The dissenters urged adoption of an original cost standard because is was easy to apply and produced stable results.

In Federal Power Commission v. Hope Natural Gas Co., 320 U.S. 591 (1944), the Court responded implicitly to the growing criticism of its constitutional standards and signaled a retreat from detailed constitutional review of maximum rate decisions. It held that an agency is "not bound to the use of any single formula or combination of formulae in determining rates.... [I]t is the result reached not the method employed which is controlling." The Court went on to explain its "end result" test:

Rates which enable the company to operate successfully, to maintain its financial integrity, to attract capital, and to compensate its investors for the risks assumed certainly cannot be condemned as invalid, even though they might produce only a meager return on the so-called "fair value" rate base.

The Court's discussion in *Hope* focused on the legality of rates under the "just and reasonable" standard of the Natural Gas Act, 15 U.S.C.A. § 717 et seq., but its opinion contained the clear implication that the era of detailed constitutional review of agency rate determinations was at an end. Thus the Court stated:

Since there are no constitutional requirements more exacting than the standards of the Act, a rate order which conforms to the latter does not run afoul of the former.

Presumably, the fifth and fourteenth amendments' prohibition on confiscatory rates retains some vitality today, but it is difficult to determine the standards through which the prohibition is enforced. Since *Hope*, the Supreme Court has not reversed any agency decision establishing a maximum rate on grounds that the rate is unconstitutionally confiscatory. The statutory "end result" test announced in *Hope* may well also be the constitutional standard for determining whether a rate is so low it is confiscatory. As applied today, the "end result" test focuses on the reasonableness of the agency's decision and the procedures used in making the decision. See section 5F.

The Court reaffirmed *Hope* in Duquesne Light Co. v. Barasch, 488 U.S. 299 (1989). It also held that legislators can require regulators to change the rules applicable to a utility's ability to recover an investment in its rates after the utility has already made that investment, as long as the amount of the investment disallowed in the utility's rates is not so large as to be of constitutional dimensions. The investment disallowed in *Barasch* was only $35 million, or 1.9% of the utility's total assets. The combination of the Court's opinion in *Barasch,* and its refusal to decide several other cases in which agencies disallowed billions of dollars in utility investments, has caused some analysts to conclude that the Court continues to lack confidence in its institutional capacity to apply meaningful substantive constitutional constraints on ratemaking in most contexts. See, e.g., Kolbe & Tye, *The Duquesne Opinion: How Much "Hope" Is There for Investors in Regulated Firms?* 8 Yale J. on Reg. 113 (1991); Pierce, *Public Utility Regulatory Takings: Should the Judiciary Attempt to Police the Political Institutions?* 77 Georgetown L.J. 2031 (1989).

The Court seems willing to apply meaningful substantive constraints on ratemaking in only one context. In Nantahala Power & Light v. Thornburg, 476 U.S. 953 (1986), the Court held that a state agency cannot "trap" a cost incurred by a state-regulated utility if a federal agency required the utility to incur the cost at issue. The state agency must allow the utility the opportunity to recover the federally-mandated cost. The Court based its holding on the Supremacy Clause, but it almost certainly was influenced by takings clause considerations as well. See R. Pierce, Economic Regulation § IIIB (1994).

Despite the apparent demise of detailed constitutional review of agency rate decisions in the federal courts, the principles announced in the cases decided between 1889 and 1944 remain important for more than historical reasons. First, many of the same principles have been carried over by modern agencies and courts as the basis for determining rates and reviewing rate determinations under typically vague statutory mandates like "just and reasonable." For instance, the "comparable risks and uncertainties" test for determining rate of return announced in *Bluefield* and the "prudently incurred" test for allowing operating expenses applied in *West Ohio* are commonly used today. See, e.g., New England Telephone & Telegraph Co. v. Public Utilities Commission, 390 A.2d 8 (Me.1978). Second, many of the statutes under which state agencies determine utility rates today were enacted when the Supreme Court was still engaged in detailed constitutional review of agency rate determinations. The legislative histories of many of these statutes indicate that the agencies are required to follow the constitutional standards for rate making in existence at the time the statutes were enacted. See e.g., Union Electric Co. v. Illinois Commerce Commission, 396 N.E.2d 510 (Ill.1979); Southwestern

Bell Telephone Co. v. State Corporation Commission of Kansas, 386 P.2d 515 (Kan.1963).

B. RATE BASE

Calculation of rate base is a critical step in establishing maximum rates, since the product of rate base multiplied by allowed rate of return is the total sum of money the agency allows to investors in the firm. A firm's rate base is the value of its capital assets that are used to produce its regulated products and on which it is permitted an opportunity to earn a return. There are four fundamental issues to be resolved in determination of a firm's rate base: (1) method of valuation; (2) property included in rate base; (3) depreciation of property in rate base.

1. METHOD OF VALUATION

In the majority of jurisdictions, the method of valuing property in a firm's rate base is no longer determined by the "fair value" principles announced in Smyth v. Ames. In a few jurisdictions, the method of valuation is dictated by statute, while in most it is an issue to be resolved in the discretion of the regulatory agencies, subject only to the "end result" test announced in *Hope*.

Smyth v. Ames no longer controls the method of valuing rate base in most jurisdictions, but the factors of valuation it required agencies to consider in determining "fair value" provide a convenient starting point for discussion of the alternate ap-

proaches to valuing rate base that are available.
The four factors suggested in Smyth v. Ames are:
(1) the market value of the firm's stocks and bonds;
(2) the earning capacity of the property under particular prescribed rates; (3) the original cost of
construction less depreciation; and, (4) the present
cost of replacing the property.

The first two methods are easily dismissed because they are circular. Assuming that all the property owned by a firm is used to produce regulated
products, the market value of the firm's stocks and
bonds will be determined largely by the maximum
rates the firm is permitted to charge. Similarly, the
earning capacity of the firm's property at prescribed
rates is dependent in large measure upon the rates
that are prescribed. Thus it makes little sense to
use either of these methods to value rate base when
the resulting value is then used to determine the
maximum rates the firm can charge. These methods
of valuation arose in the late nineteenth and early
twentieth centuries because the accounting records
of many regulated firms were so poor that they
were considered unreliable, and potentially fraudulent sources of data on the cost or value of a firm's
assets. With modern accounting practices and agency supervision of the accounts of regulated firms,
this reason for adopting either of the first two
methods of valuing a firm's assets suggested in
Smyth v. Ames has disappeared. No modern regulatory agency or reviewing court appears to use the
market value of a firm's stocks and bonds or the
earning capacity of its property under prescribed

rates as major factors in determining the value of the firm's rate base.

For most legislatures, agencies and reviewing courts, the choice of method for valuing the rate base is between original cost, reproduction cost, or some combination of the two, referred to as "fair value." Thirty-eight states rely solely upon original cost as the basis for valuing a firm's rate base. Union Electric Co. v. Illinois Commerce Commission, supra. The remainder use the "fair value" method in which a balance is struck between original cost and reproduction cost. Most federal agencies use original cost only, but the Interstate Commerce Commission traditionally used reproduction cost to value the rate base of oil pipelines until that function was transferred to the Federal Energy Regulatory Commission in 1978. See Kumar, *How Fair Is Fair Valuation of Rate Base*? 104 Pub.Util. Fort. 27 (July 19, 1979). In addition, the FCC's rules to implement the Telecommunications Act of 1996 use a version of reproduction cost . See section 15 C2.

There are several dimensions to the original cost/reproduction cost/fair value debate. Initially, it is not always clear who benefits from each method of valuation. In recent decades, most regulated firms have argued in support of reproduction cost or fair value because persistent inflation makes these methods of valuation advantageous to regulated firms unless major breakthroughs in technology reduce the cost of reproducing the functional equivalent of existing assets to an extent that offsets the effects of inflation. During some prior periods, however, regulated firms preferred the original cost method, and representatives of consumer interests argued for reproduction cost or fair value because: (1) construction costs declined since the time of initial construction, and/or (2) the original cost figures made available by the firm were unreliable. Indeed, the fair value method announced in Smyth v. Ames was supported in that case by consumer interests who wanted to take advantage of the depressed economic conditions of the 1890's to lower the rate base of a railroad whose original cost rate base was believed to be overstated. During the 1990s, cost reductions produced by technological innovation have once again induced regulated firms to support the original cost method of valuation. See section 15C2.

Originally, reproduction cost or fair value was thought to have an advantage over original cost because of relative ease of obtaining reliable measures of value. Accounting records of original cost were unreliable; inventory and appraisal of a firm's assets at current value or reproduction cost was more reliable. With the dramatic improvement in reliability of the accounts of regulated firms, however, original cost now has clear advantages in terms of certainty and ease of valuation. Application of the reproduction cost method requires inventory and appraisal of individual assets, application of construction cost indices to original cost data, or an estimate of the cost of the assets required to produce a comparable output using modern technology. All three valuation techniques are expensive, subjective, and produce widely varying results.

Notwithstanding the popularity of the original cost method and its advantages of greater certainty and ease of application, many economists continue to support the reproduction cost method. Myers, Kolbe & Tye, *Inflation and Rate of Return Regulation,* 2 Res. in Transp. Econ. 83 (1985); Navarro, Petersen & Stauffer, *A Critical Comparison of Utility–Type Ratemaking Methodologies in Oil Pipeline Regulation,* 12 Bell J. Econ. 392 (1981).

The depreciated original cost method of valuing utility assets creates enormous temporal bias in utility rates because it ignores the reality that the nominal value of an asset increases at the rate of inflation, all other things equal. Through use of the original cost method, an asset is valued at more than twice its economic value at the beginning of its life and less than half its economic value twenty years later. As a result, a regulated firm with relatively new assets charges artificially high rates, while a firm with relatively old assets charges artificially low rates. This temporal bias gives rise to many distortions and inefficiencies, including: an incentive to underuse an asset at the beginning of its life and a corresponding incentive to overuse an asset toward the end of its useful life; large intertemporal wealth transfers among consumers; distorted incentives to invest in capital assets; an incentive to use old facilities rather than more efficient new facilities; incurrence of wholesale costs so far at variance from economic costs that it is almost impossible to base a utility's retail rates on its marginal costs; and, distorted competition between or among regulated firms.

As agencies have developed increased interest in establishing utility rates based on marginal cost and in creating conditions in which competition can evolve in many sectors of regulated markets, they have frequently found it necessary to depart from the traditional original cost method of valuing the capital assets of regulated firms. For instance, FERC uses trended original cost to value oil pipelines. This valuation method reduces temporal distortion of rates by adding the inflation component of the nominal rate of return on an asset to the value of the asset each year. As a result, the value of the assets of each pipeline used for ratemaking purposes tends to correspond more closely with changes in the economic value of those assets. That, in turn, creates conditions in which a regulated oil pipeline can engage in robust competition with other pipelines and with barges and railroads. Alternatively, an agency can eliminate temporal bias in the traditional ratemaking formula by allowing the market to value the capital assets used to create a regulated product. This is now being accomplished in some industries through implementation of competitive contracting, described in section 15C.

2. PROPERTIES INCLUDED
IN RATE BASE

Independent of the method used to value a firm's rate base, controversy often arises concerning the assets that should be included in rate base. Inclusion or exclusion of a major asset from a firm's rate base can affect significantly the total sum of money allowed the firm to compensate its investors. Three aspects of this controversy—(1) the treatment of assets that are under construction but not yet in use when the firm's rates are determined (2) treatment of investments in cancelled plants, and (3) treatment of excess capacity—are so important and controversial today that they are discussed separately in the next subsections. We will discuss the other common topics of debate in this section.

Not every asset owned by a regulated firm is included in its rate base. Traditionally, there are two tests for including an asset in the rate base. Is the asset "used and useful" to the firm in making available the regulated product? Was the firm's decision to invest in the asset "prudent?" Each test has several applications, and sometimes the two overlap.

Any asset that is not used to make available a regulated product is excluded from the firm's rate base, since the firm is expected to earn a return on the value of these assets through its sales of unregulated products. Many firms make available numerous products, some regulated and some not regulated. Only those assets that are used to make available a regulated product are included in the firm's rate base. This principle has two important corollaries. First, if a single asset is used to make available both a regulated product and an unregulated product, a portion of the asset is included in rate base and a portion is not. For instance, in order to transport natural gas to market, it is usually necessary to extract liquid hydrocarbons from the gas stream. Since the liquids can be sold separately at unregulated prices, a portion of the value of the extraction plant should be included in a gas pipeline's rate base and a portion should be excluded. It is very difficult, however, to determine how much of the total value of such a jointly used asset should be allocated to the firm's rate base. Second, if an asset is used to make available products regulated by two different jurisdictions, e.g., a telephone exchange that processes both intrastate calls subject to state agency rate control and interstate calls subject to rate control by the Federal Communications Commission, the value of that asset is apportioned between the two jurisdictions for purposes of determining the firm's rate base in each jurisdiction. This apportionment typically is done independently by each agency, thereby creating the potential for double counting or the exclusion of a portion of the asset's value from the firm's rate base in both jurisdictions.

Assets that are no longer used and useful in providing a regulated product also can be excluded from a firm's rate base. It is not uncommon for an asset to lose its value in providing a regulated product over time as a result of obsolescence, a serious mechanical malfunction, or some combination of the two. When this happens before the asset has been fully depreciated, so that a portion of its value remains in the firm's rate base, the regulatory agency is likely to exclude the asset from rate base entirely as no longer used and useful. In such circumstances, however, the agency may allow the firm to include in its operating expenses the value of the asset that was previously in the rate base, since the fact that the useful life of the asset terminated before it was fully depreciated suggests that the firm and/or the agency overestimated the original useful life of the asset. In deciding whether to allow the firm to expense the undepreciated value of the asset, the agency has a choice of undesirable options. Having erred (in retrospect) in matching the cost of the asset with the revenue stream it generated, should the agency compensate for its prior error by allowing recovery of the undepreciated balance in a period when the asset is no longer productive, or should it ignore its past error and force the firm to suffer the consequences of underrecovery of capital costs? The first response seems more equitable, but the second may yield a more efficient allocation of resources.

An asset is included in rate base only if the firm's decision to invest in that asset was "prudent." An investment can be excluded in whole or in part from rate base on grounds that the firm was imprudent in making or protecting the investment in the asset.

The investment may be excluded completely if the decision to make the investment was imprudent or if the asset was managed in an imprudent way that caused it to lose its value. Alternatively, the investment may be excluded in part if the firm was imprudent in the magnitude of the investment. The first—complete exclusion—usually occurs only when the asset fails to function or to be of any value in providing a regulated product. Partial exclusion of an asset on grounds of prudence usually occurs in one of three situations—when the firm imprudently experiences cost overruns in constructing an asset, when the firm pays too much to purchase an asset, or when the firm imprudently invests in an asset with a capacity greater than necessary to provide the regulated product in sufficient quantity.

It is difficult to apply the prudent investment test in practice. Agencies and reviewing courts agree that the test is to be applied based upon the knowledge the firm had, or should have had, at the time it made the relevant decisions. Yet, agencies and reviewing courts almost invariably apply the test only after the investment has proven imprudent in retrospect—e.g., the asset has failed to perform, significant cost overruns have occurred, or significant excess capacity has arisen. In these circumstances, there is a temptation to consider the prudence of the firm's actions in light of the subsequent events.

Because of the prudent investment test, many regulated firms are ambivalent about regulatory provisions that require firms to obtain advance approval to initiate a major capital project, such as an electric generating plant. In some respects, requirements for prior approval are seen as costly nuisances because they interfere with management decisions and often delay projects. It is usually easier, however, for a firm to defend against allegations that it made an imprudent investment decision if it can show that critical elements of its decision were presented to, and approved by, a regulatory agency.

Some assets fluctuate so greatly over time that they are included in the rate base as an estimate or allowance. A firm's "working capital" is usually included in its rate base in the form of an allowance. Working capital refers to the firm's investment in cash, inventories and prepaid items, offset by its unpaid liabilities. Working capital should be included in the firm's rate base because it consists of funds that could earn a rate of return if invested in some other venture. The amount of the firm's investment in these items varies greatly from time-to-time depending on the firm's billing and collection cycle, temporal pattern of demand for its products, etc. The allowance for working capital typically is determined partly on the basis of the firm's average historical experience and partly on the basis of the agency's judgment concerning the average amount of working capital the firm needs to maintain.

a. Construction Work in Progress (CWIP)

Historically, the used and useful test precluded a firm from including an asset in its rate base until the asset was actually in use and contributing to the process of making available a regulated product. See, e.g., State v. General Tel. Co., 189 S.E.2d 705 (N.C.1972). In recent years, however, several powerful forces have combined to convince many agencies to include at least a portion of construction work in progress (CWIP) in rate base.

If CWIP is not allowed in rate base, the firm cannot earn a current rate of return on its CWIP investment, but it is permitted to use an alternative method of recovering the cost of capital invested in CWIP during the period before a new plant is placed in service. The firm can accumulate in an allowance for funds used during construction (AFUDC) an amount each year that represents the annual cost of the capital in its CWIP account. When a plant is completed and placed in service, all costs of the plant, including the accumulated AFUDC attributable to the plant, are transferred to the firm's rate base. In that way, the firm is permitted to earn a return on its CWIP, but the receipt of that money is deferred until after the plant is in service.

In theory, use of AFUDC and inclusion of CWIP in rate base should produce the same result to the firm; that is, the discounted present value of the firm's future income should be identical under either approach to the treatment of property under construction. Annual increments to a firm's AFUDC are shown as non-cash earnings on the firm's income statements. The entire AFUDC account is shown as a non-cash asset and as part of retained earnings on the firm's balance sheet.

Regulated firms almost invariably prefer inclusion of CWIP in rate base to use of AFUDC. (1) Some agencies use a lower cost-of-capital to calculate AFUDC than the rate of return they allow on rate base. (2) Some agencies do not permit compounding of annual AFUDC. (3) Because of the uncertainties associated with AFUDC, investors place a lower value on earnings represented by increases in AFUDC than they do on cash earnings. The first two potential disadvantages of AFUDC to the firm are accounting problems that, unless corrected, cause the AFUDC approach to yield a loss of present value of future earnings to the firm. The third disadvantage of AFUDC to the firm is more fundamental.

For two reasons, potential investors in the firm do not consider AFUDC earnings and assets comparable to cash earnings and assets. First, investors recognize that conversion of current AFUDC into future cash earnings is contingent upon future action by a regulatory agency in granting the firm a large rate increase to reflect transfer of the capital investment in a plant from CWIP and AFUDC to rate base. Investors also recognize that this conversion is not a certainty. If the plant does not perform as expected, if it costs substantially more than expected, if the demand for the firm's product does not grow as expected, or if political conditions simply make the grant of a very large rate increase to the firm unpalatable to the agency, all or part of the rate increase requested by the firm to reflect the transfer of the plant from CWIP to rate base may be denied or deferred. The agency can achieve this result directly by disallowing all or part of the investment in the plant as imprudent or as not "used and useful", or it can achieve the same result indirectly and sub rosa by disallowing portions of the firm's requested rate increase on other grounds. Second, investors do not consider AFUDC equivalent to cash earnings and assets because the use of AFUDC in lieu of allowing CWIP in rate base increases a firm's needs for external sources of capital. This increases the risks of investing in the firm.

In any case, the effect of AFUDC treatment is to increase the firm's cost of capital. In addition, for reasons too elaborate to warrant discussion here, AFUDC treatment can increase a firm's net liability for property and income taxes. As a result, firms see inclusion of CWIP in rate base as beneficial to them and, ultimately, as beneficial to their customers through reduction of the present value of the aggregate future rates the customers must pay.

Consumer interests generally oppose inclusion of CWIP in rate base. Their reasons for opposition include: (1) a desire to minimize current prices of regulated products; (2) concern that it may be more difficult to exclude all or a portion of an imprudent or unnecessary investment from rate base after that investment has been placed in rate base during construction than to exclude it at the time the first decision is made to include or exclude the investment; (3) the desire to avoid discrimination against present customers and in favor of future customers. The first two reasons are self-explanatory; the third requires further elaboration.

If CWIP is included in rate base, a firm's present customers must pay the capital costs of investments that are not now providing them benefits. If the firm's customers change substantially over time, due to deaths, changes in location, or changes in patterns of use of products, the firm's present customers may never derive benefits from the firm's investments in CWIP; rather, the benefits will accrue to future customers of the firm. Thus, including CWIP in rate base forces present consumers to pay for assets that will benefit only future consumers. Many consumer groups perceive this effect of including CWIP in rate base as unfair and unduly discriminatory.

On the other hand, at least if a firm's customers remain relatively stable over time, they should obtain two advantages from inclusion of CWIP in rate base. First, the present value of their future costs is reduced because of the reduction in the firm's capital costs and tax payments. Second, customer budgeting is made easier, since the firm's rates will go up gradually as a new plant is constructed instead of in one large increment when a plant is completed and placed in service.

b. Canceled Plants and Excess Capacity

A regulated firm sometimes begins construction of a major capital asset based on its expectation that the asset will be required to serve its customers and will benefit those customers, only to discover at some point in the construction process that the asset is unnecessary. A regulatory agency then must confront the issue of whether and to what extent to allow the firm to recover its investment in the partially completed capital asset if the firm terminates construction before completion of the asset. Alternatively, if the firm completes construction, the agency must decide how to deal with the resulting excess capacity.

In the 1980's, the regulatory treatment of canceled plants and excess capacity became a critically important issue in the regulated sectors of the energy industry. In particular, electric utilities canceled over one hundred partially completed nuclear generating plants, involving total capital investment losses of tens of billions of dollars. In each case, the utility filed a rate increase request following the cancelation in which it sought an increase in its rates sufficient to recover its lost investment in the canceled plant and a return on that investment. Utilities also completed scores of plants that represented expensive excess capacity. In each case, the utility attempted to recover the full cost of the plant in its rates.

The canceled or unnecessary generating plants completed in the 1980's were attributable to utility investment decisions made in the 1970's, since the lead time to construct a major generating plant in the United States was ten to twelve years. In the early 1970's, utilities forecast continued increases in demand for electricity of approximately seven percent per year, indicating that they would need to be prepared to supply approximately twice as much electricity in ten to twelve years when they could expect to complete a new generating plant. Utilities also forecast that the price of oil and gas would continue to escalate rapidly and that electricity generated through the use of nuclear power plants would be much less expensive than electricity generated in conventional oil or gas burning plants.

The utility forecasts of the 1970's proved inaccurate in the 1980's. Demand for electricity increased by less than three percent annually. Oil and gas prices declined after several years of sharp increases. Nuclear power has become much more expensive—a typical new plant completed in 1985 cost between three and five billion dollars to construct. As a result of this sharp disparity between forecast conditions and actual conditions, the over one hundred nuclear plants that were under construction in the 1980's no longer offered the prospect of reducing utility rates, conserving scarce oil and gas, and meeting new demands for electricity. Instead, most of these plants seemed imprudent in retrospect. That is to say, utilities would not have decided to begin construction of the plants in the 1970's if they had known then what they knew in the 1980's. In some cases, the remaining cost of completing a partially completed plant was so great that a decision to cancel the plant rather than to complete it served the interests of the utility, its customers, and society. In other cases, the cost of completing the plant was so low that the utility completed it, even though the result was expensive excess generating capacity.

When a utility cancels a partially completed plant, it invariably files a rate increase request in which it seeks regulatory authority to recover the cost of the plant. The cost of a plant consists of both the direct costs the utility incurred in construction and the cost of the capital the utility committed to the plant during the period of construction (to the extent that the utility was not allowed to recover its cost of capital on a current basis through inclusion of construction work in progress in its rate base.) The utility typically seeks recovery of these costs through amortization of the investment in its rates over a several-year period and through inclusion in its rates of a return on the unamortized balance of its investment. Similarly, when a utility completes a plant that constitutes excess capacity, it invariably seeks a large rate increase to reflect the addition of the plant to its rate base.

Regulatory agencies across the country struggled with the issues raised by such rate increase requests, with widely varying results. Their efforts to resolve these cases in a satisfactory manner were greatly complicated by the fact that they frequently had to choose between granting a very large rate increase to reflect an investment that may never provide benefits to consumers, or denying a rate increase and exposing the utility to a serious risk of bankruptcy. Of course, bankruptcy is the most extreme potential result of a refusal to permit a utility to recover the cost of a canceled plant. In the more typical case, such a refusal makes it more difficult for the firm to attract capital and causes a substantial increase in the firm's cost of capital—because potential investors then view the firm as a more risky investment. See Kahn, Who Should Pay for Power Plant Duds? Wall Street Journal p. 24 (Aug. 15, 1985).

Regulatory agencies responded to utility requests to recover the cost of a canceled plant or a plant that constitutes excess capacity in four ways: (1) disallowance of the cost as imprudent; (2) disallowance of the cost on the basis that the plant is not "used and useful;" (3) allowance of full recovery of the investment in the plant over a several-year period, including a return on that investment; and, (4) in the case of canceled plants, allowance of recovery of the investment in the plant over a several-year period, but disallowance of any return on that investment. The first two resolutions impose all costs associated with potential plant cancellations on the utility. The third imposes all such costs on consumers. The fourth divides the costs between the utility and consumers. In many cases, agencies divided the cost between the utility and consumers in other ways, e.g., by disallowing part of the investment as imprudent or as not used and useful.

All regulatory agencies disallow recovery of investments in canceled plants and excess capacity to the extent that they find that those investments resulted from imprudent decisions. Such a finding can result in complete disallowance if the agency concludes that the original decision to construct the plant was imprudent, or partial disallowance if the agency concludes that the original decision to begin construction was prudent, but that the utility was imprudent in failing to cancel the plant at an earlier date or that the utility was imprudent in the magnitude of the costs it incurred to construct the plant.

Even if the original decision to build a canceled plant or a plant that constitutes excess capacity is not found to have been imprudent, some agencies disallow recovery of all or part of the investment in the plant under another doctrine. Traditionally, a utility's investment in a capital asset is not included in rate base until the investment is found to be "used and useful." A canceled plant obviously never meets that standard. Moreover, a plant that constitutes excess capacity arguably is not used and useful at the time it is completed. Many agencies disallowed utility investments in canceled plants and excess capacity by applying the used and useful doctrine.

Agency treatments of investments in canceled plants and excess capacity varied in complicated ways during the 1980's. For detailed treatments of this important chapter in the history of economic regulation, see Pierce, *Public Utility Regulatory Takings: Should the Judiciary Attempt to Police the Political Institutions?* 77 Georgetown L.J. 2031 (1989); Pierce, *The Regulatory Treatment of Mistakes in Retrospect: Canceled Plants and Excess Capacity,* 132 U.Penn.L.Rev. 497 (1984). By the end of the decade, agencies had disallowed scores of billions of dollars in utility investments, thereby precipitating the bankruptcy of several utilities and imposing significant financial hardship on most electric utilities.

In one sense, the massive disallowances of the 1980s can be viewed as the inevitable consequence of routine applications of traditional utility law doctrines to unusual patterns of fact. The Court recognized the prudent investment doctrine as early as 1935. See West Ohio Gas Co. v. Public Utilities Commission of Ohio, 294 U.S. 63 (1935). It recognized the used and useful doctrine as early as 1938. See Denver Union Stock Yard Co. v. United States, 304 U.S. 470 (1938). Moreover, both doctrines were foreshadowed in passages in the Court's landmark opinion in Smyth v. Ames, 169 U.S. 466 (1898).

As viewed by utilities and prospective investors in regulated generating plants, however, the disallowances were unprecedented and represented unfair retroactive changes in the rules of the game. While the prudence doctrine long antedated the disallowances of the 1980's, it was used sparingly and to disallow only relatively modest expenses and investments prior to the 1980's. The disallowances of the 1980's accounted for more than 99 per cent of all disallowances in the history of utility regulation. Many utilities, prospective investors, and analysts believe that the unprecedented imprudence disallowances of the 1980's were a politically opportunistic reaction to consumer antipathy to high electricity rates. Similarly, while the used and useful doctrine existed for at least half a century before the 1980's, it had not been previously applied in the contexts to which it was then applied or with anything like the massive financial impact of the disallowances of the 1980's.

In some cases, agencies explicitly changed the rules applicable to rate recovery of investments during the 1980s after the investments were made. The only disallowance dispute resolved by the Supreme Court involved such a change of rules. A utility invested $35 million in the preliminary phases of construction of several generating plants. It then canceled the plants on the basis of its conclusion that they were no longer necessary or desirable because of reduced demand for electricity and changes in the relative cost of electricity generated through use of different fuels and technologies. The utility then sought a rate increase to allow it to recover its investment. The Pennsylvania PUC found that the utility had acted prudently in all respects and indicated its intent to grant the utility's rate increase. The Pennsylvania legislature then enacted a statute that prohibited inclusion of investments in canceled plants in utility rates. When the PUC interpreted the statute in a way that allowed the agency to grant the requested rate increase, the Pennsylvania Supreme Court reversed, holding that the statute prohibited the agency from authorizing the rate increase. The utility then argued that the actions of the Pennsylvania legislature, PUC, and Supreme Court constituted a taking of its property without just compensation. The U.S.

Supreme Court unanimously upheld the Pennsylvania Supreme Court. Duquesne Light Co. v. Barasch, 488 U.S. 299 (1989). The Court reaffirmed its holding in *Hope* that the methodology used to establish rates is not important to resolution of the takings issue as long as the "end result" is constitutionally permissible. It concluded that the end result in *Barasch* was constitutionally permissible because the $35 million in disallowed investment was "slight" in relation to the total value of the utility's rate base; even after the disallowance, the utility's authorized return on investment was within constitutionally permissible bounds. The Court suggested in dicta that a change in the rules applicable to rate recovery of utility investments made after a utility has already made an investment might be unconstitutional if the change in rules had a more substantial adverse effect on the utility's earnings. It is hard to attach much significance to this dicta, however, since the Court denied certiorari in cases in which state agencies disallowed investments many times larger than the investment disallowed in *Barasch*.

The massive disallowances of the 1980's, combined with the Court's refusal to reinvigorate the takings clause in *Barasch,* has created an environment in which most utilities are extremely reluctant to invest in utility-owned generating plants. They consider the regulatory risks of such investments intolerably high. See Kolbe & Tye, *The Fair Allowed Rate of Return with Regulatory Risk,* 15 Res. in L. & Econ. 129 (1992). Most utilities now prefer to purchase power from independent generating companies. This change in attitude provided a major impetus leading to the adoption of competitive contracting for wholesale power supplies, discussed in section 15C.

3.   DEPRECIATION

A firm's rate base is reduced through deduction of depreciation to reflect the declining value of many assets over time. Ordinarily, the annual deduction from rate base to reflect depreciation is accompanied by an equal addition to the firm's annual operating expenses. See Lindheimer v. Illinois Bell Telephone Co., 292 U.S. 151 (1934). Thus, depreciation both reduces a firm's revenue requirements by reducing $B(r)$ and increases a firm's revenue requirements by increasing O, in the formula: $R = O + B(r)$.

Depreciation serves two functions. It allocates to specific time periods the costs of capital assets that decline in value over time, thereby charging for constructive consumption of long-lived assets during the periods in which the assets are consumed. It allows the firm to recover in its rates the portion of the cost of such capital assets that represents the consumption of the assets during that period. If the straight line method of depreciation is used, the amount of annual depreciation appropriate for a capital asset is calculated by estimating the asset's useful life, subtracting from its original capital cost its estimated salvage value at the end of its useful life, and dividing the resulting net depreciable cost by the asset's useful life. Estimating the useful life of a capital asset is a difficult, judgmental process. It encompasses assessments of physical deterioration as well as technological, legal, and economic obsolescence.

Often, firms have the option of substituting some form of accelerated depreciation for straight line depreciation. There are several forms of accelerated depreciation, all of which have the effect of permitting a higher rate of depreciation in the early years of an asset's useful life and a lower rate of depreciation in the later years. Accelerated depreciation has its origins in the tax laws as a device for encouraging greater investment in capital assets by using depreciation to permit deferral or reduction of a firm's tax liability. The tax savings or deferral permitted regulated firms through use of accelerated depreciation has generated great controversy in rate proceedings. The debate concerning proper rate treatment of tax savings attributable to accelerated depreciation is discussed in section 5 D2.

The description of depreciation so far has focused on the approach to depreciation generally taken by the majority of agencies and courts that use original cost as the method of valuing a firm's rate base. There is an alternative approach to depreciation advocated by some economists and accepted by a few agencies and reviewing courts. This approach proceeds from the premises that: (1) depreciation should reflect the economic costs, as distinguished from the accounting costs, of using a capital asset over time, (2) depreciation should allow a firm to accumulate sufficient cash to invest in replacement assets and, (3) prices to consumers should reflect the current value of the assets consumed to make a product available. Since dollars lose value over time in periods of inflation, the advocates of this approach argue that reproduction cost should be used not only as the benchmark for valuing a firm's rate base, but also as the method of calculating depreciation of capital assets. Under this approach, the aggregate depreciation of an asset typically exceeds its original cost. Opponents of the approach argue that it gives the firm's investors a windfall.

The legal history and the debate surrounding the reproduction cost basis for determining depreciation is almost precisely analogous to the legal history and policy debate concerning the use of reproduction cost or "fair value" as methods of valuing rate base. In 1930, the Supreme Court held that the annual depreciation included in a firm's rates must be sufficient to permit the firm to restore worn out plant in order to maintain the firm's plant at its existing level of efficiency. This holding required agencies to use reproduction cost as the basis for depreciating a firm's assets as well as the basis for valuing the firm's assets in rate base. United Railways & Electric Co. v. West, 280 U.S. 234 (1930). When it announced the "end result" test for reviewing agency maximum rate determinations in *Hope*, however, the Court abandoned this constitutionally-based standard for calculating depreciation. Since *Hope*, most agencies and reviewing courts have chosen the original cost method of calculating depreciation. In recent years, however, some agencies have embraced methods of calculating depreciation that increase the convergence between economic cost and accounting cost. This roughly parallels the trend toward new methods of valuing rate base discussed in section 5B1.

C. FAIR RATE OF RETURN

With the increasing acceptance of the static, original cost method of valuing rate base and calculating depreciation, most of the change in the ratemaking formula to reflect inflation has taken the form of increases in allowed rate of return, since a change in rate of return has exactly the same effect as a change in rate base. Rate of return typically is an item of major dispute in the modern rate case. In determining rate of return, an agency must consider four primary concerns: (1) fairness to investors; (2) fairness to consumers; (3) the firm's need to attract capital; and (4) administrative simplicity.

The original constitutional test for determining a rate of return that is not confiscatory was announced in *Bluefield*:

A public utility is entitled to such rates as will permit it to earn a return on the value of the property which it employs for the convenience of the public equal to that generally being made at the same time and in the same general part of the country on investments in other business undertakings which are attended by corresponding risks and uncertainties; but it has no constitutional right to profits such as are realized or anticipated in highly profitable enterprises or speculative ventures. The return should be reasonably sufficient to assure confidence in the financial soundness of the utility and should be adequate, under efficient and economical management, to maintain and support its credit and enable it to raise the money necessary for the proper discharge of its public duties.

That test was continued as a statutory standard for determining the reasonableness of rates, with constitutional overtones, in *Hope*. In announcing the "end result" test in *Hope*, the Court held that rates, no matter how determined, need only "enable the company to operate successfully, to maintain its financial integrity, to attract capital, and to compensate its investors for the risks assumed.... "

In the "end result" test, rates are calculated using a functional approach; that is, they are adequate if they permit the firm to attract sufficient capital. Since regulated firms must compete for investment capital with other enterprises and investment opportunities, this functional approach to ratemaking continues to lead agencies and reviewing courts back to the original test for rate of return announced in *Bluefield*: the rate of return must be "equal to that generally being made ... on investments in other business undertakings which are attended by corresponding risks and uncertainties." Moreover, consumers have a right to insist that the rate of return be no more than that earned in enterprises of comparable risk. Indeed, if the rate of return allowed exceeds the firm's actual cost of capital, consumers are doubly hurt. They are hurt first by providing a windfall to those who hold equity interests in the firm when the excessive rate is permitted, but they are also harmed more indirectly by the excessive rate. Allowing a rate of return on investment higher than a regulated firm's cost of capital gives the firm an incentive to overinvest in capital assets in order to maximize its actual return on investment. See Averch & Johnson, *Behavior of the Firm Under Regulatory Constraint*, 52 Am.Econ.Rev. 1052 (1962).

There is close to unanimous acceptance of the principle of comparable return for comparable risks, and little agreement on how it can be applied in any case. There are three possible starting points for application of the comparable risk principle. The firm's allowed rate of return can be calculated based on: (1) the rate of return on low risk passive investments like U. S. Treasury Bills; (2) the rate of return earned by other regulated firms with comparable risks; or, (3) the rate of return earned by unregulated firms with comparable risks. All three benchmarks are problematic.

The risks confronted by a regulated firm are not comparable to the risks associated with a passive investment like a Treasury Bill. Regulated firms must take many risks, including: risks created by competition from substitute products (electricity competes with oil and gas, for instance); risks of technological obsolescence or major changes in the taste of the public (consider, for instance, the regulated trolley car companies that went bankrupt in the 1930's and 1940's); and regulatory risks (will the firm's next rate increase be granted?). Treasury Bills present no analogous risks. Hence, some premium must be added to the rate of return on low risk passive investments to make the return of a regulated firm comparable to the return on such competing investments, given the different risks associated with the investments. The question that remains unanswered after decades is how much of a premium must be added to the return on the passive low risk investment to meet the comparability test.

Regulated firms confronting risks comparable to those faced by the firm whose rate of return is at issue are often easy to identify. For instance, if an agency is trying to determine the rate of return appropriate for a medium-sized electric utility serving a growing metropolitan area, it often can identify a dozen or more similar firms. This application of the comparability test is circular, however. The rates of return earned by comparable regulated firms are a function of the decisions of other regulatory agencies. All agency determinations of rate of return cannot be based solely on the decisions of other agencies consistent with the functional goal of permitting regulated firms to attract capital in competition with all other investments. At least some agencies must break the circle and base their rate of return decisions on market-determined rates of return.

Almost by definition, no unregulated firm exists with risks comparable to those of a regulated firm. Society decides to regulate particular firms because they differ in significant respects from firms that are left free of regulation. Typically, a firm subject to maximum rate regulation was placed in that status because it was believed to have a high degree of monopoly power. Unregulated firms generally can be expected to confront greater risks resulting from competition than regulated firms, although regulatory risks unique to regulated firms may offset to some extent the greater competitive risks confronted by unregulated firms. Hence, if the rates of return earned by unregulated firms are used as the starting point for determining the rate of return to be allowed a regulated firm, the comparable risk test suggests the need for an adjustment to the rates of return earned by unregulated firms to reflect the differing risks to which the firms are exposed. Here the question that remains unanswered is how much of an adjustment is required to meet the comparability test. In some cases, it is difficult even to determine the direction of the adjustment, since some regulated firms confront greater risks than some unregulated firms.

Most agencies use all three of the yardsticks described above to determine the rate of return to allow a regulated firm, with upward adjustments from lower risk passive investments and, generally, downward adjustments from higher risk unregulated firms. Typically, the adjustments are based upon subjective exercise of judgment in an effort to satisfy the comparable risk test. This process is further complicated by the recognition that the risks and rates of return relevant to determining the appropriate rate of return to allow a regulated firm in the future are the *future* risks and rates of return on comparable investments. Yet, the regulatory agency has access only to historical risk and rate of return data. It must attempt to project future changes in the risk/rate of return relationship to fulfill the functional test of *Hope*.

In recent years, economists have devised sophisticated mathematical formulae for applying the comparable risk test to determine a regulated firm's allowed rate of return. These formulae typically are based on two economic models—the *capital asset pricing* model and the *discounted cash flow* model. These sophisticated tools for applying the comparable earnings for comparable risks approach attempt to measure the way in which investors perceive the risks and returns available from investment in a regulated firm relative to their perceptions of the risks and returns available from alternative investments. The discounted cash flow model is used to estimate a regulated firm's actual cost of capital— the return on investment required to entice investors into buying the firm's common stock. In simplified form, the firm's cost of capital or required rate of return on equity is calculated through the formula $R = \frac{D}{P} + g$, where D is the current dividend expected on the stock, P is the price of the stock at present, and g is the rate at which investors expect the firm's earnings and dividends to increase over time. The *g* term is particularly troublesome because it is difficult to determine investor expectations of changes in future earnings and dividends. If the *g* term can be estimated with tolerable accuracy, the formula can be useful, since the present price of the firm's stock, represented as *P* in the formula, is based on the investor's opportunity cost of equivalent risk investments. For a more detailed description of the discounted cash flow model, see Myers, *The Application of Finance Theory to Public Utility Rate Cases*, 3 Bell J.Econ. & Mgmt.Sci. 58, 65–66 (1972).

The capital asset pricing model is used to estimate a "beta" term that represents the return on risk required to convince investors to purchase the common stock of a regulated firm. The "beta" term is determined by comparing the historical returns on investment earned by comparable regulated firms with the return on investment earned over the same historical period by a hypothetical individual who invested in a diversified portfolio of securities. For a more detailed description of the capital asset pricing model, see Pettway, *On the Use of Beta in Regulatory Proceedings: An Empirical Examination*, 9 Bell J.Econ. & Mgmt.Sci. 239 (1978).

Most regulatory agencies continue to rely primarily upon subjective judgmental techniques to apply the comparable risk test, but the new mathematical formulae seem to be gaining increased acceptance. See Pettway, supra. It remains to be seen whether these formulae introduce greater precision to the process of determining rate of return or merely create the illusion of greater precision. Accurate measurement of the relevant risk variable is extremely difficult.

A firm is entitled to earn a rate of return "adequate, under efficient and economical management, to maintain and support its credit ...", Bluefield Water Works & Improvement Co. v. Public Service Commission, supra. The phrase "under efficient and economical management" is an important qualification. If an agency finds that a firm is not being managed efficiently and economically, it can lower the firm's allowed rate of return below the level otherwise required to meet the comparable risk test. See Market Street Railway v. Railroad Commission, 324 U.S. 548 (1945); D.C. Transit System, Inc. v. Washington Metropolitan Area Transit Commission, 466 F.2d 394 (D.C.Cir.1972). There are two significant problems, however, with lowering a firm's allowed rate of return based on poor quality service. First, a firm with an insufficient rate of return will have difficulty attracting the capital required to improve its performance even if its management becomes efficient. Second, agencies have difficulty determining the cause of a regulated firm's poor performance. If the actual cause of poor service is the firm's past inability to attract capital because of an inadequate rate of return allowed in the past, lowering its allowed rate of return in the future obviously is the wrong prescription for the malady. Thus, agencies at least should be cautious in reducing a firm's rate of return based on the firm's poor performance. The problem of creating incentives for good performance by regulated firms is considered more comprehensively in Chapter 8.

Up to this point, the discussion of rate of return has not distinguished among the various types of debt and equity instruments used by a firm to obtain capital. The vast majority of regulated firms obtain capital by selling bonds of various maturities and by selling preferred and common stock. When the firm obtains capital through many different types of debt and equity instruments, an agency can take one of two general approaches in determining the firm's allowed rate of return. It can determine an overall rate of return appropriate for the risks confronted by the firm, leaving to the firm entirely the mix of financing instruments it chooses to use and the return appropriate for each. Alternatively, the agency can treat as given the firm's cost of debt capital and preferred stock (in the form of interest and dividends, respectively), and determine the rate of return appropriate for the risks confronted by investors in the firm's common stock. Most agencies choose the second approach, since the firm's cost of debt and preferred stock is fixed once the financial instruments are issued, and since the common stockholders assume the bulk of the risks confronting the firm. Thus, the comparable earnings for comparable risks test typically is applied only to determine allowed rate of return to common stock based on the risks faced by the owners of common stock in the firm.

The risk confronted by the owners of common stock, and thus the return appropriate to that risk, is dependent to some extent upon the firm's capital structure. A highly leveraged capital structure, i.e., a high proportion of debt and preferred stock to common stock, creates greater risks for owners of common stock than a less leveraged capital structure. This is because interest on debt and dividends on preferred stock must be paid before owners of common stock can receive any residual earnings, and the holders of bonds and preferred stocks have a claim to the firm's assets in the event of dissolution superior to that of the firm's common stockholders. Thus, agencies often consider the firm's financial structure as one factor in determining the risk and corresponding rate of return appropriate for common stockholders.

Agencies sometimes find that a firm's capital structure is not optimum, in the sense that a different proportion of debt and equity would permit the firm to obtain capital at lower overall cost. In that situation, the agency can attribute to the firm for ratemaking purposes a capital structure different from the firm's actual structure. Agencies differ on whether, for ratemaking purposes, they should attribute to a firm a theoretically optimum financial structure or, instead, rely on the financial structure chosen by the firm's management. See Rose, *Cost of Capital in Public Utility Regulation*, 43 Va.L.Rev. 1079 (1957). The choice of policy here is determined implicitly by whether the agency believes the firm has sufficient natural incentives to adopt an optimal capital structure. In Chapter 8, we conclude that regulated firms have less incentive to be efficient than unregulated firms. Thus, agencies may be justified in reviewing the practices of regulated firms, including the capital structure they have chosen, to determine whether they are operating in the most efficient manner. On the other hand, it is difficult and expensive for agencies to engage in this type of second-guessing, and there is considerable potential for agency error. This is a problem without a clear solution.

D. OPERATING EXPENSES

1. GENERAL APPROACH

At an early date, the Supreme Court held that regulatory agencies have the power to review operating expenses incurred by a firm, and in proper circumstances to disallow those expenses in determining maximum rates. Chicago & Grand Trunk Railway v. Wellman, 143 U.S. 339 (1892). Originally, however, this power was subject to a constitutionally based limitation. In the process of holding that an agency's disallowance of a portion of a firm's advertising expenses violated the constitutional prohibition on confiscatory rates, the Court said:

> Good faith is presumed on the part of the managers of a business.... In the absence of a showing of inefficiency or improvidence, a court will not substitute its judgment for theirs as to the measure of a prudent outlay. West Ohio Gas Co. v. Public Utilities Commission of Ohio, 294 U.S. 63 (1935).

This constitutional limit on disallowance of operating expenses did not apply to past expenses the utility failed to recover in rates applicable to prior periods. Agencies were free to decline to allow future rate increases to cover prior period deficits. Galveston Electric Co. v. Galveston, 258 U.S. 388 (1922). The Court reasoned that a firm's failure to recover its costs on a current basis, whatever the cause of the failure, might justify allowing the firm a high rate of return to compensate it for the high risks suggested by its initial inability to recover its costs, but did not compel a regulatory agency to compensate the firm for its past losses through a grant of higher future rates. After *Hope*, the constitutional limits on agency power to disallow expenses in ratemaking are not clear, but again many of the principles applied originally as a matter of constitutional law continue to have vitality in modern agencies and reviewing courts both as interpretations of regulatory statutes and as guidelines for the exercise of agency discretion.

The general standard for determining whether to allow an operating expense remains basically as it was stated in Missouri ex rel. Southwestern Bell Telephone Co. v. Public Service Commission, 262 U.S. 276 (1923):

The Commission is not the financial manager of the corporation and it is not empowered to substitute its judgment for that of the directors of the corporation; nor can it ignore items charged by the utility as operating expenses unless there is an abuse of discretion in that regard by the corporate officers.

This general standard accords the management of a regulated firm considerable discretion to incur expenses and to have those expenses recognized in the ratemaking process; expenses incurred are to be allowed unless the agency or some other party can establish that they should not be allowed.

Agencies examine the expenses claimed by regulated firms, however, because of two general concerns. First, the firm may try to inflate its rates by claiming expenses that are unrelated to its regulated business and, hence, should be recovered by the firm in its revenues from unregulated sales. Second, regulation reduces a firm's natural incentive to be efficient to such an extent that the firm may relax its efforts to keep its expenses to a minimum. See generally Chapter 8.

The "abuse of discretion" basis for disallowing expenses alluded to in *Southwestern Bell* encompasses two subsidiary standards. First, an expense can be disallowed entirely if it was imprudently incurred in the sense that it does not benefit the firm's customers that purchase regulated products. Second, an expense can be disallowed in part if it is excessive in relation to the resulting benefit to the firm's customers or in relation to the cost of alternative means of providing that benefit. For instance, if an electric utility purchased fuel oil at $40 per barrel when it was available through other sources at $20, the agency would be justified in disallowing one-half of the firm's expenses of purchasing fuel oil unless the firm could explain adequately why it purchased the higher-priced oil. Partial disallowance of an expense as excessive should be based upon the circumstances and alternatives confronting the firm when it incurred the expense, but, as in the case of the imprudent investment test, there is an understandable temptation for agencies and reviewing courts to consider events after the expense was incurred that make the expense appear excessive in retrospect.

The effect of disallowance of an item of operating expense for ratemaking purposes is not to prohibit the firm from incurring the expense. Rather, the firm is not permitted to recover the expense in its rates to customers purchasing regulated products. Thus, the shareholders of the firm must absorb the disallowed expenses, with a resulting reduction in the actual rate of return earned by the shareholders. Of course, disallowance of an expense in a rate case has the effect of deterring the firm from incurring similar expenses in the future, as well as increasing the firm's cost of capital by increasing the risks of investing in the firm.

Occasionally, a regulatory agency does not stop at disallowing an expense, but goes a step further, prohibiting a firm from incurring an expense. See, e.g., New York Public Service Commission, *Statement of Policy on Advertising and Promotion Practices of Public Utilities* (1977), reproduced in R. Pierce, G. Allison and P. Martin, *Economic Regulation: Energy Transportation and Utilities* 136 (1980) (prohibiting electric utilities from engaging in certain advertising and promotional practices). But see Consolidated Edison Co. v. Public Service Commission of New York, 447 U.S. 530 (1980) (holding the New York PSC's policy unconstitutional as a violation of the first amendment).

2. SPECIFIC EXPENSES

Any item of expense is subject to potential disallowance based on an agency finding that it was excessive or did not benefit customers that purchase regulated products. In practice, however, several general categories of expenses create most of the controversy in rate cases. They are: advertising and promotional expenses, charitable contributions, executive salaries, rate case expenses, and tax savings attributable to accelerated depreciation.

The advertising and promotional expenses of regulated firms have been challenged in rate proceedings for decades. They seem to have come under increasing scrutiny in recent years, with a greater number of agencies disallowing at least a portion of advertising expenses than was the case historically. Since the arguments for and against allowance of advertising expenses vary depending on the nature and purpose of the advertising, it is useful to divide advertising into three categories initially: promotional, political, and informational.

Consumers often object to allowance of promotional advertising expenses in the rates of regulated firms on one or more of the following grounds.

First, since regulated firms typically have a legal monopoly, they do not need to engage in promotional advertising. Second, promotional advertising does not benefit the firm's customers. Third, promotional advertising may actually harm the firm's customers and the general public to the extent that it generates demand for inherently scarce products and/or creates a need to construct new facilities that are costly and that sometimes present significant health and safety risks. The third argument is particularly prevalent with respect to firms in the energy industry. Regulated firms respond with the following counterarguments. First, promotional advertising is necessary even for a firm with a legal monopoly because the products sold by the firm compete with other products, e.g., natural gas competes with oil and electricity. Second, customers of the firm benefit from promotional advertising because increasing sales permit the firm to take greater advantage of economies of scale. Third, the public is benefited by becoming aware that the products sold by the firm are superior to the products sold by other firms, even if the public should be encouraged to conserve all scarce products.

The factors relevant to allowance of expenses for political advertising are somewhat different. Political advertising refers to advertising that advocates a position on a controversial issue affecting the firm, e.g., advertising extolling the virtues of nuclear power or decrying the latest air pollution regulations. Consumer groups often oppose allowance of expenses for political advertising on the basis that the customers of a regulated firm should not be compelled to contribute involuntarily to the advancement of political views with which they may disagree. Cf. Abood v. Detroit Bd. of Education, 431 U.S. 209 (1977) (a union of public employees is prohibited by the first amendment from compelling its members to pay dues used to support political purposes). Allowance of expenses of political advertising in a firm's rates has this effect. The firms counter that the positions they take on political issues are in both their interests and the interests of their customers. Moreover, they contend that it is unfair to deter them from advocating positions on political issues by disallowing their expenses of political advertising. Cf. Consolidated Edison Co. v. Public Service Commission of New York, 447 U.S. 530 (1980) (holding that a New York PSC order prohibiting electric utilities from promoting political positions in advertising and bill enclosures violates the first amendment).

Informational advertising includes such things as explanations of how to use a product or how to conserve a product. Its allowance as an operating expense generates little controversy in rate cases. It is often difficult, however, to distinguish informational advertising from promotional or political advertising.

The recent decisions of agencies and reviewing courts do not resolve the advertising expense allowance issue in a consistent manner. Compare New England Telephone & Telegraph Co. v. Department of Public Utilities, 275 N.E.2d 493 (Mass.1971) (reversing the agency's disallowance of advertising expenses) with City of Los Angeles v. Public Utilities Commission, 497 P.2d 785 (Cal.1972) (affirming the agency's disallowance of advertising expenses).

Allowance of charitable contributions in a firm's operating expenses has also sparked considerable litigation in recent years, with conflicting results. Compare Alabama Power Co. v. Alabama Public Service Commission, 359 So.2d 776 (Ala.1978) (affirming the agency's disallowance of charitable contributions), with New England Telephone & Telegraph Co. v. Department of Public Utilities, 275 N.E.2d 493 (Mass.1971) (reversing the agency's disallowance of charitable contributions). Firms argue that charitable contributions should be allowed because: (1) firms have an obligation as good citizens to support charity; and (2) charitable contributions are essential to maintain good relations in the communities in which the firms operate. Consumer groups argue that the customers of a regulated firm should not be compelled to support charities of the firm's choice.

The issue of executive salaries typically arises in response to allegations by consumer groups that the salaries paid the top executives of a regulated firm are excessive in relation to the duties of those executives. Agencies and reviewing courts sometimes respond to such allegations by disallowing a portion of executive salaries in operating expenses and sometimes refuse to do so, either because they believe that executive salaries are a matter uniquely within a firm's managerial discretion or because they find the salaries paid by the firm reasonable in the circumstances. An agency and/or a reviewing court is more likely to disallow a portion of executive salaries when a firm is closely held and its top management also holds a substantial portion of the equity in the firm. There may be a basis for concern in this situation that the firm is disguising some monopoly profits in inflated salaries to owner/managers. Compare Latourneau v. Citizens Utilities Co., 209 A.2d 307 (Vt.1965) (reversing the agency's partial disallowance of salary of firm president), with Aberdeen Telephone Co., CCH Util.L.Rep., 18, 690 (Idaho P.U.C.1960) (disallowing portions of salary of firm president where he was also owner of firm).

In 1939, the Supreme Court addressed the issue of whether expenses incurred by a regulated firm in attempting to obtain a rate increase could be disallowed without rendering the resulting rates unconstitutionally confiscatory. The Court held that reasonable costs incurred by a firm in a rate case must be allowed:

Even where the rates in effect are excessive, on a proceeding by a commission to determine reasonableness, we are of the view that the utility should be allowed its fair and proper expenses for presenting its side to the commission. We do not refer to expense of litigation in the courts. A different case would be here if the company's complaint had been unfounded or if the cost of the proceeding had been swollen by untenable objections. Driscoll v. Edison Light & Power Co., 307 U.S. 104 (1939).

After *Hope*, the standard announced in *Driscoll* is of doubtful validity as a principle of constitutional law, since the "end result" test announced in *Hope* probably put to a stop detailed constitutional review of rate decisions by federal courts.

Many agencies and reviewing courts, however, continue to use the Court's statement in *Driscoll* as a working guideline for determining whether, and to what extent, a firm's rate case expenses should be allowed. Some agencies disallow expenses incurred in rate cases if the expenses are found to be excessive or the firm's request for a rate increase is found to be frivolous. E.g., Carolina Water Co., 32 P.U.R.3d 462 (N.C.U.C.1960); Citizens Utilities Co. of California (Cal.P.U.C.1954). If rate case expenses are allowed, the firm often is required to amortize those expenses over a future period of years, rather than to recover the expenses completely in a single year, on the theory that the benefits to the firm resulting from presenting a rate case will continue for several years in the future. See, e.g., Pacific Power & Light Co., 34 P.U.R.3d 36 (Or.P.U.C. 1960); but see Consolidated Edison Co., 54 P.U.R.3d 43 (N.Y.P.S.C.1964) (allowing rate case expenses to be included completely in the firm's operating expenses for the year in which the expenses were incurred). The decision to expense or capitalize and amortize rate case expenses should depend on the agency's judgment concerning the frequency with which rate cases are likely to occur.

Depreciation was already discussed earlier in this chapter in connection with a firm's rate base. Since the depreciation deduction from rate base and the treatment of depreciation as an expense are considered by agencies as analogous issues, that discussion will not be repeated. Rate treatment of a firm's tax savings or deferrals resulting from the use of accelerated depreciation for tax purposes, however, raises a new and controversial issue.

When a firm uses straight line depreciation of assets for tax purposes, it deducts from its taxable income an equal annual amount of depreciation in each year of an asset's useful life. The tax laws allow a firm to substitute for straight line depreciation any of several methods of accelerated depreciation. Through use of accelerated depreciation, a firm can deduct more depreciation in the early years of the useful life of an asset and less during the later years. By allowing accelerated depreciation for tax purposes, Congress encourages greater investment in new capital assets, since acceleration of depreciation deductions from taxable income allows a firm to defer a portion of its income tax liability to later years. If the firm invests in new capital assets at an increasing rate, the tax deferral effect of accelerated depreciation begins to look like an actual tax savings.

When regulated firms first began to use accelerated depreciation for tax purposes, some regulatory agencies responded by requiring the firms to "flow through" the tax advantages of accelerated depreciation in their rates. Under flow through, only the actual taxes paid by a firm are included in the firm's operating expenses. Thus, the tax advantages of accelerated depreciation accrue to the firm's customers rather than to the firm. Other regulatory agencies allowed firms to "normalize" their annual tax liabilities in their operating expenses for ratemaking purposes. Under normalization, a firm's taxes are included in its operating expenses as if the firm were using straight line depreciation for tax purposes even though the firm actually uses accelerated depreciation. As a result, the firm, rather than its customers, obtains the tax advantages of accelerated depreciation when normalization is permitted.

In 1969, when Congress passed a major tax reform act, it indicated concern about the effects of the tax flow through approach required by many agencies. First, flow through seems to defeat the purpose of allowing accelerated depreciation for tax purposes. Since flow through eliminates the advantages of accelerated depreciation to the firm, the firm does not have the incentive to invest in new capital assets that Congress intended to result from accelerated depreciation. Second, and a related point, is that regulated firms will not have any incentive to use accelerated depreciation because flow through eliminates its advantages to the firm. Third, accelerated depreciation with flow through of tax advantages was costing the U.S. Treasury large sums of money in lost tax revenues. Of course, accelerated depreciation always yields a deferral of income tax revenues, but, when combined with flow through in ratemaking, use of accelerated depreciation by regulated firms produces a second order loss of income tax revenues. Flow through of tax savings or deferrals in ratemaking reduces the firm's revenue, hence reducing still further its income tax liability.

Congress responded to these problems in the Tax Reform Act of 1969 by adding § 167(*o*) to the Internal Revenue Code. The new provision is complicated, with separate subsections providing different treatment for assets acquired before and after 1969 and different treatment for regulated firms depending on the depreciation options they used for tax purposes before 1969. A crucial subsection specifies, however, that a regulated firm cannot use accelerated depreciation for tax purposes unless it uses a "normalization method of accounting" for the tax saving or deferrals resulting from accelerated depreciation. Internal Revenue Code, § 167(*l*)(3)(G). The Internal Revenue Service, some regulatory agencies, and some reviewing courts have taken the position that regulatory agencies cannot require any flow through of the tax advantages of accelerated depreciation on post–1969 assets without rendering the firm ineligible for accelerated depreciation under the tax laws. Other regulatory agencies and reviewing courts, however, have continued to require flow through in some form because of their belief that normalization harms consumers unfairly by forcing them to pay rates that reflect tax expenses far greater than those actually incurred by regulated firms. Partial chronicles of this important and complicated controversy are contained in Dahl, *The California Remand Case: Controversy Over Normalization,* 104 Pub.Util.Fort. 13 (Dec. 20, 1979); New

England Telephone & Telegraph Co. v. Public Utilities Commission, 390 A.2d 8 (Me.1978); Los Angeles v. Public Utilities Commission, 542 P.2d 1371 (Cal. 1975).

3. PROJECTING FUTURE EXPENSES

Since utility rates typically are determined prospectively for use during a future period, a firm's future operating expenses logically should form the basis for calculating its revenue requirements and, ultimately, its rates. Most agencies, however, use historical operating expenses as at least the starting point in the ratemaking process because historical expenses can be determined with substantial certainty. Historical expenses are derived from the firm's accounts. Regulatory agencies require the accounts of most regulated firms to be maintained in a uniform manner consistent with the Uniform System of Accounts of either the Federal Energy Regulatory Commission or the National Association of Regulatory Utility Commissioners. See J. Suelflow, *Public Utility Accounting: Theory and Application* (1973).

Traditionally, a firm's actual operating costs for a specified historical period, typically a recent 12-month period denoted the "test period," less expenses that were disallowed as imprudently incurred or as not providing benefits to the firm's ratepayers, were used to calculate the firm's future revenue requirements. An expected future increase in operating expenses was included in revenue requirements only if it was known with certainty at the time the rate proceeding took place that it would be incurred. See, e.g., Central Maine Power Co. v. Public Utilities Commission, 136 A.2d 726 (Me.1957). Most agencies abandoned this traditional exclusive reliance on historical expenses, however, in response to the persistent high levels of inflation experienced in the 1970s. During periods of inflation, basing rates exclusively on a firm's historical operating expenses inevitably produces severe earnings attrition for the firm—because its future expenses will exceed the past expenses used to determine its rates, the firm earns a rate of return less than the allowed rate of return used to calculate its revenue requirements.

To avoid the earnings attrition caused by inflation, most agencies have developed one of several alternatives to total reliance on operating expenses in the historic test period. The alternatives most frequently used include: a projected future test period, a test period that is partially historic and partially future, and an historic test period with adjustments to reflect expected increases in operating expenses using a standard less stringent than the traditional "certainty" requirement. See Kamerschen & Paul, *Erosion and Attrition: A Public Utility's Dilemma*, 102 Pub.Util.Fort. 21 (Dec. 21, 1978). All of these means of accounting for inflation share the problem of the uncertain future. If future expenses are overestimated, the firm earns a rate of return greater than that allowed it in theory; if future expenses are underestimated, the firm suffers earnings attrition. Neither error can be easily remedied. Under the holding in *Galveston*, p. 145 supra, the agency need not make up for past earnings deficiencies in future rate cases, and most agencies are statutorily prohibited from changing a firm's rates retroactively. See, e.g., FPC v. Tennessee Gas Transmission Co., 371 U.S. 145 (1962). Moreover, even if an agency calculates the firm's revenue requirements and rates based upon expected future expenses, it rarely can project those expenses more than a year ahead. As a result, during periods of high inflation the firm must file for a new rate increase frequently—typically every year.

When a regulated firm has an operating cost that accounts for a high proportion of the firm's total costs, and that cost is subject to rapid escalation on an unpredictable schedule, the traditional methods of including operating costs in revenue requirements and rates are subjected to particular strain. Agencies often respond to this situation by allowing the firm to use some form of automatic rate adjustment clause. The fuel adjustment clauses frequently permitted electric utilities illustrate this situation and the typical regulatory response to it.

Fuel costs are a very high proportion of the costs of most electric utilities, and fuel costs increased at a rapid but unpredictable rate during the 1970s. If fuel costs are included in electric utility rates through use of the historic or projected future test period approach, the firm is likely to experience substantial earnings attrition and the regulatory agency must process frequent requests for rate increases. Both of these consequences can be avoided if the agency authorizes the firm to increase its rates automatically to reflect fuel cost increases incurred since the firm's rates were last determined by the agency. Of course, the automatic fuel cost adjustment clauses have had the opposite effect during much of the 1980s and 1990s as fuel costs declined.

Some consumer groups are critical of automatic adjustment clauses, however, on several grounds. First, they may provide the firm a windfall where expenses covered by the clause increase but other expenses decrease. Second, they reduce the firm's incentive to minimize costs included in the scope of the automatic adjustment clause. Third, they may encourage the firm to purchase more items covered by the clause and to reduce their purchases of functionally equivalent items not covered by the clause, even if the net effect of this change in pattern of purchases is to increase the firm's aggregate expenses and its rates. A few agencies have responded to consumer complaints about automatic adjustment clauses by eliminating the clauses entirely, but most agencies are attempting to modify the scope of the clauses or their method of implementation to reduce the problems identified by consumer groups. The modifications in use today include: allowance of only a percentage pass-through of costs covered by an adjustment clause; pass-through of costs based on a determination of what the utility should have paid, rather than what it actually paid; and systematic agency supervision or review of a firm's purchases of items included in the scope of an automatic adjustment clause. See generally, Kendrick, *Efficiency Incentives and Cost Factors in Public Utility Automatic Adjustment Clauses*, 6 Bell J.Econ. & Mgmt.Sci. 299 (1975).

Regulatory lag is both a major problem for regulated firms and a major source of incentive to be efficient. Since, under traditional ratemaking methodology, a firm is limited to a particular rate during the period from one rate increase to the next, it can increase its actual rate of return by minimizing its actual operating costs during the period of regulatory lag. Thus, regulatory lag provides one of the few sources of incentives for regulated firms to reduce their costs and enhance their efficiency.

E. TRANSACTIONS WITH AFFILIATES

Agencies exercise particularly close supervision over the inclusion of costs that are the result of purchases from the firm's affiliates. In this circumstance, agencies are concerned that the firm's transactions with affiliates may not be the product of arm's length bargaining and that the firm may be attempting to hide monopoly profits in excessive payments to affiliates. As a result, operating costs (and assets proposed for inclusion in rate base as well) that are attributable to transactions with affiliates are subjected to a special test of reasonableness before they are included in a firm's revenue requirements and rates.

Three tests have been used to police a regulated firm's transactions with its affiliates for ratemaking purposes. First, agencies compare the price at which the firm made purchases from its affiliates with the price at which it could have obtained comparable products or services from other sources. Second, agencies compare the price at which the affiliate sold the products or services to the regulated firm with the price at which the affiliate sells comparable products and services to non-affiliated firms. These are essentially tests to determine that the price paid the affiliate is market-determined. In many cases, the operating costs attributable to transactions with affiliates are allowed in the firm's revenue requirements if they pass these market tests. See, e.g., State v. General Tel. Co., 189 S.E.2d 705 (N.C.1972).

Sometimes, however, an agency disallows a portion of the costs of purchases from affiliates even if they meet the two market tests. If the affiliate does not sell in a competitive market, but instead exercises a degree of monopoly power, the agency may apply a third test to the price paid the affiliate. The third test limits the costs of purchases from affiliates allowed in the firm's revenue requirements to the affiliate's costs of providing the products or services, including a reasonable rate of return. See, e.g., Smith v. Illinois Bell Telephone Co., 282 U.S. 133 (1930). This test has the effect of indirectly subjecting the affiliate's sales to the firm to a form of rate regulation. When this third test is adopted, the agency encounters anew all the traditional problems of rate regulation as they apply to the affiliate. One of the most troublesome problems is determining the rate of return the affiliate should be allowed. Sometimes the agency limits the affiliate to the same rate of return allowed the regulated firm. See, e.g., Illinois Bell Telephone Co. v. Illinois Commerce Commission, 303 N.E.2d 364 (Ill.1973). In other cases, however, the agency recognizes that the affiliate confronts different risks than the regulated firm and, therefore, should be allowed a different rate of return commensurate with those risks. See, e.g., Application of Montana–Dakota Utilities Co., 278 N.W.2d 189 (S.D.1979).

F. AN OVERVIEW—THE ZONE OF REASONABLENESS

After describing the details of the process of determining a firm's revenue requirements, it is useful to place those details in the broader perspective of the basic test currently used by courts to review ratemaking decisions. The functional "end result" test announced in *Hope* was given further content in Permian Basin Area Rate Cases, 390 U.S. 747 (1968). There, the Court held that an agency's rate decision should be affirmed if it falls within a "zone of reasonableness." That zone is sufficiently broad to permit the agency to integrate cost factors with non-cost factors and policy considerations. American Public Gas Ass'n v. Federal Power Commission, 567 F.2d 1016 (D.C.Cir.1977). In *Permian Basin*, the Court summarized the role of the reviewing court:

It follows that the responsibilities of a reviewing court are essentially three. First, it must determine whether the Commission's order, viewed in light of the relevant facts and of the Commission's broad regulatory duties, abused or exceeded its authority. Second, the court must examine the manner in which the Commission has employed the methods of regulation which it has itself selected, and must decide whether each of the order's essential elements is supported by substantial evidence. Third, the court must determine whether the order may reasonably be expected to maintain financial integrity, attract necessary capital, and fairly compensate investors for the risks they have assumed, and yet provide appropriate protection to the relevant public interests, both existing and foreseeable. The court's responsibility is not to supplant the Commission's balance of these interests with one more nearly to its liking, but instead to assure itself that the Commission has given reasoned consideration to each of the pertinent factors.

Thus, within a wide area, agencies exercise substantial discretion to select the appropriate ratemaking methodology.

CHAPTER VI

RATES TO CUSTOMERS: PROBLEMS OF DISCRIMINATION AND CLASSIFICATION

A. INTRODUCTION

After an agency determines the aggregate revenue requirement a firm will be allowed an opportunity to earn, it must determine the rates the firm is authorized to charge in an effort to earn the allowed revenue. Typically, the firm proposes a specific set of rates to individual customers or to classes of customers with common characteristics, subject to review by the agency. In many cases, no party objects to the rate schedules proposed by the firm as long as they appear to be consistent with its allowed revenue requirements. If, however, any party objects to the proposed rate schedules, most agencies have a statutory duty to review the specific rates, not only to ensure that they are consistent with allowed revenue requirements, but also to determine that the relationship among the rates is appropriate.

The statutes under which most agencies regulate prohibit relationships between rates that are unduly discriminatory. Indeed, some major regulatory schemes were adopted for the primary purpose of eliminating undue discrimination in rates. See, e.g., Louisville & Nashville R. Co. v. United States, 282 U.S. 740 (1931). Under most regulatory schemes, a rate is unlawful if it discriminates unduly against any person, any class of customer, or any locality. These statutes also prohibit undue discrimination in the other terms and conditions under which a regulated firm provides service. See, e.g., North Carolina v. Federal Energy Regulatory Commission, 584 F.2d 1003 (D.C.Cir.1978) (holding unduly discriminatory an order allocating natural gas among geographical areas).

A rate is not unlawful merely because it differs from some other rate; only rate differentials that discriminate *unduly*, or for insufficient reasons, are unlawful. ICC v. Baltimore & Ohio R. R., 145 U.S. 263 (1892). A legal conclusion of undue discrimination can be based on a finding that one customer can purchase the same product as another customer at a different rate, unless there are distinctions between the two customers sufficient to justify the difference in rates. Rate differentials can be justified on many bases, but the personal identity of the customers is never sufficient alone to justify a difference in rates. Wight v. United States, 167 U.S. 512 (1897). Some agencies and courts also conclude that undue discrimination exists when there is a rate differential disproportionate to any difference in the costs of making a product available, unless the differential can be explained adequately on other grounds. See, e.g., Pittsburgh–Philadelphia No–Reservation Fare Investigation, 34 C.A.B. 508

(1961). Other agencies and courts, however, are not willing to consider cases of disproportionate relationships between costs and rates; they consider their responsibilities limited to review of situations in which different rates are charged for like products. See, e.g., City of Boscobel v. Wisconsin Power & Light Co., 52 P.U.R.3d 264 (Wis.P.S.C.1964).

B. REASONS FOR PROHIBITING UNDUE DISCRIMINATION

The traditional prohibition of unduly discriminatory rates is premised on the need to avoid five perceived evils—unfairness, burdens imposed on some consumers as a result of disproportionately low rates charged to other consumers, predatory pricing, "second best" problems of resource misallocation, and unjustified transfers of wealth from consumers to regulated firms. We will summarize each argument briefly after discussing the economic reasons a firm might choose to charge rates disproportionate to its costs of providing different products or serving different customers.

A firm rarely is neutral concerning the relationships among its rates even after an agency has determined the firm's allowed revenue requirements. There is only one combination of rates through which a firm can maximize its actual revenues. To understand this fundamental truism requires an introduction to the concept of price elasticity of demand.[1] The quantity demanded of any

1. See also the discussion of demand in Chapter 2.

product, or by any class of consumers, varies based on the price at which the product can be purchased. As price goes up, quantity demanded goes down, all other things being equal. The amount of change in the quantity of product demanded corresponding to changes in the price of the product varies from product to product and from customer to customer. The measure of change in quantity demanded relative to change in price for any product or customer class is referred to as the price elasticity of demand applicable to that product or class of customer. It is calculated by dividing the change in price into the resulting change in quantity demanded for each product, class of customer, and range of price change. Thus, price elasticity of demand of infinity refers to an absolutely elastic demand; any increase in a firm's price will eliminate all sales of that product or to that class of customer. Elasticity of zero refers to an absolutely inelastic demand; no change in a firm's price will change the quantity it sells of that product or to that class of customer. Price elasticities of demand of zero or infinity are very rare; most firms subject to maximum rate regulation confront elasticities of demand that vary between 0.1 (relatively inelastic) and 1.0 (relatively elastic).

The firm typically can maximize its revenues by charging rates that are higher, relative to its costs, for products that are subject to relatively inelastic demand than for products that are subject to relatively elastic demand. Similarly, the firm can maximize its revenues by charging for the same product rates that are higher, relative to its costs, to customers with relatively inelastic demand than to customers with relatively elastic demand. The firm loses fewer units of sale, and hence less revenue, by increasing the price charged for a product or to a class of customers that is subject to relatively inelastic demand than by increasing by a comparable amount the price charged for a product or to a class of customers subject to relatively elastic demand.

A simple example illustrates the significance of elasticity of demand. Suppose a firm sells two products, A and B. It is currently selling 100 units of each at $1.00 per unit. If it increases the price of A by $.10, it will sell 99 units; if it increases the price of B by $.10 it will sell 95 units. Assuming the cost of the two products is identical, and assuming a regulatory agency permits the firm to choose which product should be sold at a higher price, the firm will choose to increase the price of A (the product subject to relatively price inelastic demand) rather than B (the product subject to relatively price elastic demand). By increasing the price of A by $.10, the firm's revenues will increase by $8.90 (99 units times $1.10 per unit minus 100 units times $1.00 per unit). By increasing the price of B $.10, the firm will increase its revenues only by $4.50 (95 units times $1.10 per unit minus 100 units times $1.00 per unit).

Many allegations of undue discrimination arise in circumstances where the firm, in order to maximize its revenue, proposes rates applicable to different products or to different classes of customers that are disproportionate to the firm's costs of making products available to those customers. The firm proposes relatively high rates for products or customers subject to relatively inelastic demand and relatively low rates for products or customers subject to relatively elastic demand. The firm's attempt to maximize its revenue by charging different rates to different classes of customers can succeed only if two conditions exist—(1) price elasticity of demand varies between classes of customers, and (2) one customer cannot resell the product to another customer. Both market conditions exist for most regulated firms.

The prohibition against undue discrimination is based at least in part on the belief that it is unfair for similarly situated customers to pay different rates for the same product. Much of the impetus behind rate regulation has been, and continues to be, a concern that firms with monopoly power will charge rates that differentiate among customers unfairly—often providing one customer a competitive benefit over another customer. For instance, before the federal government began regulating the rates charged by railroads, many railroads charged the Standard Oil Trust lower rates to transport petroleum products than they charged other customers to transport the same volume of petroleum products over the same distance. This, in turn, gave the Trust a competitive advantage that permitted it to increase its degree of market power in the petroleum industry.

Concepts of basic fairness, however, do not provide much insight into what discrimination is "undue." Undoubtedly an agency or court would conclude that differential rates constitute undue discrimination when the sole motive for the differential is personal favoritism. Rarely, however, are rate differentials established solely to favor one customer or to disfavor another. More typically, rate differentials are motivated by economic considerations—either differences in costs or differences in elasticity of demand. More detailed analysis is required to determine whether rate differentials motivated by economic considerations are, or should be, labeled undue discrimination.

A second argument against undue discrimination in rates is premised on the desire to avoid "burdening" one class of customers with a portion of the costs attributable to another class of customers. This argument proceeds on the assumption a firm can make up losses on its sales to one class of customers through higher rates charged to another class of customers. It is difficult to imagine, however, circumstances in which a firm would have an incentive to engage in differential pricing that has the effect of burdening one class of customers with costs attributable to another class of customers. Two typical situations illustrate the point.

Assume first that a firm serves two classes of customers. Its fixed costs of providing service are $1,000 per day. These costs cannot be reduced by reducing the service provided either class of customers. The average fixed cost for each unit provided to

either class is $.20. The avoidable or marginal cost
of providing service to customers in either class is
$1.00 per unit, but the elasticity of demand differs
between the two classes of customers so that customers in class A will pay $1.10 per unit and
customers in class B will pay $1.25 per unit. If the
firm charges these differential rates to the two
classes of customers, it might appear at first that
the lower rate charged to class A is placing a burden
on the rates paid by class B. This is not the case,
however, since the unit rate charged class A exceeds
the marginal cost of providing one unit to class A.
Every unit sold to class A contributes $.10 toward
the fixed cost of providing service to both classes of
customers, thus reducing the rate the firm must
charge class B in order to be permitted an opportunity to earn its aggregate revenue requirements. If
members of class B object that members of class A
should be required to contribute the same amount
to the firm's fixed costs as members of class B by,
for instance, being charged $1.25 per unit, the an-
swer is that the firm has an incentive to charge
members of class A the $1.25 rate if they would pay
that rate. If members of class A would cease purchasing the service rather than purchase it at a unit
rate in excess of $1.10, the firm is maximizing the
contribution to total fixed costs available from class
A by charging class A the unit rate of $1.10, and,
through this process, the firm is also minimizing
the rate members of class B must pay to permit the
firm to recover all its fixed costs.

In the second hypothetical, assume that all costs and rates remain the same except the firm proposes to charge class A a rate of only $.90 per unit. In this situation, it is possible for the rate charged class A to burden class B with costs attributable to class A, since every unit sold to class A costs the firm $.10 more than the revenue the firm receives for the unit. Why, however, would the firm voluntarily agree to sell a unit to class A at a rate less than the marginal cost of providing that unit? Obviously it would not. Thus, this potential for one rate to burden another rate is likely to exist only when a firm is compelled by a regulatory agency to sell a product to a class of customers at a rate lower than its marginal cost of making that product available.

A third argument for prohibiting undue discrimination is to avoid predatory pricing by regulated firms. Predatory pricing refers to the sale of a product at less than marginal cost for a temporary period for the purpose of driving competitors out of business so that the firm ultimately can enhance its market power. Some regulators believe the prohibition on undue discrimination makes predatory pricing less likely because it precludes a firm from lowering price below cost selectively on one product or in one market area. Many (but not all) economists question whether predatory pricing should be a matter of concern because it appears to be a prohibitively expensive means of increasing market power. See McGee, *Predatory Price Cutting: The Standard Oil (N.J.) Case*, 1 J.Law & Econ. 137 (1958); Easterbrook, *Predatory Strategies and*

Counterstrategies, 48 U.Chi.L.Rev. 263 & n. 1 (1981) (citing conflicting authorities). These economists argue that the firm will lose more money by cutting prices to eliminate competition than it can earn by increasing prices after competition has been eliminated because the potential entry of new competition limits the price that can be charged even after existing competition has been eliminated. But see Burns, *Predatory Pricing and the Acquisition Cost of Competitors,* 94 J.Pol.Econ. 266 (1986) (empirical study showing that a dominant firm can acquire its competitors at lower cost by engaging in predatory pricing).

A fourth reason for prohibiting undue discrimination is to avoid "second best" problems. The nature of second best problems can be illustrated through a hypothetical example. Assume that two products are functionally equivalent in certain uses, say truck transport and rail transport. Assume further that the average cost (including fixed or unavoidable costs) of a unit of rail transport is $1.00 and the average cost of truck transport is $1.25, while the marginal cost of a unit of rail transport is $.70 and the marginal cost of truck transport is $.90. In this situation, if the rates charged for truck and rail transport are both based on either marginal cost or average cost, consumers are given accurate price signals indicating that rail transport is less costly than truck transport in terms of the amount of resources each requires. If, however, the rate charged for truck transport is based on marginal cost and the rate charged for rail transport is based

on average cost, consumers are given a price signal
that encourages use of the more costly truck transport. Thus, it seems undesirable from the standpoint of encouraging efficient allocation of resources
to permit functionally equivalent regulated products
to be priced on markedly different cost allocation
systems.

The second best problem can emerge from the use
of discriminatory rates in the following manner.
The trucking firm in the hypothetical may serve
two different markets—one in which it competes
with rail transport and one in which it does not.
Since its demand in the first market is likely to be
more elastic than its demand in the second market,
it has an incentive to charge a relatively low rate
(close to marginal cost) in the first market and a
relatively high rate (above average cost) in the
second market. The trucking firm can remain viable
with this pricing pattern, since it can recover most
of its fixed or unavoidable costs in the second market. The railroad may then have a serious problem.
In order to attract customers from the trucking
firm it must reduce its rates below average cost to a
level approaching marginal cost. Yet, if it serves no
market in which the elasticity of demand for its
product permits it to charge a rate at or above
average cost, it may have no means of recovering its
fixed or unavoidable costs. As a result, it may not be
able to remain viable over time as its capital assets
deteriorate and it is unable to replace those assets.
The prohibition against undue discrimination can
be used to avoid this sequence of problems by

forbidding the trucking firm from charging rates at or above average cost in one market while simultaneously charging rates approximating marginal cost in another market. This solution, however, creates collateral problems. It limits competition between firms that provide functionally equivalent products and keeps the rates of some regulated products artificially above marginal cost. As developed further in Chapter 7, many economists are critical of rate regulation that results in rates that differ from marginal cost.

Finally, some regulators and consumer groups argue that the prohibition on undue discrimination can preclude firms from obtaining unjustified transfers of wealth from consumers by charging differential rates. When a firm has a degree of market power, sells to classes of customers with different elasticities of demand, and sells a product that is difficult to resell, the firm can maximize its revenues by selling the product to customers at differential rates. The customers with relatively elastic demand are offered the product at a relatively low rate close to marginal cost, while the customers with relatively inelastic demand are offered the product at a relatively high rate at or above average cost. Thus, at least if the regulatory agency does not effectively constrain the firm's aggregate revenues, differential pricing can produce a transfer of wealth from consumers to the regulated firm.

On the other hand, differential pricing can yield economic advantages by improving the allocation of resources. Ordinarily, a firm with market power would not be willing to sell a product at a rate equal to marginal cost.[2] Therefore, some customers who are willing to purchase the product at that rate would be unable to do so. With differential pricing, at least some of the customers who are willing to purchase the product at a rate between marginal cost and the uniform rate the firm otherwise would charge all consumers will be able to obtain the product.

In summary, there are many theories underlying the prohibition against undue discrimination in rates, none of which find clear support in economic theory. This diverse and murky theoretical foundation helps to explain the difficulty agencies and courts experience in determining what discrimination is undue.

C. WHAT DISCRIMINATION IS UNDUE?

In the typical case, a party alleging undue discrimination must establish that the rate charged one customer, class of customers, or geographical area is different from the rate charged another customer, class of customers, or geographical area for the same product, and that there is no legally sufficient justification for the rate differential. A somewhat broader formulation of the standard, accepted by some agencies and reviewing courts, permits a conclusion of undue discrimination based upon disproportionality in the ratio of cost to the

2. See the discussion of monopoly pricing in section 2A2b.

price charged various customers, classes of customers, or geographical areas, if there is no legally sufficient justification for the disproportionality. Under either test, the rate differential or disproportionality between prices and costs constitutes undue discrimination only if the firm is unable to justify the differential or disproportionality to the satisfaction of the agency or reviewing court.

A rate differential usually can be justified to the satisfaction of an agency or court by demonstrating that the differential in rates is based on a corresponding differential in costs. Some agencies resolve this issue definitionally by concluding that the rates are not applicable to the same product. In addition some, though not all, agencies and reviewing courts are satisfied that a rate differential or rate/cost disproportionality is sufficiently justified if it is based on differences in the price elasticity of demand of the respective customers, classes of customers, or geographical areas.

1. COST–BASED RATE DIFFERENTIALS

Determining whether a rate differential is justified by differences in the costs of providing service to various customers, classes of customers, or geographic areas is part science and part art. As a preliminary matter, it is expensive and time-consuming to attempt to determine the cost of serving particular customers or groups of customers. For that reason, agencies and reviewing courts often permit the rate schedules proposed by firms to go into effect without detailed studies demonstrating precise cost differentials that justify rate differentials, even when a party challenges the basis for a rate differential. See, e.g., Granite State Alarm, Inc. v. New England Telephone & Telegraph Co., 279 A.2d 595 (N.H.1971).

When an agency requires detailed cost justification of rate differentials, the results frequently are not precise because the process of allocating costs to particular customers or classes of customers is far from exact. Some costs are easy to assign to particular classes of customers. Many significant costs, however, are joint, that is, they are costs that contribute to the firm's ability to provide service to several classes of customers. For instance, the primary transmission line from an electric utility's main generating unit to the utility's service area is indispensable to the firm's ability to provide service to all of its customers. Hence, the costs of constructing and maintaining that transmission line are joint costs. Economists, cost accountants and engineers have suggested many different methods of allocating joint costs among various classes of customers, but the more candid experts recognize that joint costs cannot be allocated accurately among jointly produced services. See M. Glaeser, *Public Utilities in American Capitalism* 424 (1957). Consequently, the Supreme Court has recognized that agencies and reviewing courts must be content with something short of precision in determining the relationship between rates and costs of providing service.

E.g., Colorado Interstate Gas Co. v. FPC, 324 U.S. 581 (1945).

Efforts to defend rate differentials by proving the existence of proportionate cost differentials often encounter another problem as well. What definition of the cost of providing a service should be used to determine whether the rate differential is accompanied by a corresponding cost differential? In some cases, the cost of serving customer class A exceeds the cost of serving customer class B if marginal cost is used as the basis for comparison, but the relationship is reversed if fully allocated or average cost is used to compare the costs of serving the two classes of customers. We discuss the lively debate concerning the choice between marginal cost and fully allocated cost as the primary basis for determining rates in Chapter 7.

Deciding whether a cost differential justifies a rate differential often requires careful analysis of the cost of providing different services. Assume, for instance, that a gas pipeline provides both firm and interruptible service. The pipeline incurs identical variable costs, e.g., compressor fuel, to transport each unit of gas under either form of service. The other elements of the pipeline's cost differ markedly, however, for the two types of service. Since the interruptible service is provided only when and if the pipeline has excess capacity, it accounts for none of the pipeline's fixed costs. Thus, many economists argue that the fixed costs should be borne exclusively by consumers of firm service. After decades of resistance, FERC accepted this argument in Order 636, issued in 1992.

2. RATE DIFFERENTIALS BASED ON ELASTICITY OF DEMAND (VALUE OF SERVICE RATEMAKING)

Allowing differential rates based on differences in price elasticity of demand among various classes of customers often is referred to as value of service ratemaking. Differences in elasticity of demand suggest differences in the value placed on a product or service by classes of customers.

As discussed in section B of this chapter, regulated firms have a clear incentive to use differences in elasticities of demand, or value of service, as a basis for establishing differential rates in order to maximize the revenues they actually earn. Indeed, as long as all of a firm's rates at least equal its marginal cost, the firm is benefited by using value of service as the sole criterion for establishing the relationship among its rates. Occasionally, agencies or reviewing courts have rejected, as unduly discriminatory, rate differences that were obviously predicated on value of service considerations. E.g., Wight v. United States, 167 U.S. 512 (1897) (holding that a railroad could not base a rate differential between two customers on the fact that one had access to another railroad while the other did not). Generally, however, most agencies and courts accept differences in value of service as adequate justifications for rate differentials. E.g., Northern Pacific Railway Co. v.

North Dakota, 236 U.S. 585 (1915). Indeed, agencies sometimes compel regulated firms to give greater consideration to value of service than was reflected in the firm's original rate proposal, e.g., Automobiles from Duluth to Washington, 308 I.C.C. 523 (1959), and reviewing courts sometimes require agencies to give greater consideration to value of service than was reflected in the agency's determination of lawful rate relationships. E.g., Eastern–Central Motor Carriers Ass'n v. United States, 321 U.S. 194 (1944).

When it is necessary or appropriate to allow a firm to charge rates that differ from marginal cost, the most efficient departure relies on the inverse elasticity rule. Customers with relatively high price elasticity of demand pay prices based on marginal cost, and any deficiency in firm revenues is made up by charging higher prices to customers with relatively low price elasticity of demand. This method of rate design is often referred to as Ramsey pricing. See Baumol & Bradford, *Optimal Departures from Marginal Cost Pricing*, 60 Am.Econ.Rev. 265 (1970); Ramsey, *A Contribution to the Theory of Taxation*, 37 Econ.J. 47 (1927). The efficiency of Ramsey pricing follows logically from the first principle of microeconomics: prices should be based on marginal cost. See section 7B. If authorizing a firm to base all of its rates on marginal cost would yield revenues inadequate to cover the firm's fixed costs, some customers must be charged a rate that differs from marginal cost. If customers with high price elasticity of demand confront a rate higher than marginal cost, they will respond by reducing significantly their purchases of the regulated service. That, in turn, will yield waste in the form of underutilization of the capacity of the regulated firm. By definition, customers with lower price elasticity of demand will reduce their purchases of the regulated service less in response to a higher price.

Agencies and reviewing courts have become increasingly receptive to use of Ramsey pricing. See, e.g., Burlington Northern R. Co. v. ICC, 985 F.2d 589 (D.C.Cir.1993) (approving ICC's use of Ramsey pricing in designing rail rates); Associated Gas Distributors v. FERC, 824 F.2d 981 (D.C.Cir.1987) (upholding FERC's use of Ramsey pricing for interstate transportation of natural gas). Because price elasticities of demand cannot be measured with precision, agencies usually use approximations and surrogates for actual elasticities. Generally speaking, consumers with access to economically attractive alternatives to the services available from a regulated firm have relatively high price elasticities of demand. The *Burlington Northern* case required the agency and the reviewing court to choose between two competing methods of implementing Ramsey pricing.

3. OTHER JUSTIFICATIONS FOR DIFFERENTIAL RATES

Firms use differences in costs or in elasticities of demand most frequently to justify rate differentials, but a number of other factors can sometimes justify differences in rates.

In many cases, the same firm provides service to classes of customers subject to the regulatory supervision of two or more separate agencies. Many electric utilities, for instance, provide electricity to both wholesale and retail customers. Under the Federal Power Act, the firm's wholesale rates are subject to regulation by the Federal Energy Regulatory Commission (FERC), while its retail rates are subject to regulation by a state agency. 15 U.S.C.A. § 824.

The division of regulatory responsibility for a firm's rates creates unique problems when an allegation is made that the relationship between the firm's rates in different jurisdictions constitutes undue discrimination. Some courts have held that the prohibition against unduly discriminatory rates does not apply to the relationship between rates charged in different regulatory jurisdictions, Union Electric Co. v. Illinois Commerce Commission, 396 N.E.2d 510 (Ill.1979), but the judicial resolution of this issue has not been consistent. FERC initially took the position that it has no power to consider the relationship between a nonjurisdictional and a jurisdictional rate and no power to correct any undue discrimination inherent in such a relationship. The Supreme Court reversed FERC, holding that FERC has the power and the duty to consider such relationships, at least where the effect of the undue discrimination is to create an anticompetitive situation in which the wholesale customers of the electric utility are placed in a price squeeze that precludes them from competing with the utility for retail customers. FPC v. Conway Corporation, 426

U.S. 271 (1976). If FERC finds that the relationship between the firm's jurisdictional and nonjurisdictional rates is unduly discriminatory and anticompetitive, its power to correct the relationship is constrained by the fact that it has jurisdiction over only one of the rates at issue. Presumably, it must either correct the relationship by ordering a change in the jurisdictional rate or obtain the cooperation of the state agency to change both rates.

Under many regulatory statutes, a firm has limited ability to increase the rates it charges a customer it has agreed to serve under a long-term, fixed rate contract. See, e.g., FPC v. Sierra Pacific Power Co., 350 U.S. 348 (1956). The firm has greater power to increase the rates it charges a customer in the absence of contractual constraints. Richmond Power & Light v. FPC, 481 F.2d 490 (D.C.Cir.1973). If, however, the firm serves similar customers under different forms of contracts, the firm's limited power to raise the rates charged some of those customers creates the potential for substantial rate differentials to evolve over time. If the rate differentials are attributable solely to differences in the firm's contractual power to increase its rates, the differential does not constitute undue discrimination, but if any other factor contributes to the differential, it may be considered unduly discriminatory. See Boroughs of Chambersburg v. FERC, 580 F.2d 573 (D.C.Cir.1978).

Sometimes firms or regulatory agencies defend rate relationships that otherwise would be considered unduly discriminatory on the basis that a particular customer or class of customers cannot afford to purchase service at cost-based rates. This rationale has been invoked to defend unusually low rates for particular industrial customers (Calvert Wire Co. v. Pennsylvania Power Co., 51 P.U.R.(ns) 248 (Pa.P.U.C.1943)), irrigation farmers (Utah Power & Light Co., 22 P.U.R.4th 351 (Idaho P.U.C. 1977)), small-volume residential consumers of natural gas and electricity (Gas & Electric Utilities Rate Structure, 24 P.U.R.4th 332 (Cal.P.U.C.1978)), and youthful airline passengers (Domestic Passenger Fare Investigation, Phase 5—Discount Fares, CCH Aviation L.Rep. 22,096 (C.A.B.1972)). When proposed by a regulated firm, particularly low rates based on a customer's inability to pay higher rates may be motivated more by differential elasticities of demand than by any desire to benefit customers with limited financial resources. When, however, an agency attempts to force a firm to provide service to a financially disadvantaged customer at a particularly low rate, value of service considerations probably are not a significant factor in the decision.

There is no consistent trend of agency and court decisions concerning the legal adequacy of relative ability to pay as a justification for rate differentials. Compare American Hoechest Corp. v. Department of Public Utilities, 399 N.E.2d 1 (Mass.1980) (rejecting argument that a particularly low rate for electric service to the elderly poor constitutes undue discrimination), with Mountain States Legal Foundation v. Public Utilities Commission, 590 P.2d 495 (Colo.1979) (holding unduly discriminatory a particularly low rate for electric service to poor residential customers.) Of course, a legislature can resolve all serious doubt concerning the legality of rates based on ability to pay by authorizing such rates by statute. See, e.g., Gas & Electric Utility Rate Structure, 24 P.U.R.4th 332 (Cal.P.U.C.1978) (implementing a California statute requiring particularly low rates for certain residential customers on the assumption that most of those customers are poor).

CHAPTER VII

RATES TO CUSTOMERS: PROBLEMS OF ALLOCATION

A. FULLY DISTRIBUTED COSTS AND RATES

Regulatory agencies often emphasize the need for rates to be based on costs, but cost is an ambiguous word that takes on meaning only when combined with an adjective. For decades, regulated firms and agencies have debated which measure of cost is most appropriate as a basis for setting rates. Most frequently, the debate focuses on the choice between average, or fully distributed, cost and marginal cost. The concept of average cost can be understood most easily by considering a firm that produces only one product. If the firm produces 1000 units of the product at a total cost of $1000, its average cost is $1 per unit. If the firm produces more than one product, calculating the average cost of any of its products is more troublesome. To the extent that some of its costs are joint, that is they contribute to the production of more than one product, those joint costs must be allocated among the products to which they are jointly attributable in order to calculate the average cost of any of the firm's products. After decades of study by accountants, economists and regulators, no satisfactory method of allocating joint costs has been found. All of the twenty or more methods currently in use have elements of arbitrariness. The courts have recognized the inherent inability to allocate joint costs in accordance with any generally accepted formula, and, for that reason, they tend to allow agencies considerable discretion to calculate average cost through any of several methods of allocating joint costs. See, e.g., Colorado Interstate Gas Co. v. FPC, 324 U.S. 581 (1945); Groesbeck v. Duluth, S. S. & A. Ry. Co., 250 U.S. 607 (1919).

Use of average cost has the advantage of producing a set of rates that should yield to the firm aggregate revenues equal to its allowed revenue requirements. Since the firm's total costs for ratemaking purposes are the same as its allowed revenue requirements, average cost based rates multiplied by the number of units of each product expected to be sold will yield total revenue equal to the firm's allowed revenue requirements. Use of average cost has two significant disadvantages, however. First, joint costs must be allocated among products in a somewhat arbitrary manner in order to calculate average cost. Second, use of average cost is likely to produce a misallocation of resources. This allocative effect of average cost based rates is discussed in the analysis of rates based on marginal cost.

B. MARGINAL COST RATES

Marginal cost is the avoidable cost a firm must incur to produce one more unit of a product at a given level of output. Marginal cost may be greater or less than average cost. As explained in Chapter 2, prices in a competitive industry are determined by marginal cost.

Most economists argue that the rates charged by regulated firms should be based on marginal cost. Indeed, the equation of marginal cost and price frequently is referred to as "the central policy prescription of microeconomics." 1 A. Kahn, *The Economics of Regulation* 65 (1970). Prices based on marginal cost permit efficient allocation of resources among competing activities, products and consumers. If the price of a product is determined by its marginal cost, consumers confront a price that reflects the amount and value of the resources required to produce the last, or marginal, unit of that product. They then make the decision to purchase or not to purchase an additional unit based on a comparison of the price of a unit of that product with the price of a functional alternative to the product, say, a unit of natural gas versus a unit of insulation. If the prices of all functional alternatives were based on the marginal cost of those alternatives, consumer choice among alternatives would be based on a comparison of the actual resource costs of producing an additional unit of each functionally equivalent product. By contrast, prices based on average cost provide consumers with false price signals that do not reflect the cost of the resources required to produce an additional unit of a product. If average cost is above marginal cost, consumers purchase less of the product than they would if they confronted a price representing the resource costs of producing an additional unit; the opposite problem results when average cost is below marginal cost.

Notwithstanding its desirability as a means of furthering allocative efficiency, marginal cost pricing has not been embraced by all regulated firms or regulatory agencies. There are several significant problems with the use of marginal cost as the primary determinant of the rates charged by regulated firms.

1.   PROBLEMS IN MEASURING MARGINAL COST

Calculating the marginal cost of a product is not easy. Accountants often differ on what costs can be avoided by producing one less unit of a product. Indeed, whether a cost is avoidable or fixed depends on the relevant decision-making period. In the very short run, all costs are fixed; in the very long run, all costs are avoidable. Experts often disagree on the time horizon appropriate for use in calculating marginal cost. Moreover, it is often difficult as a practical matter to isolate the avoidable cost of producing one unit less of a product because the factors of production frequently are not divisible into units that correspond to a single additional unit of a product. As a result, some agencies use incremental cost as a more practical surrogate for marginal cost. Incremental cost refers to the avoidable cost incurred to produce an additional increment of a product. The increment need not be a single unit of the product; rather it can be some larger number of units that reflects logically the way in which additional units of the product would be produced.

The opinion of the Wisconsin Public Service Commission in Madison Gas & Electric Co., 5 P.U.R.4th 28 (Wis.P.S.C.1974), illustrates some of the problems of measuring marginal cost. The Commission decided to use marginal cost principles to determine the rates the firm could charge, but it then had to decide which of four possible methods of applying marginal cost principles was most appropriate—short run marginal cost, short run incremental cost, long run marginal cost, or long run incremental cost. Short run incremental cost and long run marginal cost seemed to offer few relative advantages, so the Commission narrowed its choice to short run marginal cost or long run incremental cost. In the context of an electric utility, short run marginal cost consists primarily of the cost of the fuel used to generate an additional kilowatt hour of electricity. That cost depends on the kind of fuel used and the source of that fuel, both of which are likely to vary from season to season, day to day, and even hour to hour. Thus, using short run marginal cost has the advantage of providing consumers price signals that reflect the resource cost of the fuel their decisions to consume electricity force the utility to use. Short run marginal cost has two disadvantages, however. First, it varies so much over relatively short periods of time that the firm has difficulty reflecting it accurately in its rates, and consumers are confronted with highly volatile and unpredictable rates. Second, the short run focus precludes any reflection in the firm's rates of the costs of adding future generating or transmission capacity; yet, any significant increase in consumption of electricity today will force the firm to incur substantial future costs to expand its capacity. The Wisconsin Commission selected long run incremental cost rather than short run marginal cost to avoid these two disadvantages of short run marginal cost. Other agencies, faced with the same decision, have come to the opposite conclusion. See, e.g., Potomac Electric Power Co., 31 P.U.R.4th 219 (D.C. P.S.C.1979).

2. SECOND BEST PROBLEMS

As described in section 6B, second best problems can result from the use of marginal cost to determine the price of one product and average cost to determine the price of a functional equivalent to that product. In such circumstances, the relationship between the prices charged for the two products may mislead consumers into purchasing the product with higher marginal cost, thereby increasing unnecessarily the resources society must devote to serving the function that either of the products performs. The second best problem can be solved by basing all prices on marginal cost, but for two reasons agencies often try to avoid the problem by using average cost as the basis for determining the rates appropriate for a regulated firm. First, rates applicable to the functionally equivalent product often are not in the agency's jurisdiction. Second, even if the agency has the power to determine the rates applicable to both products based on marginal cost, it may decline to do so because marginal cost rates often conflict with the regulatory goal of permitting the firm an opportunity to earn its allowed revenue requirements.

3. CONFLICTS WITH REVENUE REQUIREMENTS

It would be purely fortuitous if the revenues earned by a firm through rates based on marginal cost equalled the allowed revenue requirements calculated by the agency through the use of the traditional formula: $R = B(r) + O$. If average cost exceeds marginal cost, rates based on marginal cost will yield revenues less than allowed revenue requirements, thereby threatening the firm's long run financial viability. If marginal cost exceeds average cost, rates based on marginal cost will yield revenues greater than allowed revenue requirements—a result arguably in conflict with the agency's statutory mandate and one which at least can be expected to make the agency unpopular with the consuming public. This potential divergence between aggregate revenues resulting from rates based on marginal cost and allowed revenue requirements is often referred to as the revenue constraint. If an agency wants to use marginal cost as the basis for calculating the rates of a regulated firm, it must devise some method of accommodating the revenue constraint.

If marginal cost is less than average cost, the problem is one of insufficient aggregate revenues which eventually can threaten the viability of the regulated firm. The problem of inadequate revenues yielded by rates based on marginal cost can be accommodated in any of four ways—a subsidy, use of a multi-part rate, use of the inverse elasticity rule, or reliance on the principle of diminishing marginal utility. We discuss multi-part rates in the next section.

The most simple and direct solution to the inadequate revenue problem is to provide the firm a subsidy equal to the difference between revenues resulting from marginal cost rates and the firm's allowed revenue requirements. However, this solution is usually not available because regulatory agencies rarely have the power to grant subsidies.

A second method of responding to the inadequate revenue problem is to structure the firm's rates in accordance with the inverse elasticity rule. If one group of customers is characterized by price inelastic demand and another group is characterized by price elastic demand, the goals of marginal cost pricing can be furthered by charging the customers with elastic demand rates based on marginal cost. The resulting revenue deficiency then can be made up by charging the customers with inelastic demand rates in excess of marginal cost. The supra-marginal cost rates confronted by consumers with inelastic demand have little adverse effect on allocative efficiency because, by definition, consumers with inelastic demand respond to price changes with only slight changes in quantity demanded. See section 6C2. The ability to accommodate the revenue constraint through reliance on the inverse elasticity rule is, however, dependent upon the ability to identify groups of consumers with widely divergent elasticities of demand. It is difficult and costly to determine elasticities of demand applicable to various customer classes, and efforts to make such determinations often produce unreliable results. See, e.g., Taylor, *The Demand for Energy: A Survey of Price and Income Elasticity*, in *International Studies of the Demand for Energy* (W. D. Nordhaus ed. 1977).

A third approach to the problem of inadequate revenues is to devise rate patterns that reflect the principle of diminishing marginal utility. This economic principle states that each consumer values the next unit of a product slightly less than the value the consumer placed on the prior unit. See section 2 A1a. Hence, the allocative goal of marginal cost pricing can be served by establishing a price equal to marginal cost for the last units of a commodity purchased by each consumer, with the revenue deficit made up by charging supramarginal cost prices for the preceding units. This method would work well if agencies could identify the marginal utility curve for each consumer and construct individualized rate schedules corresponding to each consumer's curve. In practice, the principle can be applied only crudely through declining block rates applicable to general classes of consumers with marginal utility curves that are believed to be approximately the same.

If marginal cost exceeds average cost, the problem is reversed—rates based on marginal cost will yield aggregate revenues in excess of allowed revenue requirements.[1] This excess revenue problem can be accommodated through methods analogous to those available to solve the problem of inadequate revenues.

The difference between revenues derived from charging rates based on marginal cost and the firm's allowed revenue requirements could be taxed.

1. If a firm's marginal cost exceeds its average cost, it is difficult to find a good reason to regulate the firm. A firm whose marginal cost exceeds its average cost at current output levels is no longer able to take advantage of economies of scale by increasing its output. In the absence of economies of scale, the firm is not a natural monopoly, and competition should be effective as a means of controlling price, profit and output level. Yet, agencies often find that a regulated firm has marginal cost above average cost. There are four possible explanations for these findings: (1) the agency has miscalculated average cost; (2) the agency has miscalculated marginal cost; (3) the firm, though once a natural monopoly, no longer has cost characteristics consistent with a natural monopoly; or (4) the firm is regulated for reasons other than its perceived monopoly power, e.g., to preclude it from earning excessive rents or windfall profits. See section 2 B3.

Like the subsidy, however, this option is not normally within the power of a regulatory agency.

The inverse elasticity rule could be applied, in this case by charging marginal cost rates to the customers with the most elastic demand and rates less than marginal cost to customers with the most inelastic demand. Here again, the problem of identifying customers with substantially different elasticities of demand must be confronted.

Finally, the principle of declining marginal utility can be relied upon to avoid excess revenues resulting from marginal cost pricing, with the same limitations that apply to use of this principle to avoid inadequate revenues. To avoid the excess revenues that can result when marginal cost exceeds average cost, the principle of declining marginal utility dictates selection of rate schedules that confront consumers with a rate based on marginal cost for the last units they purchase and that accommodate the revenue constraint by charging rates less than marginal cost for the preceding units. The result is a series of increasing block rates applicable to classes of customers whose marginal utility curves are believed to be approximately the same.[2]

Often, the divergence between a firm's allowed revenue requirements and the revenues it would earn if it based all of its rates on marginal cost is

2. For more detailed discussion of the available techniques for reconciling marginal cost pricing with a firm's allowed revenue requirements, see Pierce, *Marginal Cost Pricing of Energy— But How?*, 102 Pub.Util.Fort. 24 (Dec. 7, 1978); Pierce, *Natural Gas Rate Design: A Neglected Issue*, 31 Vand.L.Rev. 1089 (1978).

attributable primarily to use of inappropriate methods of valuing the firm's assets for ratemaking purposes. As agencies increasingly shift to valuation methods that yield a greater convergence between the actual economic value of a firm's assets and the value of those assets used to calculate a firm's allowed revenue, conflicts between marginal cost pricing and revenue requirements will decline in significance. See section 5B1. Ideally, rates should be based on marginal social cost, including the environmental costs of a production process that are borne by society but not by the firm. Until recently, an agency could not base a firm's rates on marginal social cost without creating an intolerably large gap between the firm's allowed revenues and the revenues it would earn by charging rates based on marginal social cost. The trend to use market-based methods of environmental regulation, discussed in section 15D, is eliminating this impediment to adoption of rates based on marginal social cost.

C. THE AVERAGE COST VERSUS MARGINAL COST DEBATE

In many regulated industries, marginal cost and average cost differ significantly. As a result, the choice between average cost and marginal cost as a primary basis for establishing rates is one of the most important and controversial issues confronting a regulatory agency. The argument for marginal cost pricing finds strong support in economic theory; marginal cost pricing should produce a more efficient allocation of resources because it forces consumers to confront prices equal to the avoidable cost of making available an additional unit of a regulated product. The arguments against marginal cost pricing are premised on the practical problems created by any attempt to reflect marginal cost in the rates of a regulated firm consistent with the goal of constraining the firm's aggregate revenues. This debate has been active in virtually every regulated industry for decades. The following account of the recent highlights of the marginal cost/average cost debate in the context of railroads should help to explain the significance and complexity of this issue.

Railroads have high fixed costs and joint costs represented by their investment in roadbed and, to a lesser extent, their investment in rolling stock. These costs are not affected by decisions to provide one more unit of rail service over any particular route. As a result, the marginal cost of a unit of rail service (consisting primarily of fuel, the cost of the personnel required to operate a train, and the opportunity cost of using the rolling stock on some other route) typically is substantially below the average cost of a unit of rail service (including some proportion of fixed and/or joint costs). The Interstate Commerce Commission, the courts and Congress have been considering for many years whether rail rates should be based on marginal cost or average cost. The dispute that produced the Supreme Court decision in American Commercial

Lines, Inc. v. Louisville & Nashville R. Co., 392 U.S. 571 (1968), illustrates a typical situation in which this issue arises.

Traditionally, ingot molds had been transported from Pittsburgh, Pennsylvania, to Steelton, Kentucky, by a combination of truck and barge at a joint rate of $5.11 per ton. The railroad proposed to provide the same service at an identical rate. Since rail transport would provide service advantages over the barge-truck combination, all of the ingot molds eventually would be shipped by rail if the railroad were permitted to charge its proposed rate.

Owners of trucks and barges serving the route protested the rate proposed by the railroad, claiming that it would eliminate the "inherent advantage" of barge-truck service in providing this transportation service. The ICC was required by statute to establish rates that preserved the inherent advantages of one mode of regulated transport over another.

The ICC found that the marginal cost of the rail service was $4.69 per ton, while the average cost of the rail service was $7.59 per ton. It found that the average and marginal costs of the barge-truck service were approximately equal, at $5.19 per ton. Thus, the issue before the ICC was whether the inherent advantage of a mode of transport should be determined with reference to its relative marginal cost or its relative average cost. If relative marginal cost is the proper measure, the railroad should be allowed to charge its proposed rate, thereby taking the traffic from the barge-truck combination. If average cost is the proper measure, the railroad should not be permitted to charge a rate based on marginal cost since that would destroy the inherent advantage of the barge-truck combination.

The railroad presented several expert witnesses who testified that marginal cost was the proper basis on which to compare competing services and that rates based on marginal cost provide significant economic advantages. In outline form, the advantages of permitting the railroad to charge marginal cost rates included: (1) marginal cost rates enhance allocative efficiency by confronting consumers with rates that reflect the resource costs attributable to a decision to make available one unit of a product; (2) marginal cost rates benefit the customers who confront the rates by providing them service at a lower price; (3) marginal cost rates benefit the railroad and its other customers by maximizing the potential contribution to joint and fixed costs made by the customer confronted with marginal cost rates; (4) the railroad can remain viable by charging marginal cost rates to customers with elastic demand attributable to the existence of competitive alternatives and charging rates above marginal cost to customers with inelastic demand; (5) permitting marginal cost rates encourages effective competition among alternative modes of transport.

The owners of trucks and barges countered with the following arguments against marginal cost pricing: (1) allowing the railroad to set its rates at marginal cost eventually is self-defeating because the railroad must recover its fixed and joint costs somehow to remain viable; (2) it is unfair both to competitive alternatives and to shippers without access to competitive alternatives to allow the railroad to charge rates equal to marginal cost on routes where they face competition and to recover most of their fixed costs by charging rates in excess of marginal cost on routes where they do not face competition; (3) permitting the railroad to charge rates based on marginal cost provides only short-lived benefits to shippers of ingot molds because the railroad can increase its rates above marginal cost once the truck-barge competition is eliminated.

The ICC agreed with the barge-truck owners, holding that average cost is the proper benchmark for determining which mode of transport has an inherent advantage. It rejected the railroad's proposed marginal cost rate because it would deprive the truck-barge mode of its inherent advantage. The agency also stated, however, that it was reconsidering its general position on this issue in a pending rulemaking.

A district court reversed the ICC, holding that marginal cost was the proper basis for determining inherent advantage as a matter of law. However, the Supreme Court reversed the district court and affirmed the ICC. It held only that the ICC had the discretion to defer resolution of the issue until it completed its rulemaking. The Court's discussion, however, suggested that it found the intent of Congress unclear and that it ultimately was likely to defer to any ICC resolution of the issue.

Since *American Commercial Lines*, much of the debate over marginal cost versus average cost rates has taken place at the ICC and in Congress. In 1979, the ICC permitted railroads to charge rates above average cost to shippers with inelastic demand in order to allow the railroads an opportunity to recover a portion of their revenue deficit, but the ICC explicitly refused to allow the railroads "to make up their entire short fall by extracting monopoly profits from captive shippers." San Antonio v. Burlington Northern, 361 I.C.C. 482 (1979). In 1980, Congress enacted legislation that allows railroads substantially more flexibility to establish rates based on competitive conditions. Much of the opposition to deregulation of rail rates was by coal shippers who objected strenuously to the railroads' proposal to apply the inverse elasticity rule and to recover much of their fixed costs through disproportionately high rates for shipping coal. This dispute ultimately yielded a complex compromise. Any railroad can charge up to 180 percent of variable costs for any service. In addition, railroads that are not making a reasonable return on investment can charge an additional 6 percent until 1984, and 4 percent thereafter. Staggers Rail Act of 1980, 94 Stat. 1895. ICC ultimately decided to use a variation of marginal cost pricing, Ramsey pricing, to implement the statute, with the blessing of reviewing courts. See section 6C2. Agencies and courts have become increasingly receptive to marginal cost pricing in most regulated industries.

D. MULTI–PART RATES

Most products are sold at a particular price per unit purchased. Multi-part pricing refers to a system of rates in which each customer is charged both a price per unit and a separate price independent of the number of units purchased by the customer. Multi-part pricing is common in many regulated industries. For instance, electric and gas utilities typically charge large volume customers a commodity charge based on the units of electricity each actually consumed during the entire billing period and a demand charge based on the maximum amount of electricity the customer used during a particular brief segment of time within the billing period. Thus, a customer might be charged $.05 per kilowatt hour of electricity used during a month plus $2.50 per kilowatt of electricity demand at the utility's time of greatest demand during that month.

Since multi-part rates have the effect of making the same product available at different unit rates, they can only be charged by a firm with monopoly power for a product that cannot practically be resold. Many regulated firms sell under these conditions.

From the firm's perspective, multi-part rates often are desirable. They permit the firm to increase its revenues vis-a-vis the revenues it could earn by charging a one-part rate. The potential for the multi-part rate to increase the firm's revenues follows from the principle of diminishing marginal utility. A multi-part rate has the effect of making the last units purchased by a customer available at a price less than the average unit revenue the firm obtains under the rate schedule. Thus, the customer purchases more units than it would if it were forced to pay a one-part unit rate equal to the firm's average revenue per unit, while the firm's total revenue from the customer exceeds the revenue it would obtain if it charged only the commodity rate.

Customers purchasing products under multi-part rates pay different effective unit rates depending on their load factor. Load factor is calculated by dividing a customer's units of consumption on an average day by its units of consumption on a peak day. Thus, a customer with a low load factor, suggesting a wide variation in the quantity it uses from time to time, pays a higher effective rate per unit than a customer with a high load factor. This, in turn, encourages all customers subject to multi-part rates to control their consumption patterns to minimize their variation in use over time. To the extent that customers create more even patterns of demand, the regulated firm has less need to increase its capacity to provide a particular number of units at a specific time. This reduces the firm's investment in capital equipment, thereby reducing its costs and its rates.

The desirable effect of the multi-part rate in terms of reducing a firm's investment in capacity occurs only if the demand charge encourages a reduction in the aggregate maximum demand on the utility system. Thus, if the maximum period of demand for a particular customer differs significantly from the period of maximum aggregate demand on the system, a demand charged based on the individual customer's maximum demand will not assist the firm by reducing its investment in capacity. For this reason, the demand charge often is based on the number of units consumed by the customer at the time the regulated firm was experiencing its maximum aggregate demand.

Economists have long argued that all of a firm's capacity costs, e.g., generating plant, transmission lines, pipelines, should be included entirely in the demand charge of a two-part rate. A firm's decision to invest in additional capacity is based on increases (or expected future increases) in the maximum aggregate demand for the firm's product. Therefore, capacity costs are attributable entirely to customers who require service during periods of maximum aggregate demand in proportion to the units demanded by each customer at that time.

Regulators, however, traditionally were unwilling to allocate capacity costs entirely to the demand charge. In FPC Opinion No. 225, Atlantic Seaboard Corp., 11 F.P.C. 43 (1952), the Commission ordered all costs that vary with units of output and 50 percent of capacity costs included in the commodity charge, with the other 50 percent of capacity costs included in the demand charge. The Commission considered, but rejected, the testimony of economists urging it to allocate all capacity costs to the demand charge. The Commission reasoned that it would be unfair to relieve customers who do not purchase during periods of maximum demand from all capacity costs, since those customers also benefit from existence of the firm's investment in capacity.

After the *Atlantic Seaboard* decision, the 50–50 division of capacity costs became common. It was not unusual, however, for regulators to vary this allocation to further other policies. For instance, the proportion of capacity costs allocated to the commodity charge often was reduced to permit a firm to compete more effectively for high load factor customers with access to competitive alternatives. See, e.g., FPC Opinion No. 430, United Fuel Gas Co., 31 F.P.C. 1342 (1964). Allocating a smaller proportion of capacity costs to the commodity charge reduces the effective unit rate charged high load factor customers. Conversely, other policies, such as a shortage of a product that eliminates pipeline capacity as an effective constraint, have sometimes influenced regulators to decrease the proportion of capacity costs allocated to the demand charge. See, e.g., FPC Opinion No. 792, Texas Gas Transmission Corp., 11 F.P.S. 5–923 (1977). Disputes concerning allocation of capacity costs between demand and commodity charges often are vigorously contested, since they can have significant economic effects on regulated firms, suppliers of competing products, and customers with differing load factors. Recently, agencies have been more willing to enhance efficiency by allocating all capacity costs to the demand charge. After fifty years of debate and vacillation, FERC finally adopted that approach to natural gas pipeline rate regulation in Order 636, issued in 1992.

Many regulated firms use a three-part rate. In addition to the demand and commodity charges, the three-part rate typically includes a customer charge. The customer charge is usually a fixed amount billed to each customer in a class for a particular period in which the customer was entitled to receive service. It is independent of both the units of product purchased during the period and the maximum demand imposed by the customer during the period. The customer charge allows the firm to recover those costs that do not vary with quantity purchased or with maximum demand, but rather with the number of customers served by the firm. Typically, these include meter reading, billing, and collecting.

E.   SEASONAL AND PEAKLOAD RATES

Another increasingly common variation on the uniform unit rate is the seasonal or peakload rate. The cost of providing a unit of many products, such as electricity and natural gas, varies depending on the time when the unit is provided. For many firms, the unit cost of providing a product is higher during periods of high demand than during periods of low demand.

Temporal cost differences are attributable to at least three different sources. First, the raw materials used to make the product sometimes vary in nature and source depending on the amount of demand for the product at a particular time. For instance, a natural gas utility might have access to a fixed quantity of natural gas each day at an average cost of $3.00 per thousand cubic feet. If demand exceeds that quantity on any day, the utility must supplement its relatively inexpensive supply of natural gas with a propane-air mixture or synthetic gas that costs over $5.00 per thousand cubic feet. Second, units purchased at a time of high demand may strain the firm's physical capacity, thereby forcing it to increase its capacity in the future at great cost. An example is an electric utility that must construct new generating units or transmission lines solely because demand for electricity has increased at the periods of highest demand. Third, the opportunity cost of a firm's decision to provide a unit of product is higher during periods of high demand. To illustrate this, consider the railroad that has idle rolling stock during some periods, so that the opportunity cost of using an item of rolling stock during such periods is zero. At other times, demand for the firm's rolling stock exceeds its supply, so that the opportunity cost of using the rolling stock for one purpose (e.g., transporting coal) is the lost revenue to the firm resulting from the inability to use the rolling stock for a competing purpose (e.g., transporting grain).

These temporal differences in unit costs can be substantial. Reflecting such differences in rate differentials furthers allocative efficiency by confronting consumers with the resource costs of their decisions to purchase units of a product at times when those units are particularly costly. In addition, some temporal rate differentials are based on application of the inverse elasticity rule, since demand may be more inelastic during periods of high demand than during periods of low demand.

Rates that vary temporally can take many forms. One of the most common is the two-part demand-commodity rate discussed in section 7D. The two-part rate furthers efficiency if the demand charge is based on the customer's demand at a time the firm is experiencing particularly high aggregate demand. To be true to the economic principles underlying temporal rate differentials, the demand charge should reflect all of the firm's capacity costs of providing service during periods of high demand.

Seasonal rates provide a relatively simple means of reflecting temporal differences in costs where demand for a product varies substantially from one season to another. Examples of seasonal demand variations include the high demand for electricity for air conditioning in the summer, the high demand for natural gas for heating in the winter, and the high demand for railroad rolling stock during the grain harvesting season.

The decision of the Wisconsin Public Service Commission in *Madison Gas & Electric*, 5

P.U.R.4th 28 (Wis.P.S.C.1974) provides a good illustration of seasonal rates for electric utilities. The Commission ordered into effect higher rates for the summer months than for the winter months. Since the regulated firm experienced higher demand in the summer attributable to air conditioning, its unit costs were higher in the summer. The Commission reasoned that consumers should be made aware of the differential unit costs they were forcing the firm to incur through their consumption decisions during different seasons. The firm would then receive more accurate signals to aid it in planning future capacity and in making fuel acquisition decisions based on seasonal demand levels that reflect the differential costs of making the product available in seasons of high and low demand.

A somewhat different application of the seasonal or peak load pricing principle is illustrated by the controversy in Fuels Research Council, Inc. v. FPC, 374 F.2d 842 (7th Cir.1967). Two gas pipelines proposed to vary their rates substantially depending upon period of use by placing the bulk of their capacity costs in the demand charge of a two-part rate. Through this device, the pipelines could make sales to large-volume interruptible customers at relatively low rates reflecting the short-run variable cost of providing the gas plus a small share of the pipelines' capacity costs. Interruptible customers are required by contract or tariff to cease taking gas whenever the pipeline experiences demand in excess of its capacity.

The pipelines argued that interruptible customers should not be required to bear a proportionate share of the pipelines' capacity costs, since their use of gas does not contribute to the need for the pipeline to install additional capacity. Moreover, by allocating only a small fraction of capacity costs to these off-peak uses, the pipelines could compete effectively for large-volume interruptible customers, thereby obtaining at least some additional contribution to the pipelines' capacity costs. Coal producers opposed the proposed rates because of the loss of customers they would experience if gas were available to large volume interruptible customers at rates that reflect only a small portion of capacity costs. The coal producers argued that it was unfair to vary rates based on time of use.

The Commission approved the pipelines' proposed peak/off-peak rate differential, and the court of appeals affirmed the Commission. Both the Commission and the court accepted the pipelines' arguments that temporal differences in unit cost should be reflected in differential unit rates to further economic efficiency. *Fuels Research* illustrates the way in which temporal cost differences and elasticity differences can merge to justify peak/off-peak rate differentials.

Seasonal differences in demand and unit cost can be reflected in rates approximately by charging relatively high or low rates for uses in which demand tends to correlate with periods of high or low aggregate demand, respectively. For instance, most electric utilities experience greater aggregate demand in summer than in winter, while demand for electricity for heating exists only in the winter. Thus, the principles underlying seasonal rate differentials also can support particularly low rates for space heating use of electricity. See, e.g., Mathews v. Jersey Central Power & Light Co., 2 P.U.R.4th 515 (N.J. Bd. of Util. Comm.1974) (approving proposed low rates for all electric houses in order to encourage greater off-peak use of electricity for space heating.)

The demand for, and unit cost of, some products also varies frequently during a single day. Demand for electricity, for instance, usually reaches its peak each day during the late afternoon or early evening hours. Thus, the fuel costs, capacity costs, and opportunity costs of providing electricity tend also to peak at that time. If this difference in aggregate demand and the corresponding difference in unit cost is reflected in rates that vary by time of day, consumers receive more accurate price signals; the costly variations in demand experienced by the firm diminish; and economic efficiency is furthered. In recent years, some agencies have required firms to adopt time-of-day rate schedules. See, e.g., Rate Design for Electric Corps., 15 P.U.R.4th 434 (N.Y.P.S.C.1976).

Direct load management techniques are a further extension of the peak load pricing principle. Recently, some firms have begun to offer electric service to members of some classes of customers at particularly low rates if the customer agrees to allow the firm to control the customer's access to electricity through a master switch. This method of load control offers the advantage of permitting the firm to reduce the demand on its system at any time it experiences excess aggregate demand, instead of relying on rate differentials that reflect only approximately the periods of peak demand.

Use of time-of-day pricing and load management techniques is limited by transaction costs. Meters that record usage by time of day and remote control switches that allow a utility to turn off equipment when it experiences peakload conditions are expensive. The technological revolution in telecommunications and computing is rapidly reducing these obstacles, however. Eventually, it may be both feasible and desirable to establish rates that change constantly as demand and supply conditions change. Some large customers already receive service on this basis.

F. JUST AND REASONABLE RATES

Regulatory agencies typically have considerable discretion to select the methodology most appropriate for determining the individual rates a regulated firm can charge. Under most statutes, a reviewing court can upset an agency order establishing a rate only if it is unduly discriminatory or unjust and unreasonable. The rate order has a "presumption of validity," and anyone challenging it must carry "the heavy burden of making a convincing showing that it is invalid." The agency is "not bound to the use of any single formula or combination of formulae in determining rates." Federal Power Commission v. Hope Natural Gas Co., 320 U.S. 591 (1944). Thus, most rate design disputes are won or lost at the agency level.

CHAPTER VIII

REGULATION OF SERVICE
LEVEL AND QUALITY

In a sense, regulation of the level and quality of service provided by a firm is essential to further the goals of maximum revenue and rate regulation. If a firm's rates are constrained, it can increase its revenues by lowering the quality of the service it provides. Thus, regulatory agencies must attempt to control quantity and quality of service through some means.

A. LEVEL OF SERVICE

Many regulated firms are subject to a statutory duty to provide adequate service to anyone requesting service within the franchise area in which the firm is authorized to provide service. The firm can be compelled to provide service even when doing so requires an additional investment that is unprofitable, as long as it will not render the business as a whole unprofitable. See New York ex rel. New York and Queens Gas Co. v. McCall, 245 U.S. 345 (1917). This duty to provide service to the public is considered a quid pro quo for the monopoly conferred on the firm by its franchise. Regulatory agencies often authorize firms to decline requests for service in specified circumstances, such as where initiation of service requires an expenditure above a given level or where the firm is experiencing a supply or capacity shortage.

The level of service a firm is required by statute to provide often is described merely as "adequate"—a standard so imprecise that it is not subject to uniform definition by agencies and courts. The general adequacy standard usually is supplemented by more precise service obligations contained in a firm's franchise or in certificates authorizing it to provide service to particular customers. Regulating the adequacy of a firm's service is fraught with problems of determining whether the service level is adequate, identifying the reasons for inadequate service, and devising incentives for firms to improve their quality of service. See section 8D.

B. RESTRICTIONS ON EXIT

Most firms that are subject to maximum rate regulation also are subject to statutory limits on their power to cease providing service. These limits on the ability of a regulated firm to exit a market are based on several arguments: (1) on grounds of equity, regulated monopolies should not be permitted to terminate service just because the service has become unprofitable; (2) in some cases, termination of service can create health and safety problems, e.g., termination of natural gas service to a residence in the winter; (3) customers of a regulated firm without supply alternatives frequently invest substantial capital in reliance upon continued availability of service; (4) some services that are not profitable to the firm provide substantial external benefits to a region or locality.

A common restriction on exit forbids a firm from ceasing to provide a service previously begun without first obtaining permission from a regulatory agency. Typically, the agency can grant permission to abandon the service only if it finds that abandonment is consistent with the present or future public convenience and necessity—a standard broad enough to encompass virtually any decisional factor the agency wants to consider. See, e.g., FPC v. Moss, 424 U.S. 494 (1976).

Traditionally, most regulated firms were permitted to cease providing service to an individual customer if the customer refused to pay its bills within a specified time. In recent years, however, many agencies have imposed limits on the power of firms that provide essential services like natural gas and electricity to cut off service for nonpayment of bills. The inability of many low income families to pay rapidly rising energy prices and the potential for freezing to death have combined to support these restrictions on termination of service. In 1978, Congress passed a statute requiring all state regulatory agencies to consider restricting the power of electric utilities to terminate service to residential customers for nonpayment of bills when such termination is likely to create a health hazard. Public Utility Regulatory Policies Act of 1978, 16 U.S.C.A. § 2625(g). To the extent that a firm is required to continue service to non-paying or late-paying customers, the firm must incur additional costs that ultimately are reflected in the rates charged to the firm's other customers. Assuming (as we do) that government has an obligation to protect the health of poor people, it is at least questionable whether this protection should be provided through utility regulation rather than through the welfare system. See generally, Posner, *Taxation By Regulation*, 2 Bell.J.Econ. & Management & Sci. 22 (1971).

An agency's power to restrict a regulated firm's exit from a market is limited by the Due Process Clause and the Fifth Amendment's prohibition on taking property without just compensation. A firm cannot be compelled to continue operating an entire regulated business at a loss, Railroad Comm'n v. Eastern Texas R.R., 264 U.S. 79 (1924), nor can it be compelled to continue a regulated business that is unprofitable by subsidizing the regulated business with revenues from unregulated businesses, Brooks–Scanlon Co. v. Railroad Comm'n, 251 U.S. 396 (1920). On the other hand, a firm can be compelled to continue to operate an unprofitable portion of a regulated business as long as the entire regulated business is not unprofitable. Puget Sound Traction, Light & Power Co. v. Reynolds, 244 U.S. 574 (1917). The firm can be compelled to maintain the unprofitable parts of the business even when it must make large new investments to do so. Fort Smith Light & Traction Co. v. Bourland, 267 U.S. 330 (1925).

Regulatory restrictions on exit have several economic effects. First, the existence of such restrictions encourages increased investments in reliance upon continued availability of regulated services. Of course, this result could also be obtained through negotiation of long term contracts between regulated firms and their customers, but the regulatory controls imposed on rates and other terms and conditions of service limit the ability of customers to negotiate long term contracts with regulated firms.

Second, restrictions on exit can produce net benefits to the economy by forcing a firm to continue to provide a service that is unprofitable to it but that provides large benefits to a community that are not reflected in the firm's revenues. For instance, a freight line serving a textile mill might be unprofitable because the mill will pay only $1000 per month for freight service that costs the railroad $1200. Merchants and mill employees in the town may, however, derive an additional $400 of economic benefit a month from the continued operation of the freight line. This benefit cannot be captured by the railroad in its revenues since it has no way of compelling the merchants and mill workers to pay for continued freight service to the mill. In this circumstance, general economic welfare is furthered by keeping the unprofitable line in operation, since the total economic benefits of the line to society ($1,400) exceed its total cost ($1,200).

Existence of beneficial externalities is a major economic justification for forcing regulated firms to continue unprofitable services. There are two major problems with the theory, however. First, it is very difficult to measure external benefits; many commentators believe that regulatory decisions refusing to permit exit from a market are based on nonexistent or trivial external benefits. See Bowman, *The New Haven: A Passenger Railroad for Nonriders*, 9 J.Law & Econ. 49 (1966). Second, if a firm is required to maintain many unprofitable services based on the existence of external benefits, its financial viability may be imperiled over time, since external benefits by definition cannot be captured by the firm in its revenues.

Restrictions on exit can delay or preclude reallocation of productive resources from activities with low or negative economic benefits to activities with high positive benefits. Returning to the hypothetical rail line serving a textile mill, if there actually are no external economic benefits associated with continued service to the mill, forcing the railroad to continue service has three undesirable economic effects. First, the railroad is compelled to devote $1,200 worth of resources to yield $1,000 worth of economic benefits, when those resources could be reallocated to an activity that yields benefits of more than $1,200. Second, keeping the railroad from abandoning a service whose marginal cost exceeds its marginal revenue forces the railroad to engage in internal cross-subsidization of one activity by another activity. For instance, the $200 loss on the service to the textile mill must be recouped through higher rates charged for other services, thus truly "burdening" the railroad's other customers with high rates necessary to offset losses on the unprofitable activity. See section 6B. Those higher rates, in turn, reduce the quantity of the profitable services provided by the firm, thereby producing a misallocation of resources. Finally, the firm's overall financial viability is jeopardized if it has insufficient profitable lines available to subsidize the unprofitable activities it is required to continue. A good case can be made that the economic plight of many firms in the railroad industry has been attributable largely to these adverse economic effects of forcing railroads to continue to provide unprofitable services. See Senate Committee on Commerce, S.Rep.No. 94–499, 94th Cong., 2d Sess. (1974).

Restrictions on exit also cause regulated firms to be very cautious in initiating new services, since they have no assurance that they can withdraw a new service it it becomes unprofitable. As a result, regulatory restrictions on exit are powerful barriers to entry into a market. Thus, regulatory restrictions on exit also insulate regulated firms from competitive pressures that otherwise would force them to increase their efficiency and reduce their prices. See Bailey, *Contestability and the Design of Regulatory and Antitrust Policy,* 71 Am.Econ.Rev. 178 (1981).

In recent years, commentators, legislators, and regulators have recognized the adverse economic effects of the traditionally strict standards for allowing regulated firms to abandon unprofitable (and often uneconomic) services. Several regulatory statutes have been amended to make it easier for firms to cease providing unprofitable services. This easing of restrictions on exit often is accompanied by innovative methods of attempting to determine whether an unprofitable service should be continued because it produces external benefits and permitting regulated firms to internalize the external benefits associated with otherwise unprofitable services. The recent changes in methods of regulating the attempts of railroads to withdraw service illustrate this trend.

In 1976, Congress amended the statutory standard for permitting railroads to abandon unprofitable services. Railroad Revitalization and Regulatory Reform Act of 1976 (4R Act), 49 U.S.C.A. §§ 10903–10904. The ICC has interpreted the new standard in a manner that permits abandonment of rail service in a larger class of cases. See, e.g., Abandonment of Railroad Lines—Use of Opportunity Costs, 360 I.C.C. 571 (1979) (approving use of opportunity costs as a factor in deciding whether to authorize abandonment of rail lines); Chicago & North Western Transportation Co.—Abandonment Between Sanborn and Wanda, 354 I.C.C. 1 (3d Div.1977) (holding that a service that is unprofitable at present and likely to remain unprofitable in the future can be abandoned even if abandonment results in inconvenience and higher costs to shippers.) At the same time it authorized the use of less stringent standards for abandonment of service, Congress also established in the 4R Act an elaborate mechanism through which private parties, states and the federal government could subsidize the continuation of otherwise unprofitable rail services to the extent necessary to avoid abandonment. 49 U.S.C.A. § 1654.

These statutory changes in the approach to abandonment of rail service have produced several improvements in economic efficiency. First, easing the standards for abandonment reduced the misallocation of resources, cross-subsidization, and deterioration of financial condition of the railroads resulting from continuation of unprofitable services. Second, substitution of direct subsidies for internal subsidies has created incentives for subsidization of unprofitable services only when the services generate significant external benefits. Third, use of direct subsidies reduced the financial burden on railroads resulting from continuation of services that otherwise would be unprofitable. Fourth, the greater ease of exit encouraged railroads to become more venturous in providing new services. The new standards are complex, however, requiring the ICC to balance profitability against a plethora of other factors, such as impact on employment, shippers, the local economy, and the environment. As a result of the difficulty of measuring these countervailing factors and political pressure to continue rail services, it is likely that railroads still will be required to continue some uneconomic services.

C. UNINTENDED EFFECTS OF REGULATION ON PRODUCT QUALITY AND EFFICIENCY

Regulation can affect product quality and the efficiency of regulated firms in a variety of ways. Before describing the ways in which regulators can attempt to improve efficiency and quality, some of the unintended adverse effects of regulation on efficiency and quality are described.

Maximum rate regulation tends to reduce the incentive for firms to operate efficiently. Since firm revenues and rates are determined through a cost-plus methodology, firms have less incentive to minimize costs through efficient operating and purchasing practices. It is important to recognize, however, that regulation only reduces incentives for efficiency; regulated firms still are affected by some incentives for efficiency. First, regulatory lag is a potential source of efficiency; since the rates a firm can charge are fixed for some time between rate cases based on the firm's historical or projected costs, it can increase its profits between rate cases by reducing its actual costs. Second, even with cost-plus rate regulation a firm may have an incentive to reduce its costs in order to avoid a loss of sales; the strength of this incentive depends on the price elasticity of customer demand for the firm's product. Third, the management of a firm may have an incentive for efficiency resulting from professional training, pride and personal advancement.

A second potential inadvertent source of inefficiency in regulated firms is referred to as the A–J effect, after the scholars who detected it, Averch and Johnson. If a firm is allowed a rate of return on its capital investment greater than its actual cost of capital, it has an incentive to overinvest in capital assets, thereby increasing its total costs. See Averch & Johnson, *Behavior of the Firm Under Regulatory Constraint*, 52 Am.Econ.Rev. 1052 (1962). The A–J effect has been criticized, however, as being inconsistent with empirical evidence of firm behavior and ignoring the actual manner in which regulators determine allowed rate of return. See Joskow, *Inflation and Environmental Concern: Structural Change in the Process of Public Utility Price Regulation*, 17 J.L. & Econ. 291 (1974).

Rate regulation also can create inefficiency by discouraging coordination among firms that operate in different jurisdictions. For instance, regulators in one state might fear partial loss of control over a firm if the firm uses the facilities of firms in other states or operates facilities jointly with them. As a result, the state agency might erect barriers to such coordination. Yet, coordination might enable the firm to take advantage of substantial economies. It has been argued forcefully that jurisdictional impediments to greater coordination among firms has increased substantially the total cost of electricity in the United States. 2 A. Kahn, *The Economics of Regulation* 70–77 (1971).

Finally, economic regulation sometimes impairs efficiency and improved quality of service by retarding the development and use of superior new technologies. For instance, when railroads and trucking firms devised a more efficient method of combining the two modes of transport by placing loaded trailers on flat cars, the new method could not be implemented until it was approved by the ICC which was slow in responding. Owners of other modes of transport objected to the proposed innovation, with delay in its implementation the inevitable result of protracted litigation. See Ex parte No. 230, Substituted Service—Charges and Practices of For–Hire Carriers and Freight Forwarders, 1964 WL 8725, 8736 (I.C.C.1964).

D. REGULATORY ATTEMPTS TO IMPROVE EFFICIENCY AND PRODUCT QUALITY

Regulatory agencies have the power to order improvements in efficiency or quality of service. Examples from the natural gas and electricity industries illustrate some of the ways in which agencies can exercise direct control over efficiency and quality of service.

In the early 1970's, New York City residents complained that a natural gas company was not effectively avoiding and controlling leaks. The state utility commission responded by instituting an inspection program and by issuing general regulations governing the firm's procedures for avoiding, detecting and repairing leaks. See Jones, *An Example of A Regulatory Alternative to Antitrust: New York Utilities in the Early Seventies*, 73 Colum.L.Rev. 462 (1973).

Most agencies have some power to order regulated firms to improve their quality of service or their efficiency by changing their methods of operation in various respects. Agencies experience great difficulty exercising those powers effectively, however. Improving the operating efficiency of a firm or the quality of service it provides typically requires a complicated series of actions, expenditures and investments in related areas. Devising such an integrated program to improve efficiency or service quality requires a detailed knowledge of the firm's present facilities, operating procedures, expected future needs, and available options. Most agencies do not have sufficient skilled personnel or detailed knowledge of the firms they regulate to order firms to make major changes in their facilities or methods of operation with confidence that significant improvements in efficiency or service quality will result. It is possible, of course, to increase an agency's staffing and funding to enable it to assume a greater role in supervising the activities of regulated firms. It is doubtful, however, that the increased funding and staffing would pay for itself in increased efficiency or quality of service. For a discussion of the problems an agency would encounter if it attempted to improve the efficiency of the electricity industry through pervasive direct regulation of investment planning and operating procedures, see S. Breyer & P. MacAvoy, *Energy Regulation By the Federal Power Commission* 89–121 (1974).

In addition to the power to affect a firm's efficiency and quality of service through direct regulation, agencies can create incentives for efficiency and improved service quality indirectly through their actions in rate cases. An agency can reduce the rates a regulated firm can charge below the level the firm otherwise would be entitled to charge without violating the constitutional prohibition on confiscation of property if the reduction is based on a finding that the quality of service provided by the firm is so low that a rate reduction is warranted.

In Market Street Ry. v. Railroad Commission, 324 U.S. 548 (1945), the agency reduced the rate the firm could charge from seven cents to six cents. The agency conceded that the firm could not earn an adequate rate of return on its investment at the new six cent rate, but it found that the service quality provided by the firm was so low that consumers should be required to pay no more than six cents for the service. The agency's rate reduction order was upheld by the Supreme Court against the firm's contention that the order resulted in an unconstitutional confiscation of private property. The Court based its affirmance of the agency order in part on the agency's finding that the firm's service had deteriorated after its last rate increase. The significance of this basis for affirmance is questionable, however, because of the other reasons given by the Court for its decision. The Court emphasized that the firm could not earn an adequate rate of return on its investment by charging any conceivable rates. Indeed, the Court strongly suggested that the firm could not remain economically viable under any set of rates. Thus, it is not clear how the reasoning in *Market Street Railway* would apply to an agency order reducing the rates charged by an economically viable firm that provides low quality service.

In D.C. Transit System v. Washington Metropolitan Area Transit Commission, 466 F.2d 394 (D.C.Cir.1972), the agency refused to consider the firm's request for rate increase until the firm took actions designed to improve its quality of service, specifically, the acquisition of new buses at a cost of $6.4 million. The firm appealed, contending that the agency order was confiscatory. The firm also argued that it could not attract enough capital to purchase the buses without first obtaining a rate increase. The court affirmed the agency's order, holding that a firm's rates could be held hostage to a service improvement. That is, its allowed rate of return could be held to a level that otherwise would be confiscatory based on a finding that the firm is providing low quality service.

The approach to improved quality of service reflected in *Market Street Railway* and *D.C. Transit* has superficial appeal. If firms know that they will be punished in rate cases for providing low quality service (and conversely rewarded for providing high quality service), this knowledge should create an incentive to provide service of acceptable quality. There are, however, two significant problems with this approach. First, agencies and reviewing courts have great difficulty distinguishing the causes of low quality service. If the service provided by the firm is poor because the firm has been allowed an inadequate rate of return in the past, the proper remedy is to permit the firm to increase its rates rather than to refuse to increase its rates or to order a rate reduction. Second, even if poor management is a primary cause of the firm's low quality service, the firm rarely can improve its service under more efficient management without charging rates that allow it a competitive rate of return. Improvements in service usually require large capital expenditures, and a firm's ability to generate capital or to attract it from outside investors is dependent on its rate of return. Not surprisingly, the trolley company whose rates were reduced in *Market Street Railway* declared bankruptcy and the bus company whose rates were at issue in *D.C. Transit* was sold to the City of Washington at a low price. Reduction of the rates a firm can charge based on its low quality service may create a general incentive for *other* regulated firms to improve the quality of service they provide, but such an action frequently causes the ultimate demise of the particular firm that was the subject of the rate order.

Rewarding a firm that provides particularly good service with a higher than normal rate of return also creates problems. The A–J effect is likely to cause firms with a rate of return higher than their actual cost of capital to overinvest in capital assets to the ultimate detriment of their customers.

Askew v. Bevis, 283 So.2d 337 (Fla.1973), illustrates a different method of relating rates to quality of service. The agency found that the firm was providing low quality service. Instead of declining to grant the firm's rate increase, however, the agency granted the increase and required the firm to place the additional revenues in an escrow account until the firm improved its service quality. As a result, the firm had a clear incentive to improve its service, but it also could obtain the capital necessary to improve its service by borrowing against the escrow account, at least if it could convince investors that it could improve its service through additional capital investments. The approach taken in *Askew* seems more promising than the draconian measures taken in *Market Street Railway* and *D.C. Transit*. Even under this approach, however, the agency has the unenviable task of determining the level of service that is satisfactory and, where service falls below this level, the cause of the low quality service.

Rate regulation of a firm decreases the firm's incentive to operate efficiently and to provide high quality service. Regulatory agencies have attempted to ameliorate this problem through a variety of direct and indirect means. To date, no satisfactory solution to this problem has been identified. It is likely that economic regulation simply can not replicate the natural incentives to efficiency and high quality service created by competition.

We discuss more sophisticated and systematic ways of improving the performance of regulated firms in chapter 15.

CHAPTER IX

MINIMUM RATE REGULATION

Many industries are subject to minimum rate regulation instead of, or in addition to, maximum rate regulation. Minimum rate regulation prohibits a firm from providing a product or service at less than the specified minimum rate. The most common justifications for minimum rate regulation are: to avoid destructive competition; to ensure quality, safety and sufficient capacity; to avoid predatory pricing; to protect an existing regulatory scheme; and, to permit internal cross-subsidization of socially desirable activities.

A. AVOIDING DESTRUCTIVE COMPETITION

The justification advanced most frequently in support of minimum rate regulation is the need to avoid destructive competition. The term destructive competition is used loosely to refer to many conditions, including markets in which normal competition causes the demise of some of the less efficient firms. When used in this sense, avoidance of destructive competition is an exceedingly weak argument for regulation. As noted in section 2A, competition provides great economic advantages in part

234

because it encourages efficiency by eliminating the least efficient firms.

Destructive competition also is used in a more narrow sense, however, to describe the unfavorable potential results of competition among firms with particular cost characteristics. In a competitive market, firms sell at a price equal to marginal cost. If competitive firms have high fixed costs and excess capacity, and they sell all their products at marginal cost, they will not earn revenues sufficient to cover all their fixed costs. See generally, 2 A. Kahn, *The Economics of Regulation* 172–178 (1971). With excess capacity, the marginal cost of a product is below its fully allocated cost because marginal cost does not include the cost of capacity when a firm already has excess capacity. The cost of the excess capacity is a sunk cost that is ignored for pricing purposes. Eventually, the financial condition of firms in this circumstance deteriorates; they are not able to maintain their assets in good condition; the quality of products and services they provide declines; and their customers may suffer as a result.

Minimum rate regulation, eliminating or greatly restricting price competition among the firms, is a typical response to the problem of destructive competition. If minimum rates are set equal to the firm's average or fully allocated cost of providing goods and services, its revenues will be sufficient to permit it to recover all its fixed costs.

Railroads are a good example of an industry in which the potential for destructive competition exists, since many railroads have high fixed costs and excess capacity. Assume, for instance, two railroads with identical costs that provide service only on a single route on which they compete for traffic. Each has fixed costs of $1,000 and a marginal cost of $1 per unit of transportation service provided. Total demand for transportation service at a unit price of $1 is 3,000 units. Competition between the two railroads would force each to charge a unit price of $1, equal to the marginal cost of a unit of service. Assuming that the traffic is divided evenly between them at the identical $1 unit price, each railroad will earn $1,500 in revenues. This level of revenue will permit each railroad to recover its variable costs, but not its fixed costs. With minimum rate regulation, each railroad could charge a price based on its fully allocated unit cost of $1.67, and each could earn revenues of $2500—enough to permit recovery of both fixed and variable costs. Actually, the unit rate would have to be set above $1.67 to achieve this result, since the number of transportation units demanded would fall below 3,000 as a result of the increased unit price. At some point, the railroads would lose revenues as a result of further rate increases, depending on the price elasticity of demand for rail transport. This effect of elasticity of demand is one of the major weaknesses of minimum rate regulation.

Use of minimum rate regulation to avoid destructive competition can be criticized on many grounds. The destructive competition rationale has formed the basis for minimum rate regulation in many industries in which there is no potential for destructive competition. For instance, minimum rate regulation of the trucking industry was justified largely by fear of destructive competition. The primary evidence to support the contention that destructive competition exists in the trucking industry is the high rate of business failures by trucking firms during the 1930's. See Report of the Federal Coordinator of Transportation, H.R.Doc.No. 89, 74th Cong., 1st Sess. 113–17 (1934). This evidence is scarcely persuasive, however, since the generally depressed economic conditions of the 1930's produced a high number of business failures in many industries. Trucking is not an activity that involves high fixed costs, so it has little potential for destructive competition.

Minimum rate regulation eliminates price competition and substitutes for it a set of administered prices higher than the prices competition would yield. The minimum rates often are set at a level high enough to permit the least efficient firms to earn an adequate rate of return. These higher prices have three adverse effects. They cause an artificial reduction in the quantity of the product or service demanded; they transfer wealth from consumers to the regulated firms; and they eliminate incentives to use the products and services of the most efficient firms. The net effect often is serious misallocation of resources.

Minimum rate regulation based on avoidance of destructive competition has been imposed on many industries whose cost structures suggest no real potential for destructive competition, including airlines (Air Freight Rate Investigation, 9 C.A.B. 340 (1948)), dry cleaners (State Board of Dry Cleaners v. Thrift–D–Lux Cleaners (Cal.1953)), and milk producers (Nebbia v. New York, 291 U.S. 502 (1934)). Even when real potential for destructive competition exists, as with railroads, minimum rate regulation is a questionable response to the problem. In this situation, imposition of minimum rates still results in considerable economic inefficiency. Higher prices reduce the quantity of the product or service demanded. This reduction in quantity demanded increases the amount of idle capacity in the industry. The higher prices overstate the actual resource costs required to make another unit of the product available by placing a value on fixed costs that are already sunk in an industry with excess capacity. The lack of price competition reduces incentives for efficiency and keeps consumers from choosing the most efficient firms in the industry.

There are two alternative ways of responding to the potential for destructive competition that offer significant economic advantages over minimum rate regulation—allow the destructive competition to take place or reimburse the industry's fixed costs with a direct subsidy. If destructive competition is simply allowed to occur, the end result may be quite tolerable. Permitting firms with high fixed costs and excess capacity to sell at prices based on relatively low marginal cost encourages full use of the capacity of the industry, gives consumers price signals that reflect the existence of the excess capacity, and gives the firms price signals indicating they should not invest in new capacity. Some firms in the industry undoubtedly would go out of business, but they would be the least efficient, highest cost firms. As the least efficient firms withdrew from the market, the amount of excess capacity would decline, and the more efficient firms would survive. The process of permitting a return to competitive equilibrium through this sequence of events could be painful and protracted, but it may be preferable to the alternative of accepting the high economic costs of minimum rate regulation indefinitely.

Providing direct subsidies to firms confronting potential destructive competition to cover their high fixed costs is another alternative to minimum rate regulation. It avoids the allocative inefficiency of minimum rate regulation, since the firms would be encouraged to use their capacity fully and to sell at prices based on marginal cost. Compared with the alternative of doing nothing, the subsidy has the advantage of avoiding the protracted period required to permit the industry to return to competitive equilibrium. It has the disadvantage, however, of not providing a natural mechanism for eliminating inefficient firms and for channeling demand to the most efficient firms.

B. ASSURING QUALITY, SAFETY AND SUFFICIENT CAPACITY

Minimum rate regulation often is imposed as a method of assuring that an industry supplies an adequate quantity of high quality, safe products or services. This rationale for minimum rate regulation is based on the premise that price competition will create incentives for firms to save money by reducing their spending on safety, quality and adequate capacity, thereby hurting the consuming public. Minimum rate regulation eliminates this incentive and provides firms sufficient revenues to earn an adequate rate of return while continuing to maintain an adequate supply of safe, high quality products. This rationale has been used as a justification for minimum rate regulation of taxicabs, trucking (American Trucking Associations v. United States, 344 U.S. 298 (1953)), airlines (Air Freight Investigation, 9 C.A.B. 340 (1948)), milk producers (Nebbia v. New York, 291 U.S. 502 (1934)), and dry cleaners (State Board of Dry Cleaners v. Thrift–D–Lux Cleaners, 254 P.2d 29 (Cal.1953)).

It is not at all clear that minimum rate regulation actually improves the safety or quality of an industry's products, or that it assures adequate capacity. There is no empirical evidence to support a correlation between minimum rate regulation and safety, quality or adequate capacity. Moreover, the theoretical premises to support such a correlation are suspect. Why not rely on consumer expressions of preference through purchase decisions to ensure a level of quality, safety and capacity desired by consumers? If there are important safety or quality features that consumers are not likely to recognize, why not require those features through direct safety regulation instead of relying on the indirect effects of minimum rate regulation?

Even the intermediate link between minimum rate regulation and greater financial stability of the firms in an industry is weak. Not all firms are aided by minimum rate regulation; the largest, most efficient firms often lose revenues to smaller, less efficient firms that otherwise would not be able to compete effectively. Minimum rate regulation does not eliminate the inefficient firms with precarious financial situations that may tend to cut corners on safety; indeed, it may permit such marginal firms to remain in business when competition would force them out of the market.

The presumed link between a firm's financial situation and the safety of its products is also suspect. Some firms earn increased revenues as a result of minimum rate regulation, but there is no assurance they will spend any portion of those increased revenues on safety or quality. The unavailability of price competition may create an incentive for firms to spend more on quality features that are highly visible to consumers, e.g., plush upholstery and good liquor on airplanes, but there is no increased incentive to spend on quality and safety features consumers cannot detect, since these features cannot possibly attract more customers. Thus, if the rationale for minimum rate regulation is concern that consumers cannot identify important safety and quality features, that rationale seems weak indeed.

While the benefits of minimum rate regulation are unclear at best, its adverse effects are well-documented; minimum rate regulation results in higher prices, transfer of wealth from consumers to producers, reduced industry output, lower use of available capacity, and retention of inefficient firms in the industry. See Levine, *Regulating Airmail Transportation*, 18 J.Law & Econ. 317 (1975). Over the last two decades, the U.S. has eliminated minimum rate regulation of airlines, trucking and railroads. Over the last two decades, the U.S. has eliminated minimum rate regulation of airlines, trucking, and railroads.

C. AVOIDANCE OF PREDATORY PRICING

Another common justification for minimum rate regulation is to preclude firms from engaging in predatory pricing. Predatory pricing refers to an attempt by a firm to obtain market power in an industry by reducing its prices just long enough to drive its competitors out of the market. After competition has been eliminated, the firm can exercise monopoly power to raise its prices above competitive levels.

The basic weakness of the predatory pricing rationale is the evidence that predatory pricing is not a significant problem. See Isaac & Smith, *In Search of Predatory Pricing,* 93 J.Pol.Econ. 320 (1985). Predatory pricing is not an effective way of obtaining market power. Is is very expensive for a firm to reduce its prices enough over a sufficient period of time to force competitors out of business. Moreover, even if a firm is willing to incur the high cost of eliminating competitors through predatory pricing, once it begins to exercise monopoly power by charging super-competitive prices, it creates incentives for new firms to enter the industry. The potential for new entrants limits the price the firm can charge and, hence, the magnitude of its monopoly profits. Economists have demonstrated consistently that predatory pricing does not pay. See McGee, *Predatory Price Cutting: The Standard Oil (N.J.) Case*, 1 J.Law & Econ. 137 (1958); Easterbrook, *Predatory Strategies and Counterstrategies*, 48 U.Chi.L.Rev. 263 (1981). *See also* Matsushita Electric Industrial Co. v. Zenith Radio Corp., 475 U.S. 574 (1986) (finding implausible alleged conspiracy to engage in predatory pricing because such a conspiracy would make no economic sense). Since predatory pricing seems to be a chimerical concern, and minimum rate regulation imposes demonstrable economic costs, imposition of minimum rate regulation to avoid the potential for predatory pricing does not appear to be a defensible decision.

D. PROTECTION OF AN EXISTING REGULATORY SCHEME

Often minimum rate regulation of an industry evolves indirectly from maximum rate regulation of another industry through a series of policy decisions. The history of regulation of the transportation industry illustrates this phenomenon. First, maximum rate regulation was imposed on an industry (railroads) because the industry was perceived to have monopoly power. The maximum rate regulation was implemented in a manner that produced rates based on average or fully allocated costs, rather than marginal costs, to enable the regulated firms to earn aggregate revenues that provided an adequate rate of return on their capital investments.

Then a new industry (trucking) emerged that competed for some of the customers of the regulated industry. The new industry had a natural incentive to charge prices based on marginal cost to attract customers from the regulated industry. If a regulated (railroad) firm responded by lowering its rates to marginal cost where it was confronted with competition from the new unregulated industry, it would lose revenues, and its pattern of rates would become uneven. Where it faced competition, its rates would tend to be based on marginal cost; where it did not face competition, it would seek permission to charge rates above average cost in order to make up the deficiency in aggregate revenues caused by the necessity to charge rates less than average cost in circumstances where it confronted competition. If it did not lower its rates below average cost to meet the new unregulated competition, it would lose customers, and its revenues would decline even more than they would have if the firm reduced its rates to marginal cost in order to retain customers. Thus, in this situation the regulated firm will pressure the regulatory agency to permit it to charge higher

rates in markets where it does not face competition in order to maintain its aggregate revenues at an acceptable level.

Thus, whether or not the previously regulated firms respond to competition by reducing prices, the introduction of unregulated competition disrupts the pre-existing methods of regulating the rates charged by the industry that originally had monopoly power. A typical response to this disruption of the pre-existing regulatory scheme is to extend regulation to the new industry, with primary emphasis on imposition of minimum rates. If the new industry is prohibited from engaging in effective price competition with the previously regulated industry, the old methods of regulating the industry might remain viable.

At this point in the process, however, serious problems develop. Where they are in competition with each other, firms in both the new and the old industry place pressure on the agency to permit them to charge rates low enough to attract most of the customers for which the firms are competing. This enmeshes the agency in the difficult administrative task of determining which regulated firm *should* serve each group of customers, and then establishing minimum rates that produce that result. In the case of transportation, Congress determined that selection of the firm to serve the market should be based on the firms' relative costs of providing service to the market. This, in turn, forced the agency to decide whether marginal cost or average cost should be used as the basis for determining which firm could serve the market at least cost. The foregoing is a history in outline form of the sequence of events that led to the controversy in American Commercial Lines v. Louisville & Nashville R. Co., concerning the use of marginal cost versus average cost to determine which mode of transport has an inherent advantage in serving a market. See section 7C.

Since we believe that marginal cost provides the superior method of comparing the advantages of two competing industries, and since unregulated competition would yield prices based on marginal cost, the preferred response to potential disruption of a regulatory scheme by the emergence of new competition for the regulated industry would seem to be deregulation of the previously regulated industry. Once the regulated industry is faced with effective competition, the original natural monopoly rationale for regulating the industry disappears. At this point, continued regulation of the old industry and extension of regulation to the new industry can only be predicated on one of the other justifications for minimum rate regulation. Since all the other justifications for minimum rate regulation are, upon close analysis, theoretically weak and empirically unsupported, deregulation of the competing industries seems far superior to extension of regulation to the new industry.

This conviction is strengthened by the realization that new competitive forces constantly will threaten the preexisting scheme for regulating the original industry, and efforts to preclude entry of, or to extend regulation to, all potential new entrants in the competitive fray are unlikely to succeed. The inevitable efforts to evade minimum rate regulation through new forms of competition and the attempts of regulators to block new forms of competition impose significant costs on society.

E. PERMITTING INTERNAL CROSS–SUBSIDIZATION

Providing revenues from which regulated firms can be expected to subsidize unprofitable activities is a final justification for minimum rate regulation. As discussed in section 8B, regulated firms sometimes provide services that are unprofitable to them but provide benefits to individuals outside the firm that are not reflected in the firm's revenues. Where these external benefits, combined with the benefits reflected in the firm's revenues from providing the service, exceed the cost of the service, continuation of the unprofitable service provides net benefits to society. Restrictions on market exit can be used to force firms to continue these unprofitable but socially desirable services. There is a limit, however, to the extent of the ability of a regulated firm to provide unprofitable services, since the firm experiences a net loss on each such service.

Minimum rate regulation arguably allows firms to continue to provide unprofitable but socially desirable services by increasing artificially the firm's revenues from other services to offset revenue deficits from the unprofitable services. This justification for minimum rates also is subject to criticism on several grounds. First, minimum rate regulation does not uniformly increase firm revenues. If demand for the firm's product or service is relatively elastic, minimum rate regulation may actually decrease firm revenues. Second, many of the unprofitable services firms are required to continue do not generate sufficient external benefits to offset the cost of the service; thus, they should be discontinued rather than subsidized. See section 8B supra. Third, even if some unprofitable services should be continued, direct subsidies probably provide a better means of accomplishing this result than internal subsidization made possible through minimum rate regulation, given all the adverse effects of minimum rate regulation described above.

F. METHODS OF MINIMUM RATE REGULATION

It is difficult to generalize concerning the methodology used to establish minimum rates, since the stated and unstated purposes of minimum rate regulation vary from industry to industry and from case to case. One relatively common technique is to set a single uniform rate as both the maximum and minimum any firm can charge, with the rate based on average cost to permit firms to earn their allowed revenue requirements. Since regulated firms with different cost characteristics often serve the same market, the uniform rate must be based on some approximation of the average cost of the competitive firms. See, e.g., General Passenger–Fare Investigation, 32 C.A.B. 291 (1961). Often, however, the agency feels compelled to set the minimum rate below average cost in order to permit regulated firms to compete effectively against unregulated firms. See, e.g., Railway Express Agency v. CAB, 243 F.2d 422 (D.C.Cir.1957).

Some agencies consider protection of the economic viability of all regulated firms their primary obligation in setting minimum rates. Consistent with this goal, they prohibit any rates lower than the average cost of the least efficient firm serving the market. See, e.g., Petroleum Products in Illinois Territory, 280 I.C.C. 681 (1951). Statutory amendments and judicial opinions have tempered the power of agencies to pursue this goal. See, e.g., ICC v. New York, New Haven & Hartford R.R., 372 U.S. 744 (1963) (holding that a rate reduction could not be rejected solely because it would have the effect of diverting traffic to the firm offering the reduced rate). There is little doubt, however, that some agencies continue to establish minimum rates at levels designed to protect the economic viability of all regulated firms.

G. RECENT TRENDS IN MINIMUM RATE REGULATION

In recent years, some agencies and legislatures have recognized that minimum rate regulation often creates more problems than it solves. Some agencies have reduced their use of minimum rate regulation, and legislatures have reduced or eliminated the statutory power of some agencies to impose minimum rates. The best example of this trend to date is the airline industry. In the mid–1970's, then CAB Chairman Alfred Kahn announced the Board's intention to allow airlines to reduce their rates significantly below the minimum rates previously imposed by the Board. This relaxation of minimum rate regulation by the agency was followed by passage of a statute virtually eliminating the Board's power to set minimum airline rates. Airline Deregulation Act of 1978, 49 U.S.C.A. §§ 1301–1729.

In the Railroad Revitalization and Regulatory Reform Act of 1976 (4R Act), Congress also narrowed the power of the ICC to set minimum rates for railroads. 49 U.S.C.A. §§ 10701–10786. The 4R Act prohibits the ICC from finding any proposed rate too low if it contributes to the going concern value of the proponent railroad. Any rate that equals or exceeds variable costs is presumed to contribute to the firm's going concern value. 49 U.S.C.A. § 10701.

The federal government has eliminated its role in minimum rate regulation in almost all contexts except agriculture and ocean shipping. Many state and local governments continue to implement minimum rate regulation in a variety of contexts, however, with significant adverse effects on consumers.

CHAPTER X

RESTRICTIONS ON ENTRY

A. CONSTITUTIONAL LIMITS

Beginning in the nineteenth century and extending into the early part of the twentieth century, the Supreme Court limited the power of legislatures to control entry into markets. The Court held in a series of cases that regulatory barriers to entry were permissible under the Due Process Clause only when there was a demonstrable failure of the market affected by the regulatory scheme, for example, the market was monopolized. See chapter 2 and its analysis of the "business affected with a public interest" and substantive due process tests. With the demise of substantive due process in the 1930's, however, the federal courts no longer required proof of market failure to justify regulatory restrictions on entry. Such restrictions are now upheld routinely, subject only to the need to establish a reasonable relationship between the restriction and some plausible governmental interest. See, e.g., New Motor Vehicle Board v. Orrin W. Fox Co., 439 U.S. 96 (1978) (upholding California statute limiting entry into the business of selling automobiles). But see, Mashaw, *Constitutional Delegation: Notes Toward a Public, Public Law*, 54 Tul.L.Rev.

849 (1980). Some state courts continue to hold unconstitutional restrictions on market entry that seem to the Court to be anticompetitive. See, e.g., Aston Park Hospital, Inc., 193 S.E.2d 729 (N.C. 1973) (holding that legislative restrictions on construction of new hospitals are not reasonably related to the public health and, therefore, violate the Due Process Clause of the state constitution). Moreover, federal courts continue to hold restrictions on market entry unconstitutional where the restrictions have the effect of discriminating unnecessarily against interstate commerce. See, e.g., Dean Milk Co. v. City of Madison, 340 U.S. 349 (1951) (holding unconstitutional a city ordinance making it unlawful to sell milk in the city unless the milk was processed in the city on grounds that the ordinance discriminated against out of state milk when nondiscriminatory measures would serve the public purposes as well).

B. REASONS FOR RESTRICTING ENTRY

There are four common reasons for restricting entry into a market: (1) to protect consumers from firms that may provide low quality services; (2) to continue the advantages of a natural monopoly; (3) to allocate inherently scarce resources; and (4) to sustain a system of minimum rate regulation.

1. ASSURANCE OF SERVICE QUALITY

Regulatory restrictions on entry into some otherwise unregulated markets are based entirely on the perceived need to protect the public from firms or individuals who are not qualified to provide a product or service. Restrictions on admission to many professions and skilled trades, such as law and medicine, are based on the premise that there is a minimum level of knowledge or skill required to perform tasks adequately, and the public should be protected from individuals who do not possess the minimum skill level. Of course, restrictions on entry of this type must also be founded on the belief that members of the consuming public are not capable of determining for themselves whether an individual possesses the skills requisite to the service offered. To the extent that restrictions on entry into professions or skilled trades preclude individuals from providing services for which they are qualified, the effect of such restrictions is to decrease the supply of the service, increase its price, and render it unavailable to some segments of the public.

All restrictions of this type have the potential for manipulation by individuals who have an interest in increasing the price of a service in order to enhance their income. In a few cases, the courts have limited the power of members of a profession to limit entry under authority delegated by statute. See, e.g., Gibson v. Berryhill, 411 U.S. 564 (1973) (holding that a board composed entirely of optometrists in private practice could not decide whether optometrists employed by corporations could practice optometry because the board members had too great a personal stake in the decision); see also, Withrow v. Larkin, 421 U.S. 35 (1975). But see, e.g., Friedman v. Rogers, 440 U.S. 1 (1979). In most cases, however, restrictions on entry into professions or skilled trades have been upheld as reasonably related to the permissible goal of protecting the public from unqualified individuals. See, e.g., Hackin v. Lockwood, 361 F.2d 499 (9th Cir.1966) (holding that a state can prohibit an individual from practicing law solely on the basis that the individual did not graduate from a law school accredited by the American Bar Association).

Many comprehensive regulatory schemes also impose threshold barriers to entry into a regulated industry based on the need to screen out unqualified firms. Regulatory statutes often preclude firms from entering a regulated industry unless they can establish that they are "able ... properly to do the acts and perform the service proposed." Natural Gas Act, Section 7(e), 15 U.S.C.A. § 717f(e). In some statutes, the threshold for entry is particularized to include standards of financial responsibility designed to protect the public from firms that otherwise might enter an industry, cause harm to individuals, and then have inadequate financial resources to compensate for the damage they have done. For instance, any trucking firm must carry at least $1,000,000 in liability insurance as a prerequisite to entry into the regulated market. Motor Carrier Act of 1980, 49 U.S.C.A. § 10927(b)(3).

2.   PROTECTING NATURAL MONOPOLY

A natural monopoly is a situation in which high fixed costs yield economies of scale so great that the relevant market can be served at lowest cost by a single firm. In this situation, two or more firms attempting to compete in the market would produce undesirable economic consequences. See section 2B1 supra. Competition between the firms would be unstable, with each firm tending to sell at marginal cost, but none able to cover all fixed costs at this price level. The firms would be required to duplicate each other's major facilities, such as telephone, electric, or natural gas lines. This duplication of facilities would increase the cost of service to the public by limiting the extent to which each firm could take advantage of economies of scale. Moreover, duplication of facilities would cause unnecessary environmental and aesthetic harm. To avoid these potential adverse consequences of competition and to permit firms to take full advantage of economies of scale, entry is restricted in markets that are natural monopolies. In theory, rate regulation of the firm that is allowed to serve a market free of competition ensures that consumers receive the benefits of the economies of scale enjoyed by the firm.

Entry restrictions typically are enforced by granting a single firm an exclusive franchise to serve a particular market or by requiring that all firms obtain a certificate or license to enter the market. Regulatory restrictions on entry premised on the desirability of permitting consumers to enjoy the advantages of economies of scale and avoiding unnecessary duplication of facilities have been upheld consistently by the courts against attacks on their constitutionality. See, e.g., Idaho Power & Light Co. v. Blomquist, 141 P. 1083 (Idaho 1914).

When entry into a regulated industry is restricted, the agency typically allows a firm to enter a new market only if it finds that entry is consistent with the present or future public convenience or necessity. Entry is not permitted simply because the agency believes that competition is preferable in the abstract; the agency must find that competition will provide benefits to the public in the particular market. See Hawaiian Telephone Co. v. FCC, 498 F.2d 771 (D.C.Cir.1974). Thus, where the reason for limiting entry is to permit consumers to enjoy the full benefits of economies of scale, the agency must determine administratively the extent of the potentially available economies of scale relative to the size of the market at issue. See Carroll Broadcasting Co. v. FCC, 258 F.2d 440 (D.C.Cir.1958). This is a difficult task. There are numerous examples of cases in which an agency or a reviewing court refused to permit entry of a new firm even though the economies of scale seemed modest relative to the aggregate demand in the market. See, e.g., FCC v. RCA Communications, Inc., 346 U.S. 86 (1953) (holding that FCC could not authorize a new firm to enter the radiotelegraph market between the United States, Portugal and the Netherlands, even when such entry would not require substantial investment in new facilities, because FCC did not specifically find that competition would benefit the public).

If entry is prohibited where the cost characteristics of the industry would permit two or more firms to compete effectively in a market, the public loses potential benefits. Regulation cannot create as strong incentives for efficiency as can competition. See section 8 C.

There are two related grounds for criticizing regulatory restrictions on entry based on the need to protect the advantages of a natural monopoly. First, because of the difficulty of determining the potential economies of scale available in a relevant market, entry often is restricted when competition between two or more firms would be effective without sacrificing economies of scale. In these circumstances, consumers lose the potential efficiency-enhancing value of competition.

Second, when economies of scale are sufficient to justify precluding a firm's entry into a market, regulatory restrictions on entry are unnecessary because the existence of the economies of scale will deter new firms from entering the market anyway. If a potential entrant sees a market that is being served by a single firm whose cost characteristics cause it to have a natural monopoly in that market, the potential entrant rarely will have an incentive to invest the large amount of capital necessary to enter the market. It will recognize that it has little opportunity to earn a return on its investment in the unstable competitive market that would be created by entry of a second firm.

It is possible for a market structure to develop in which several firms are in unstable competition for a market that should be served by a single firm. Typically, this occurs in industries in which economies of scale have increased over time; the market originally was appropriate for competition among several firms, but increasing economies of scale now have rendered it a natural monopoly. Market structures of this type were common in the electricity and natural gas industries in the early part of this century. When inappropriate market structures evolve in this manner, however, they cannot be avoided through restrictions on entry, and unstable competition between the firms ultimately will produce a single firm market structure in any event. Restrictions on entry would be ineffective because the increased future economies of scale cannot be foreseen any better by regulators than by the firms that entered the market originally under very different cost conditions. Unstable competition ultimately will produce a single firm market because the competing firms will have a natural incentive to merge to avoid losses resulting from unstable competition and to take full advantage of the newly available economies of scale. See generally G. Brown, *The Gas Light Company of Baltimore* (1936).

There are two limited circumstances in which a new firm has an incentive to enter a market that was previously served by a natural monopolist— when the firm is attracted by the potential for "cream-skimming," and when it can use a new technology that allows it to provide service at prices lower than those charged by the natural monopolist. Both circumstances are illustrated in Specialized Common Carrier Services, 29 F.C.C.2d 870 (1975).

In that case, several firms requested authority to construct microwave facilities to provide specialized communication services in various parts of the country. At the time, microwave communications was a relatively new technology with the potential to provide better service at lower cost than the traditional transmission by wire used by the dominant firm in the market, AT & T. The rates charged by AT & T reflected the high cost of its pre-existing equipment. It was in the process of replacing that equipment gradually with microwave equipment, but the original cost of much of its traditional equipment had not yet been fully depreciated and reflected in its prior rates. The new firms had no pre-existing capital goods to depreciate. Thus, the new firms could charge compensatory rates below those charged by AT & T if they were permitted to enter the market. Yet, if AT & T lowered its rates in response to the competition from the new firms, it would never be able to recover the full cost of its pre-existing capital assets. In this circumstance, an argument can be made that it is inequitable to allow new entrants where the effect is to preclude the pre-existing firm from recovering the cost of its prior investments under depreciation schedules previously approved by the agency. It must be recognized, however, that restricting entry in this situation reduces the incentive to develop new technology and reduces the speed with which that technology is introduced in the market. Thus, a high social cost must be paid to avoid arguable inequity.

The *Specialized Common Carrier Services* case also illustrates the "cream skimming" incentive for market entry. The new firms did not propose to provide communications services for all potential users; rather they proposed only to serve certain high density geographic areas and high volume users. AT & T complained that the specific markets proposed were particularly profitable, and that other users of AT & T's services would suffer increased rates if the new firms were allowed to "skim the cream" from AT & T's market. The potential for cream-skimming can exist only, however, if the rates charged by the pre-existing firm yield subsidization of some markets and consumers by others. The FCC previously has established a rate structure for AT & T that required internal cross-subsidization of low volume, low density markets by high volume, high density markets, because the FCC perceived significant societal advantages in a structure of uniform rates based on average cost of service. In this situation, if new firms are allowed to serve the subsidizing markets, and the pre-existing firm is left only with the subsidized markets, the pre-existing firm must increase the rates it charges the subsidized markets in order to continue to earn a fair return on its investment. Thus, the decision to permit new entry in this circumstance reflects an implicit judgment concerning the desirability of the internal cross-subsidization required by average cost ratemaking—if continued cross-subsidization is desirable, entry should be prohibited; if continued cross-subsidization is undesirable, entry should be permitted and the pre-existing firm should be allowed to depart from a rate structure based on average cost.

3. RATIONING LIMITED RESOURCES

In some circumstances, an agency has no apparent choice but to limit entry because the available resources will not physically permit more than a discrete number of firms to participate in a market. The classic example of entry limitations based on scarce resources is the broadcasting industry. Because of electrical interference, there are a limited number of broadcasting frequencies available in any geographic area. In the absence of an effective market for broadcasting frequencies, available frequencies must be allocated administratively through regulatory restrictions on entry. Restrictions on entry based on the need to allocate limited resources have been upheld consistently. See, e.g., FCC v. Sanders Bros. Radio Station, 309 U.S. 642 (1940). Where two competing firms each apply for a mutually exclusive license to enter a market, a regulatory agency cannot grant a license to one without first conducting a hearing in which the proposals of the competing applicants are compared. Ashbacker Radio Corp. v. FCC, 326 U.S. 327 (1945). The basis for selecting the firm that is permitted to enter the market in this situation is discussed in section 11 C.

Changes in technology can undermine the factual premises that support restrictions on entry based on limited resources. For instance, the advent of ultra high frequency (UHF) TV broadcasting and cable television have at least arguably transformed TV broadcasting into an industry in which there is no effective resource constraint on the number of firms that can compete. But see Red Lion Broadcasting Co. v. FCC, 395 U.S. 367 (1969) (upholding constitutionality of FCC's "fairness doctrine" on grounds that broadcast frequencies are inherently limited).

4. PROTECTING MINIMUM
RATE REGULATION

The effectiveness of any regulatory scheme for establishing minimum rates depends on the power to limit entry into the market. Requiring all firms in a market to charge rates above the level that otherwise would result from competition permits many firms to earn supracompetitive profits, which in turn attracts potential new entrants to the market. If unlimited entry is permitted, and the new entrants are allowed to charge rates of their own selection, they will siphon business from the firms previously in the market or force those firms to charge rates lower than the previously established minimum rates, thereby destroying the effectiveness of the minimum rate structure. If unlimited entry is permitted and the new entrants are subjected to the pre-existing minimum rates, the industry soon will be characterized by excess capacity. Thus, minimum rate regulation invariably is coupled with regulatory limitations on market entry.

In order to limit entry into a market, it is first necessary to define the market. Regulatory statutes typically limit a firm's right to enter a market by providing services for others, but rarely limit the right of consuming firms or individuals to provide services for their own consumption. Consumers of services that are subject to minimum rate regulation have an incentive to find sources of the service that are not regulated, since the cost of the service typically is well below the minimum rate applicable to the service. Thus, consumers often attempt to purchase services in a form that disguises the fact that they are purchasing services. Two cases from the trucking and airline industries illustrate the problems encountered by agencies in their attempts to preclude disguised entry into markets.

The most superficial method of entering a transportation market in a manner that avoids minimum rate regulation was through a buy-sell arrangement. Instead of purchasing transportation service from a regulated trucking company, for instance, a firm desiring transportation service simply sold its goods to another firm that transported the goods to the ultimate purchaser for resale. The transporting firm thereby arguably avoided all regulatory constraints since it was only providing service for its own consumption. It could make a profit by charging rates (in the form of the difference between its buying and selling price) above its costs but below the minimum rate applicable to regulated firms that provided transportation for hire.

The ICC attempted to avoid these disguised methods of entering the regulated trucking business through application of its "primary business test." A particular application of this test was disputed in Red Ball Motor Freight, Inc. v. Shannon, 377 U.S. 311 (1964). There, the firm purported to engage primarily in the purchase of livestock in Texas for resale in Louisiana. It transported the livestock in its own trucks, and purchased sugar in Louisiana for resale in Texas. It also transported the sugar in its own trucks. The firm argued that its transport of the sugar was exempt from regulation, since it was not a service provided for hire. The ICC, however, contended that the firm was engaged in disguised provision of for hire transportation service that was particularly advantageous to the firm because its trucks otherwise would return to Texas empty. Hence, the firm's cost of transporting sugar on the backhaul portion of its trips was particularly low, well below the minimum rate applicable to for hire transportation over that distance.

The ICC maintained that the firm was attempting to divert business from regulated truckers by using its available backhaul capacity. It argued that Congress had adopted a rule of per se illegality for all operations by unregulated truckers that involved use of backhaul capacity. The Court rejected that argument, holding that the ICC must apply the traditional form of its primary business test. This test required consideration of the following criteria:

> the large investment of assets or payroll in transportation operations; negotiating the sale of goods transported in advance of dispatching a truck to pick them up; direct delivery of the transported goods from the truck to the ultimate buyer, rather than from warehoused stocks; solicitation of the order by the supplier rather than the truck owner; and inclusion in the sales price of an amount to cover transportation costs.

Applying these criteria, the Court concluded that the firm was in the general mercantile business of buying and selling commodities, and that its transportation was incidental to that business. Hence, ICC could not prohibit the firm from transporting its sugar; nor could it impose minimum rate regulation on that service.

Voyager 1000 v. CAB, 489 F.2d 792 (7th Cir. 1973), illustrates another attempt by consumers to circumvent restrictions on entry into a market in order to avoid the effects of minimum rate regulation, and another attempt by a regulatory agency to protect its minimum rates by prohibiting disguised entry. At the time *Voyager* was decided, the Federal Aviation Act prohibited entry into the commercial airline business without first obtaining the permission of the CAB, but it did not prohibit members of clubs from chartering airplanes. Voyager was a travel club with a large membership and an extensive schedule of charter flights. Voyager claimed it was a club exempt from regulation; CAB argued that Voyager was unlawfully engaged in common carriage of air passengers in competition with scheduled airlines. The court accepted the CAB's contention, holding that an operation is unlawfully competing with commercial airlines if it "holds itself out as ready and willing to undertake for hire the transportation of passengers or property from place to place, and so invites the patronage of the public." The court found sufficient evidence that Voyager was holding itself out to the public to provide air transport based on the nature of Voyager's advertisements for new members. The advertisements emphasized that the primary purpose of the club was to provide air travel and that membership was not limited to people with common interests independent of air travel. The court left open the possibility that an organization could be a travel club exempt from regulation if it limited its membership to individuals with a common interest other than travel, e.g., employees of a corporation, members of a union, alumni of a university. Incidentally, with the deregulation of airline passenger service, charter services as separate entities have declined significantly, suggesting again that they were products of regulation and efforts to avoid its inefficient costs.

The more effective a minimum rate regulation scheme is at maintaining rates above marginal cost, the greater the incentive it creates for consumers of the regulated service to avoid regulation through various devices, such as transporting their own goods, providing their own service through a group or cooperative effort, or fitting within some other statutory exemption from regulation (for instance, many statutes exempt from regulation transportation of agricultural commodities). The more service that is diverted from firms subject to minimum rate regulation, the less effective the minimum rate scheme becomes in terms of its furtherance of any of the putative goals of minimum rate regulation. Thus, consumers of services subject to minimum rate regulation constantly are searching for new ways to avoid regulation, and agencies charged with responsibility for implementing minimum rate regulation constantly must attempt to eliminate or limit the diversion of customers from regulated firms to exempt services.

If a firm attempts forthrightly to enter a market subject to minimum rate regulation, it must first convince an agency that its entry into the market will serve the public convenience or necessity. When there already is a regulated firm serving that market, the potential new entrant can anticipate that its request for permission to enter will be contested vigorously. The history of the ICC's standards for permitting entry into transportation markets illustrates the classic approach to entry taken by agencies that restrict entry in order to protect a minimum rate regulation scheme.

The basic test for determining whether entry of a new carrier will serve the public convenience or necessity was stated by the Supreme Court in Chesapeake & Ohio Ry. v. United States, 283 U.S. 35 (1931). A potential entrant must establish that the additional service it proposes is necessary to provide adequate service to the market. The Court did not define adequate service, but it affirmed an agency order permitting entry based on the agency's conclusion that, at least in some circumstances, competition can be expected to stimulate better service.

The original test for permitting entry of a new firm has been explained further in several cases since *Chesapeake & Ohio*. In Bowman Transportation Inc. v. Arkansas–Best Freight System, Inc., 419 U.S. 281 (1974), the Court held that potential harm to pre-existing firms serving a market is not sufficient alone to preclude entry of a new firm. The ICC could permit entry in the face of resulting harm to other firms based on a finding that the gains to the consuming public as a result of permitting entry of the new firm far outweigh the adverse effects on existing firms. The Court seemed to suggest that the new entrant must prove that existing service in the market is inadequate in some respect as a necessary condition to justify its entry into the market. It also held, however, that the agency need not provide the existing firms an opportunity to improve their level of service before permitting a new firm to enter the market.

Since *Bowman*, the ICC has modified its test for permitting entry in subtle ways that seem to make it easier to enter a market. In Liberty Trucking Co., Extension—General Commodities, 131 M.C.C. 573 (1979), the ICC restated its test for entry, but with emphasis on the burdens imposed on firms who are opposing entry. In order to block entry of a new firm into a market, existing firms must establish that (1) entry of the new firm will hurt the existing firms; (2) as a result of the harm the existing firms suffer, the public will be harmed; and, (3) the harm to the public outweighs public benefits that will flow directly from entry of the new firm and indirectly from the increased competition created by the new firm. A test similar to that stated by the ICC in *Liberty Trucking* was announced by the Supreme Court in the context of entry into the broadcasting industry. In FCC v. Sanders Bros. Radio Station, 309 U.S. 470 (1940), the Court held that harm to existing firms in a market could not be considered in determining whether to allow a new firm to enter the market, but that harm to the public as a result of excessive competition in the market could form the basis for a refusal to permit entry.

It is difficult to see how the public could be harmed by entry of a new firm into a market absent very large economies of scale, but even under the modern tests for determining whether to permit a firm to enter a market, entry often is barred by a finding that entry would harm the public. In many cases, the agency seems to base its finding of public harm almost entirely on a finding that entry will harm existing firms. See, e.g., Colonial Refrigerated Transportation, Inc., Extension—Florida to 32 States, 131 M.C.C. 63 (1978). It is quite possible— even likely—that entry will harm existing firms while simultaneously benefitting the consuming public through the effects of competition, so the leap of logic reflected in decisions denying entry on these grounds is difficult to accept.

Since the primary reason for restricting entry into markets like trucking was to protect a scheme of minimum rate regulation, it is not surprising that the ICC declined to grant entry based on a firm's promise to provide service at lower rates. Until 1979, the ICC refused to consider an offer to provide service at lower rates as a factor in favor of permitting entry into a market unless the existing rates are "so high as to constitute a virtual embargo." Porter Transp. Co. Common Carrier Application, 74 M.C.C. 675 (1958). The ICC modified that policy to some extent in Change of Policy Consideration of Rates in Operating Rights Application Proceedings, 359 I.C.C. 613 (1979). The Commission announced that it would consider promises of reduced rates as a factor in favor of entry under specified conditions, including: (1) the proposed rate reduction must be substantial; (2) shippers sponsoring the new entrant must describe any negotiations they conducted with existing firms in an effort to obtain reduced rates; (3) the proposed lower rates must be attributable to real operational efficiencies or cost advantages as opposed to "false economies" such as lower wages, reduced proportional payments to owner operators, or reduced spending on safety; and, (4) the order authorizing entry may be conditioned on the new entrant's commitment to continue providing service at the reduced rate for a specified time. Fortunately, Congress abolished regulation of the trucking industry and the ICC in the 1990s.

When a firm in one regulated industry proposes to enter a market in competition with firms in another industry regulated by the same agency, the decision whether to allow entry often is more complicated. The problem is illustrated by Schaffer Transportation Co. v. United States, 355 U.S. 83 (1957). A trucking firm applied for a certificate authorizing it to transport granite between two locations previously served only by railroads. The trucking firm's application was supported by granite shippers, who contended that existing rail service was inadequate. Rates for carload shipments were as low as the rates offered by the trucking firm. Less than carload rates were, however, much higher than the proposed truck rates, and the granite shippers objected to shipping delays caused by their economic need to defer shipment until they had a full carload.

The ICC denied the application of the trucking firm, finding that rail service was adequate and that the true basis for the shippers' support of the application was a desire for lower rates—a basis the ICC did not consider sufficient to support entry. The Supreme Court reversed and remanded. It held that the ICC could not deny one mode of transport entry into a market served by another mode of transport without first determining which mode possesses an inherent advantage in serving that market, since the National Transportation Policy formulated by Congress requires the Commission to preserve the inherent advantages of each mode of transport. The Court left to the Commission the initial task of selecting the criteria on which the required determination of inherent advantage was to be made. *Schaffer* laid the foundation for a protracted dispute concerning the use of average cost versus marginal cost as a means of measuring inherent advantage. That dispute eventually was considered by the Court in *American Commercial Lines*. See section 7C.

It is impossible to consider restrictions on market entry in the abstract without relating those restrictions to the rationales underlying minimum rate regulation. Since, as set forth in chapter 9 supra, all of the justifications for minimum rate regulation are weak and insubstantial, and because minimum rate regulation produces substantial economic harm, the lack of enthusiasm for restrictions on market entry logically follows. In addition to all of the other adverse consequences of minimum rate regulation, the need to restrict entry in order to preserve a scheme of minimum rate regulation creates three significant problems. First, the very effort to restrict entry imposes high transactions costs. Second, given the substantial incentives for consumers to avoid the effects of minimum rate regulation, firms constantly devise new methods of disguising entry into markets, and agencies cannot police effectively all forms of disguised entry. As a result, profitable segments of the market regularly are diverted from regulated firms to unregulated providers of service. Thus, even if one were to accept the goals of minimum rate regulation, the inability of agencies to prohibit all forms of disguised entry into regulated markets jeopardizes the effectiveness of the regulatory scheme in serving its putative goals. Third, restrictions on entry into markets in which regulation keeps rates well above costs create incentives for consuming firms to use less efficient, more costly means of meeting their needs. If, for instance, ICC rate regulation keeps the rates for commercial truck transportation twenty percent above costs, shippers benefit by transporting their own goods at costs higher than those incurred by commercial trucking firms as long as the additional costs are less than the twenty per cent differential between the costs and rates of the commercial firms.

C. RECENT TRENDS

Restrictions on entry into the commercial airline industry were largely eliminated by the Airline Deregulation Act of 1978, 49 U.S.C.A. §§ 1301–1729. Elimination of most regulatory barriers to entry in the airline industry followed logically from the abolition of CAB power to establish minimum rates contained in the same legislation. The Motor Carrier Act of 1980, the 4R Act, the Staggers Rail Act, and the Trucking Industry Regulatory Reform Act of 1994 ultimately eliminated regulatory restrictions on market entry in the rail and trucking industries.

Agencies have relaxed regulatory restrictions on entry even in markets that once were considered classic natural monopolies. In Order 436, issued in 1985, FERC greatly reduced regulatory barriers to entry in the natural gas transportation market. Reviewing courts have consistently upheld those policies. See, e.g., Cascade Natural Gas Corp. v. FERC, 955 F.2d 1412 (10th Cir.1992). FERC's policies are premised on its well-supported belief that competition, or the threat of competitive entry, can improve the performance of a market even when the market incumbent enjoys large economies of scale. See Broadman & Kalt, *How Natural Is Natural Monopoly? The Case of Bypass in Natural Gas Distribution Markets,* 6 Yale J.Reg. 407 (1992). The FCC began relaxing regulatory restrictions on entry into the telecommunications market as early as 1975. See Washington Utilities & Transportation Commission v. FCC, 513 F.2d 1142 (9th Cir.1975). In the Energy Policy Act of 1992, Congress greatly reduced the barriers to entry in the electric generation market. It created a new category of exempt wholesale generators (EWGs) and made numerous other changes in law designed to allow EWGs to compete against each other and against electric utilities. That change in policy was influenced by the realization that electricity generation is no longer a natural monopoly function. See section 2B1.

CHAPTER XI

RATIONING RESTRICTED RESOURCES

A. RESOURCES SUBJECT TO REGULATORY RATIONING

Regulatory agencies often confront the need to determine administratively which of two or more parties desiring a regulated resource are entitled to that resource. The need for regulatory rationing can arise for a variety of reasons and in many different contexts.

The classic reason for administrative allocation of a resource is illustrated by allocation of broadcast frequencies. Because of the potential for electronic interference, there are only a discrete number of broadcasting frequencies available. Since the number of parties desiring to use frequencies typically exceeds the number of frequencies available, the FCC has been given the responsibility to ration available broadcast frequencies among competing applicants through a licensing process.

Another typical reason for regulatory rationing is the existence of cost characteristics that suggest the desirability of permitting only one firm or facility to serve a particular market.

A third typical situation giving rise to the need for regulatory rationing is encountered when the perceived need to avoid destructive competition induces an agency to limit the number of firms competing in a market.

Finally, regulatory constraints on the maximum price that can be charged for a product can produce a situation in which the quantity of the product demanded exceeds the supply available at the maximum rate. When this occurs, as it did from time to time in the natural gas and petroleum industries during the 1970's, a regulatory agency must ration the limited supply among competing claimants.

When the resource sought by two or more competing applicants consists of a specific mutually exclusive regulatory authorization such as a license to broadcast on a frequency the successful applicant is chosen through a comparative hearing. In Ashbacker Radio Corp. v. FCC, 326 U.S. 327 (1945), the Court held that an agency cannot grant one application that is mutually exclusive with another without first conducting a consolidated comparative hearing in which the proposals of both applicants are considered. At the conclusion of the consolidated hearing, the choice of the successful applicant is based on the agency's comparison of the characteristics of the applicants and their proposals that are relevant to the public interest.

Agencies can use generally applicable rules governing the allocation of restricted resources to supplement, or even to supplant, comparative hearings. In the context of rationing regulatory authorizations like licenses or certificates, rules often are used to resolve in advance issues that otherwise could be raised in a comparative hearing. See, e.g., United States v. Storer Broadcasting Co., 351 U.S. 192 (1956) (upholding FCC rules stating that an application for a broadcast license will not be granted if the applicant has an interest in more than a specified number of broadcast stations of various types). In the context of pervasive rationing schemes, such as regulatory allocation of crude oil and petroleum products, the extremely broad scope of the effort dictates that the agency rely almost entirely on generally applicable rules rather than individual comparative hearings.

The need to engage in regulatory rationing of resources has diminished greatly in recent years. Technological breakthroughs have expanded the number of broadcast frequencies available and have created myriad functional alternatives. The demise of minimum rate regulation in most of the markets in which it once held sway has reduced the need to ration transportation routes. Changes in technology and resulting changes in cost structures have eliminated the natural monopoly rationale for authorizing only one natural gas pipeline or electric generating company to operate in a given area. Finally, greater willingness to allow price to allocate commodities like oil and natural gas has eliminated the need to ration those resources administratively.

B.   CRITERIA FOR ALLOCATION

The statutory criteria for regulatory rationing of restricted resources are stated with varying degrees of specificity. Many statutes require the agency to act in a manner consistent with the public convenience and necessity and, within that very broad framework, leave to the agency the task of determining the comparative criteria relevant to its selection of competing applicants. This is typically the case where the agency is required to determine which of one or more applicants is entitled to a mutually exclusive license or certificate to construct or operate a broadcast station, pipeline, truck route, airline route or financial institution. The broad statutory public interest standard sometimes is supplemented by a statutory obligation to consider one or more specified criteria. For instance, the National Environmental Policy Act requires any federal agency to consider the environmental impact of any "major Federal action significantly affecting the quality of the human environment." 42 U.S.C.A § 4332(2)(C).

Other statutes granting agencies authority to ration restricted resources contain lengthy decision-making criteria. Sometimes these lists of detailed criteria leave the agency as much effective discretion as a general public interest standard because the criteria are comprehensive, inconsistent and not accompanied by any indication of legislative preference. See, e.g., Emergency Petroleum Allocation

Act, 15 U.S.C.A. § 753(b)(1) (specifying that crude oil and petroleum products are to be allocated based on a consideration of approximately thirty factors). In other cases, however, the detailed statutory criteria for rationing are specific and binding on the agency. See, e.g., Natural Gas Policy Act of 1978, 15 U.S.C.A. § 3391 (requiring that residential and essential agricultural users receive preferential access to natural gas during times of shortage).

Whether allocation criteria are determined by the legislature or by the agency, the specific criteria vary depending upon the nature of the resource being allocated. When regulatory authority to construct or operate a facility is at issue, the decisional criteria focus on the comparative public benefits or detriments promised by the competing applicants. Where two or more applicants compete for a license to operate a broadcasting station, the criteria include a comparative evaluation of the competing applicants' legal and character qualifications, financial ability, equal employment opportunity record and promise, multiple ownership status and program design to meet ascertained community needs. See generally, G. Robinson, E. Gellhorn & H. Bruff, *The Administrative Process* 280–285, 324–345 (4th ed. 1993). Of these, the last two have been the most important. See Ascertainment of Community Problems by Commercial Broadcast Applicants (F.C.C. 1976); FCC v. National Citizens Committee for Broadcasting, 436 U.S. 775 (1978). The Commission's record in applying these criteria, however, has been consistently criticized as unprincipled, ad hoc and arbitrary, and it has moved in recent years toward reliance on more objective (e.g., lottery) rules as a first step toward deregulation. See, e.g., FCC v. WNCN Listeners Guild, 450 U.S. 582 (1981); further implemented by the FCC's rule partially deregulating radio broadcasting, see *Office of Communication of United Church of Christ v. FCC*, 707 F.2d 1413 (D.C.Cir.1983).

When an agency is required to allocate a regulated commodity that is in short supply, it (or the legislature) has a choice of several possible approaches. It can rely on traditional patterns of consumption, giving preference to those who have used the commodity historically. It can use a legal right analysis, relying principally on the terms of pre-existing contracts, certificates and tariffs. It can use time and patience as an implicit basis for allocation, by resort to a first come, first served queuing system. It can attempt to replicate the allocation produced by a free market by measuring through some means the value placed on the commodity for various uses. Or, it can allocate the commodity among competing groups of consumers based on some hierarchy of socially preferred activities or goods. In fact, most allocation schemes reflect all of these fundamental bases of allocation in some measure, with changes in the degree of significance attached to each occurring over time.

C. THE MARKET ALTERNATIVE

Almost all resources are scarce in the sense that a greater quantity is demanded than can be supplied if the resource is made available at zero cost. In the United States, most scarce resources are allocated among competing consumers through prices determined by the market. The advantage of the market as an allocational device is described in Chapters 1 and 2.

The market allocates scarce resources to those individuals that place the greatest value on the resource as measured by the price they are willing to pay to obtain an additional unit of the resource. Absent price regulation, the market would allocate commodities like natural gas or petroleum products according to this criterion. Moreover, the government could use the market to allocate resources like broadcasting licenses or certificates authorizing construction of pipelines by conducting an auction among the competing applicants and allowing such licenses and certificates to be treated as transferable property rights. Through such a system, the market should maximize the aggregate consumer welfare produced by the resources. The market would allocate a resource like a broadcasting license to the competing applicant that placed the greatest monetary value on the license. The value placed on the license by each applicant should, in turn, reflect the amount of money each applicant expects to earn through use of the license, which should ultimately reflect the aggregate value consumers place on the use each applicant makes of the license.

The decision to substitute regulatory allocation of scarce resources for the market necessarily reflects at least implicit dissatisfaction with the expected results of using the market as an allocational device. There are at least three plausible reasons for rejecting the market in favor of regulatory allocation.

First, sometimes there are reasons to believe that the market will not function as theory suggests because of the absence of one of the assumed conditions underlying effective operation of the market. For instance, in theory, any firm's bid for a broadcasting license would be based on its desire to maximize the return on its investment. The amount of money bid, then, would depend on the firm's expected revenues from operating a radio or TV station. If, however, some firms or individuals base their bids in whole or in part on some goal other than profit maximization—for instance, a desire to spread a particular political philosophy—the allocation of broadcast licenses produced by the market would not necessarily maximize the aggregate welfare of consumers of radio and TV broadcasts.

Second, in some circumstances use of the market to allocate a resource may interfere with the goal of limiting the revenues of the firms or individuals that produce the resource. For instance, as described in Chapter 2, the prices charged by oil and gas producers were constrained primarily to limit the "windfall profits" or excessive rents producers could earn by selling low cost gas or oil discovered long ago at prices reflecting the much higher marginal cost of finding new gas and oil today. Permitting price to be used as a method of allocating oil and gas among competing consumers would interfere with this goal, unless the windfall profits were limited through some other method.

Third, the allocation of a scarce resource produced by the market depends to some extent on the distribution of wealth among consumers. If society concludes that the current distribution of wealth is in some sense wrong, it can use regulatory allocation of scarce resources at less than the market value of the resources as a partial means of redistributing wealth from disfavored to favored groups of consumers.

Even if the market sometimes produces an allocation of resources that seems inequitable, it is difficult to accept administrative allocation of scarce resources as a superior alternative. Administrative allocation invariably yields large reductions in aggregate social welfare. Studies by economists show that administrative allocation of oil cost the nation $500 million annually and administrative allocation of natural gas cost $1 billion annually. K. Arrow and J. Kalt, *Petroleum Price Regulation: Should We Decontrol?* 15 (1979); P. Merrill, *The Regulation and Deregulation of Natural Gas* 60 (1981).

CHAPTER XII

ALTERNATIVES TO COST
OF SERVICE RATE
REGULATION

In Chapters 4 through 7, we described the most common method of regulating rates. Each firm's rates are based primarily on the costs incurred by the firm to make available a regulated product or service, with the goal of permitting each firm to earn a return on its invested capital sufficient to permit it to continue to attract the capital necessary to provide the regulated product or service. In this chapter, we will describe five other methods that have been used to control prices or profits in various contexts.

A. RATES BASED ON OPERATING RATIOS

The ICC traditionally used a firm's operating ratio rather than its return on investment as the primary basis for establishing maximum and minimum rates applicable to commercial trucking firms. A firm's operating ratio is calculated by dividing the firm's total revenues by its operating costs. Generally, the ICC set trucking rates at a level that produced an operating ratio of 93 per cent. See

Class and Commodity Rates, New York to Philadelphia, 51 M.C.C. 289 (1951). The Commission was urged repeatedly to use return on investment rather than operating ratio as its primary benchmark for setting rates, but it consistently refused to do so until 1969, when it began to use both return on investment and operating ratio as determinants of proper rates. See, e.g., General Increase, Middle Atlantic and New England, 322 I.C.C. 820 (1969).

The ICC stated its reasons for preferring operating ratio to return on investment in Middle West General Increases, Interstate Commerce Commission, Division 3, 48 M.C.C. 541 (1948). There, several trucking firms requested rate increases based on a showing that their operating ratios exceeded 93 per cent, and their claim that as a result, they were unable to attract capital. The Department of Agriculture opposed the rate increases, contending that rate of return on investment is a better indicator of a firm's ability to attract capital than operating ratio, and that the firms were earning a rate of return sufficient to attract capital. The ICC rejected the Department's argument and held that operating ratio was the preferred method of determining a trucking firm's ability to attract capital for several reasons: (1) much of a trucking firm's investment is in working capital that varies constantly in amount; thus, basing rates on return on investment would produce rate instability; (2) trucking firms, unlike regulated monopolies, have relatively low investments in capital assets; therefore, use of return on investment would not provide sufficient revenues to such firms; (3) the primary risk to which a trucking firm is exposed is inability to cover operating expenses; therefore, operating expenses should be used as the primary basis for establishing the rates charged by trucking firms.

It is difficult to find any support in economics for the use of operating ratio as a basis for determining rates. As described in Chapter 5, a firm's ability to attract capital is a function of its rate of return on investment relative to the rate of return earned by firms with comparable risks. To the extent that operating ratio has any relationship to a firm's ability to attract capital it is as a crude measure of risk, but risk is only important as a comparative device to determine the rate of return necessary to compensate investors for taking a risk. Thus, even if operating ratio correlates with risk, operating ratio alone provides no basis for determining the revenues a firm must earn in order to attract capital. An operating ratio of 93 per cent may provide a rate of return on investment of 2 per cent or 100 per cent depending on the magnitude of the firm's capital investment.

One speculation is that the ICC used operating ratio as its primary basis for setting truck rates because the ICC considered assurance of high profits to trucking firms one of its most important goals; yet it did not want reviewing courts and the public to detect the very high rate of return on investment in commercial trucking produced by its method of rate regulation.

B. STANDARD COST RATES

Several agencies have adopted a variation on traditional cost-of-service ratemaking in which rates are based on calculation or approximation of standard costs applicable generally to an entire industry or to a class of product, rather than on costs unique to a specific firm. Standard cost ratemaking was used extensively in regulation of the airline industry (see General Passenger–Fare Investigation, 32 C.A.B. 291 (1961)) and the natural gas production industry (see FPC opinion No. 699, National Rates for Natural Gas, 51 F.P.C. 2212, 4 P.U.R.4th 401 (1974)).

A brief description of standard cost ratemaking as it has evolved in the natural gas production industry will illustrate its salient characteristics. The Federal Power Commission began trying to regulate natural gas producers by establishing separate maximum rates applicable to each producer based on the producer's cost of service. It soon abandoned this approach primarily because there were too many producers for the Commission to establish separate rates for each based on an analysis of the costs incurred by each.

It replaced its system of individual maximum rates based on cost of service with a few maximum rates that applied to all gas produced from a specified geographical area. Within some of the production areas, the Commission established several different maximum rates applicable to gas supplies with common characteristics that could be expected to correlate generally with cost of production. The factor used most often to distinguish supplies within an area for maximum rate purposes was the vintage of the gas—the time when the gas was first produced.

The area wide maximum rates were not determined based on the cost of service of any particular producer. Rather, the Commission (1) divided the cost of producing gas into its major components; (2) collected data on the average cost of each production activity, either on an area or a national basis; and, (3) determined the maximum rate for the production area by aggregating the historical figures on the average cost of each production activity. See generally, Permian Basin Area Rate Cases, 390 U.S. 747 (1968) (affirming the FPC's area wide approach to establishing maximum rates for natural gas producers).

The standard cost approach to determining maximum rates for natural gas producers evolved through two more stages. In 1974 and 1976, the Commission established new maximum rates that applied to all producers nationwide. The national rates were calculated for differing vintages of gas based on the national average cost of finding and producing gas during each relevant time period. See FPC opinion No. 699, National Rates for Natural Gas, 51 F.P.C. 2212, 4 P.U.R.4th 401 (1974); FPC Opinion No. 770, National Rates for Natural Gas, 10 F.P.S. 5–293 (1976).

In 1978, Congress enacted the Natural Gas Policy Act, 15 U.S.C.A. §§ 3301–3342, containing a third version of standard cost pricing for natural gas producers. That statute divided gas supplies into approximately thirty categories based on factors such as vintage, depth of well, and amount of production from well, that Congress believed to be correlated with cost of production. Each category of gas was subject to a different rate ceiling, with the ceiling applicable to each category rising over time with inflation and, in some cases, with an additional percentage adjustment based on expected increases in real costs attributable to the fact that gas is a depleting resource.

Maximum rates based on standard costs offer three significant advantages over maximum rates based on each firm's cost of service. First, where a regulated industry contains a large number of firms, it is much easier and less expensive to establish a few maximum rates applicable to general categories of products based on industry cost data than to establish separate maximum rates for each firm based on the costs incurred by each firm. Delay, the bane of the administrative process, is thereby reduced.

Second, if an agency is charged with setting rates applicable to firms that compete with each other, often it has little practical choice but to establish uniform rates based on standard costs. Different rates applicable to firms in competition would be likely to channel the bulk of the market to the firm with the lowest rates. In an industry typified by recurring periods of excess capacity, such as commercial air transport, establishing different rates for firms in competition for the same market would not yield a rate regulation system that would be effective in avoiding the effects of "destructive competition." Thus, CAB felt it had little choice but to establish uniform rates for all airlines competing in the same market. See General Passenger–Fare Investigation, 32 C.A.B. 291 (1961).

Finally, maximum rates based on standard cost create incentives for efficiency. A firm whose maximum rates are based on its own costs has a reduced incentive to control its costs, since any change in its costs is likely to be reflected eventually in an analogous change in its rates. When, however, a firm's maximum rates are based on industry wide costs, it benefits by minimizing its costs. Hence, it has a more powerful incentive to operate in an efficient manner.

Notwithstanding these significant advantages, standard cost ratemaking does not respond to all the problems inherent in maximum rate regulations, and in some cases it creates significant new problems. Congress deregulated airlines in 1978 and natural gas producers in 1989, based on its well-founded belief that a competitive market would yield better results than standard cost ratemaking.

C. PRICE FREEZE WITH COST PASSTHROUGH

The pervasive price control program initiated by the Nixon Administration in 1971 was implemented through an entirely different method than cost of service rate regulation. The methods of price control used in that program survived the eventual demise of economy-wide price controls in 1974 and were used as the basic method of controlling the prices of petroleum products until 1981. Those methods of price control continue to be of considerable interest because they are proposed for economy-wide application from time to time by influential politicians and economists.

The basic purpose of the price control program implemented in 1971 was to control a six percent level of general inflation that was considered intolerable at the time and that was producing distortion and individual hardships in the economy. Price controls were considered a method of stabilizing inflation superior to traditional monetary and fiscal policies because they affected prices independently and directly, and they responded to institutional and psychological forces that some observers believed to be major factors in producing high inflation. The institutional forces included labor unions with the power to bargain for wages above market levels (hence, the price controls were accompanied by wage controls) and major markets dominated by a few firms that could set prices above the levels that atomistic competition would produce. The psychological forces that price controls were designed to combat consisted primarily of the belief by consumers and workers that prices would continue to increase at an increasing rate. Therefore, goods should be purchased immediately in order to avoid the effects of future inflation, and wages must be increased immediately in order to offset the effects of future inflation. This inflationary psychology was believed to be driving inflation; it could do so through imperfections in the operation of the market created by collective bargaining and oligopolistic markets.

The price control program responded to the problem of inflation through direct constraints on prices. In its first brief stage, the program froze prices throughout the economy. In later phases, price increases were permitted, but only in specified circumstances. The circumstance used by firms most frequently as a basis to increase prices was an increase in costs. See generally, T. Morgan, *Economic Regulation of Business* 332–367 (1976).

When the economy wide price control program lapsed in 1974, the basic approach to regulating prices adopted in that program was continued in effect for the petroleum industry. Underlying this extension of price controls was the theory that the enormous increases in the price of foreign crude oil placed in effect by OPEC threatened (1) to permit U.S. producers of crude oil to earn windfall profits by selling at the prices established by OPEC; (2) to disrupt the operation of the U.S. petroleum market by placing refiners who purchase from foreign producers at a competitive disadvantage; and (3) to force precipitous increases in the price of petroleum products to U.S. consumers. To avoid these results, (1) price controls were imposed on domestic crude oil; (2) refiners with access to disproportionate quantities of price controlled domestic crude oil were forced to share the economic advantages of such access with less fortunate refiners through the entitlements program; and (3) price controls were imposed on all refiners and resellers of petroleum products in an effort to insure that they would not reap the windfall profits that would be available to domestic crude producers but for the regulation of the price of domestically produced crude oil. The price controls on refiners and resellers of petroleum, although extremely complex in their details, consisted primarily of a base price plus cost passthrough approach. Refiners and resellers could sell petroleum products at a price no greater than the price they charged on a specified date before the OPEC price increases, plus increases in costs allowed by the agency after that date. See Phase IV Price Regulations, 6 C.F.R. § 150.351 et seq., 38 Fed.Reg. 22536 (Aug. 22, 1973). See generally, P. MacAvoy, *Federal Energy Administration Regulation* (1977).

Price controls based on a price freeze subject to cost passthrough differ significantly from cost of service rate regulation. Price controls of this type are not based on calculations of revenue requirements necessary to earn a particular return on investment. The prices charged by each firm on the date of the freeze, and implicitly the rate of return corresponding to that price, are accepted in the price control scheme. The price changes only to the extent of increased costs allowed by the agency. The rate of return earned by the firm can change, however, as a result of changes in any number of factors, including refusal of the agency to allow passthrough of costs actually incurred and changes in the amount of capital invested by the firm.

There is now a broad consensus among economists and politicians that price controls are a poor way of attempting to deal with the problem of inflation. The case against wage and price controls is summarized in the 1969 report of President Johnson's Council of Economic Advisers, which stated:

> Mandatory price and wage controls ... freeze the market mechanism which guides the economy in responding to the changing pattern and volume of demand; they distort decisions on production and employment; they require a huge and cumbersome bureaucracy; they impose a heavy and costly burden on business; they perpetuate inevitable injustices. They are incompatible with a free enterprise economy and must be regarded as a last resort appropriate only in an extreme emergency such as all-out war.

In addition, temporary price controls often are followed by a period of very rapidly increasing prices, and the potential for imposition of price controls often induces firms to increase their prices in order to begin the price control period with a favorable base price.

D. GOVERNMENT OWNERSHIP

Partial or complete government ownership is an alternative to economic regulation of an industry. If the competitive market is not producing results deemed socially desirable because of some type of market failure—monopoly, destructive competition, externalities, etc.—it is theoretically possible to obtain improved results by substituting government ownership for private ownership and commanding the government officials to operate the industry in a manner that furthers socially desirable goals. Since the government presumably does not respond to the profit maximization motive of private firms, it will not be influenced by market imperfections that distort the incentives confronted by private firms.

Complete government ownership of an industry occurs only rarely in the United States—the postal system is the classic example—but it is employed much more frequently in Europe, where in many countries basic industries like electricity, oil and natural gas are largely government owned. The primary disadvantage to total government ownership as an alternative to government regulation of privately-owned firms lies in the uncertain incentives to which government decisionmakers respond. While they are not necessarily influenced by distorted market forces created by imperfect markets, government decisionmakers may respond to other incentives that interfere with their furtherance of statutorily mandated goals. In particular, many critics of government ownership argue that, because government decisionmakers have little incentive to respond to market forces, they also have little incentive to innovate or to minimize costs.

Partial government ownership of an industry can be used as an alternative to economic regulation through the concept of yardstick competition. Under this approach, the government enters an industry as a partial supplier of a good for the purpose of providing a yardstick against which the performance of the private firms in the industry can be measured. Even if the government does not compete in the same geographic market as the private firms, if the government can provide a higher quality product at lower price, it brings political and public relations pressure on the private firms to improve their performance.

Critics of yardstick competition maintain that government entry into an industry creates unfair pressures on private firms because the government entity often is given significant advantages over its private counterparts. For instance, even though government must incur costs to borrow the capital required to invest in the business, the governmental entity rarely is required to internalize those costs; rather, they are absorbed by the government as a whole. Moreover, the government often alots to itself particularly advantageous markets or resources that permit it to provide a product at lower cost than its private counterparts.

Yardstick competition through partial government ownership of an industry has been used in various industries, but the Tennessee Valley Authority is the classic example of this approach. The TVA was established as a government agency with the authority to generate, transmit and distribute electricity in the Tennessee Valley. The agency was established in part to put pressure on private suppliers of electricity to lower their rates and/or to become more efficient. Whether properly or through use of unfair advantages, TVA clearly has had that effect. See Hardin v. Kentucky Utilities Co., 390 U.S. 1 (1968) (refusing to enjoin TVA from competing for markets with a privately owned company whose rates were 2½ times those charged by TVA). The Supreme Court consistently has rejected contentions that government entry into a previously private industry violates the fifth, ninth, tenth, and fourteenth amendments to the Constitution. See Tennessee Electric Power Co. v. TVA, 306 U.S. 118 (1939); Ashwander v. TVA, 297 U.S. 288 (1936); Jones v. City of Portland, 245 U.S. 217 (1917). In recent years, however, many of the government participants in markets, including the TVA, have charged prices as high as, or higher than, many private market participants.

CHAPTER XIII

ANTITRUST AND REGULATION

Up to now we have focused on the substantive administration of government regulation of business, including the policies and rationales underlying this scheme that substitutes administrative control for the perceived inadequacies of the private market. In addition to regulatory regimes specifically regulating rates, service and quality, or controlling the degree of permissible competition—a system of government oversight initially reserved for natural monopolies and later extended to serve other social goals—an alternative, less intrusive approach has been taken under the antitrust laws. In general, this alternative (at least theoretically) relies on free enterprise and the private market to assure consumer welfare. Antitrust therefore intervenes in private markets only when necessary to promote competition through laws and rules prohibiting those practices which impair rivalry and deny consumers the benefits of competition. For example, predatory pricing is made illegal when used to exploit or expand monopoly power. Price fixing and other market sharing arrangements are similarly proscribed because they deny interfirm rivalry for consumer purchases.

The theoretical difference between the two approaches is stark and simple. Industry regulation is based on the conclusion that private market pressures are inadequate and will continue to be so, and that government must supply the missing ingredients, invariably by limiting private firm freedom of choice or action. Antitrust, on the other hand, assumes that market place rivalry is possible and that in this circumstance legal regulation should be limited to those steps necessary to assure the openness of markets.

However, neither system is complete nor comprehensive. The federal antitrust laws apply only to private action not regulated by state governments or federal agencies, and even then they may be confined by other policies such as those favoring freedom of speech or petitions to government. Moreover, administrative regulation is seldom designed to embrace every market decision made by regulated firms and thus it often supplements rather than substitutes for antitrust requirements. This interplay between antitrust and government regulation is the focus of this chapter. Identifying the boundaries between the two, especially where other policies such as federalism are also present, can be exceedingly difficult. We therefore focus on the primary principles and leave the details of particular applications to specialized texts.

A. STATE ACTION[1]

The "state action" doctrine is an effort to resolve the conflict between the federal policy stated in the antitrust laws in favor of competition and an individual state's decision to regulate a segment of its economy in order to further distinctive economic, social or political goals.

The doctrine originated in the Supreme Court's landmark decision in Parker v. Brown, 317 U.S. 341 (1943), which ruled that the Sherman Act was intended by Congress to regulate only private practices restraining trade. *Parker* involved a California statutory program designed to eliminate competition by allowing raisin producers to petition the state director of agriculture to establish an "orderly marketing" plan for the purpose of promoting price stability and limiting excess supply from going on the market. Since the California raisin crop accounted for 95 percent of the nation's and half of the world's production, the effect of the proposal on competition was not insignificant. Nonetheless, the California director had found that the plan would conserve the state's agricultural wealth and yet not permit producers unreasonable profits. In unanimously upholding this scheme against challenge under the Sherman Act, the Supreme Court stated:

1. While the focus here is on the difficult legal issues of implied antitrust immunity, express exemptions from antitrust for state regulation are not uncommon. See, e.g., McCarran–Ferguson Act, 15 U.S.C.A. § 1012(b) (exempting state regulated insurance from the antitrust laws) discussed in Part B.

[The program] derived its authority and its efficacy from the legislative command of the state and was not intended to operate or become effective without that command.... The state in adopting and enforcing the ... program made no contract or agreement and entered into no conspiracy or restraint of trade or to establish a monopoly but, as sovereign, imposed the restraint as an act of government which the Sherman Act did not undertake to prohibit.

Thus the *Parker* Court determined that state legislatures were not prevented by the federal antitrust laws from regulating market practices within their states.

However, this exemption from the Sherman Act did not apply, according to the Court, unless the competitive restraint was imposed as a government action. In other words, even though private individuals in fact engaged in price fixing and other anticompetitive conduct, all actions were attributed to the state and exempt from antitrust liability if mandated and supervised by a state agency. *Parker* thus held that the antitrust laws do not prevent the states from substituting economic regulation for the free market preference of the Sherman Act.

The rule in Parker v. Brown was ostensibly based upon Congress' intent in adopting the Sherman Act. Although the Court was undoubtedly accurate when it said that nothing in the Act or its history supported a conclusion that the purpose was to restrain state action,[2] it could just as well have reached a contrary conclusion had it started from the opposite premise (that nothing in the Act permitted contrary state action) as the Justice Department had urged to the Court. The Supreme Court's interpretation of the Sherman Act was clearly affected by considerations of federalism. The Court reflected this concern in its express reliance on a rule of statutory construction that "an unexpressed purpose to nullify a state's control over its officers and agents is not lightly to be attributed to Congress." Thus, the state action doctrine was undoubtedly meant to be an accommodation to important state interests.

While not stated so directly, the Court must also have been sorely pressed by the possibility that unrestrained application of the Sherman Act could be used by lower federal courts to overturn state occupational licensure and other state or federal market regulation programs with which they did not agree. That is to say, the 1943 Supreme Court surely viewed the *Parker* case as an opportunity to seal the demise of substantive due process that had until the mid 1930's been frequently used to overturn state and federal economic regulation on constitutional grounds. See section 3A. Without the state action rule of *Parker*, courts could have relied on the Sherman Act to overturn such regulation. Such a possible intrusion into state matters would have introduced confusion and discord in economic

   2.   317 U.S. at 351: "The Sherman Act makes no mention of the state as such, and gives no hint that it was intended to restrain state action or official action directed by a state."

affairs and could not have seemed consistent with the purpose of the antitrust laws or with sound policy—especially in the midst of World War II.

These underlying policy concerns help explain that despite numerous requests that it do so, the Supreme Court refused for over three decades to consider further the reach of the state action doctrine. Left without much guidance, lower courts often gave the rule a very broad reach. The high water mark was probably the decision in Washington Gas Light Co. v. Virginia Elec. & Power Co., 438 F.2d 248 (4th Cir.1971), where a utility's tie-in arrangement was ruled to be within the *Parker* exception because a state regulatory commission was aware of the arrangement—even though the agreement had never been either formally submitted to or approved by the commission. In the court's words, it was "sensible to infer that silence means consent, i.e., approval."

In 1975, the Supreme Court broke its silence on the state action doctrine and began a search for a solution to the problem of state or local abuse of this exception to antitrust requirements. In Goldfarb v. Virginia State Bar, 421 U.S. 773 (1975), the Court considered whether a minimum fee schedule for lawyers approved by a county bar association (itself part of an integrated state bar, where membership of all attorneys was mandated by the state supreme court) was exempt from antitrust attack. Overturning the Fourth Circuit's "silence is golden" interpretation of the *Parker* doctrine, the Court held that greater state control was required. "It is

not enough that, as the County Bar puts it, anticompetitive conduct is 'prompted' by state action;
rather, anticompetitive activities must be *compelled
by direction* of the State acting as a sovereign." Id.
at 791 (emphasis added). Since neither the Supreme
Court of Virginia nor the state legislature had mandated minimum legal fees, it was not state "compelled" activity and therefore was within the reach
of the Sherman Act.

Over the next ten years, the Court returned to
this issue eight times, trying to apply *Goldfarb's*
clear but simple standard to more ambiguous fact
situations. The result was a welter of complex and
confusing rules that generally exempted lawyer regulation from antitrust review while holding cities
subject to potential treble damage liability. Lawyer
activities were ostensibly regulated by bar groups
acting under delegated authority from their state
supreme courts. Cities, on the other hand, were
usually acting independently without significant
state oversight. Despite the requirement of state
compulsion set forth in *Goldfarb*, other cases
seemed to require something more. A consistent
rationale did not develop and the rule began to
falter.

For example, *Goldfarb* was quickly followed by
two decisions further narrowing the state action
exception. In Cantor v. Detroit Edison Co., 428 U.S.
579 (1976), a divided Court decided that an electric
utility's program exchanging new light bulbs without charge for burned-out bulbs could be challenged
under the antitrust laws despite the fact that the

program was included in the public tariff filed by
the utility with the state commission and approved
by it. Redefining the concept of compulsion, the
Court relied on the fact the state had sought to
regulate only the distribution of electricity, not the
marketing of light bulbs. The exchange program
had been initiated by the utility in order to increase
the consumption of electricity and it was seemingly
free to file a tariff and abandon it at any time.
Similarly, two years later the Court held that a city-
owned electric light system could be sued for antitrust violations since there was no indication that
the state had required its cities to engage in the
challenged conduct. City of Lafayette v. Louisiana
Power & Light Co., 435 U.S. 389 (1978).

The next two cases, however, firmly reestablished
the continuing life of the state action doctrine. In
Bates v. State Bar of Arizona, 433 U.S. 350 (1977),
the Court held that a state supreme court rule
prohibiting lawyer advertising could not be challenged under the Sherman Act because the state
court imposing the rule was "the ultimate body
wielding the State's power over the practice of
law."[3] That is, even though the rule was initially
proposed by the state bar and adapted from an ABA
proposal, the rule itself had been approved by the
state court which actively supervised its application.
Next, in New Motor Vehicle Bd. v. Orrin W. Fox

3. The prohibition on lawyer advertising, however, was found
to be a violation of the first amendment commercial speech
doctrine. See also, Zauderer v. Office of Disciplinary Counsel, 471
U.S. 626 (1985); Virginia State Bd. of Pharmacy v. Virginia
Citizens Consumer Council, Inc., 425 U.S. 748 (1976).

Co., 439 U.S. 96 (1978), the Court upheld a California regulatory scheme which allowed auto dealers to ask a state board to review a manufacturer's decision to place a competing dealer nearby. Conceding that the regulation was designed to "displace unfettered business freedom," nonetheless it was part of an "articulated and affirmatively expressed" design and thus was within the state action exemption.[4]

The difficulty with both the *Bates* and *Fox* decisions, however, was their failure to explain the degree to which private control will be tolerated under the guise of state regulatory action. The difference in the degree of state regulation involved in the prohibition of bar advertising in Bates or in restricting auto dealer location in *Fox* (which were state action) and the state's recognition of minimum fees in *Goldfarb* or the light bulb exchange in *Cantor* (which were not state action) seemed more formalistic than real. What seemed to count, apparently, was whether the state or a private party *appeared* to have formulated and implemented the scheme. The stakes (of potential private antitrust liability) are high, yet the outcome seems unpredictable. In each instance the guiding hand of private self-interest was likely to be evident in the state regulatory program.

Subsequent decisions reflected this concern in their limitation on private opportunities to use state

4. Earlier that term, in Exxon Corp. v. Governor of Maryland, 437 U.S. 117 (1978), the Court upheld state laws protecting "independent" service station dealers (from stations owned by oil companies) against constitutional (substantive due process) challenge.

regulation for protecting private marketing arrangements and narrowing of state discretion to overturn antitrust policy. In California Retail Liquor Dealers Ass'n v. Midcal Aluminum, Inc., 445 U.S. 97 (1980), the Court limited any suggestion that the state action doctrine had returned to its pre–1975 prominence. There the Court declared that when wine producers and wholesalers set a dealer retail price in compliance with a state command to do so, they can be held to have violated the Sherman Act even though the challenged restraint meets the first requirement of *Parker*, namely that it was clearly articulated and affirmatively expressed in state policy. The reason, according to the Court, was that the second branch of the *Parker* doctrine had not been satisfied:

> The State simply authorizes price-setting and enforces the prices established by private parties. The State neither establishes prices nor reviews the reasonableness of the price schedules; nor does it regulate the terms of fair trade contracts. The State does not monitor market conditions or engage in any "pointed reexamination" of the program.

Thinly disguised state support for private market controls went too far, allowing the Court to stop further abuse of the *Parker* rule. It therefore held that "[t]he national policy in favor of competition cannot be thwarted by casting such a gauzy cloak of state involvement over what is essentially a private price fixing arrangement."

In applying *Parker's* first requirement of a "clearly articulated and affirmatively expressed" state policy, in Community Communications Co. v. City of Boulder, 455 U.S. 40 (1982), the Court held that cities were not sovereign entities within the *state* action immunity even when operating under a home-rule charter granted by a state constitution. Thus, Boulder's "emergency" ordinance declaring a moratorium on expansion of a cable television system could be reviewed under the antitrust laws as a possible conspiracy to restrict competition.[5] As a consequence, virtually every action by a municipality or other state subdivision could be challenged as an antitrust violation—and the lawsuits quickly became a flood. Congress stepped in, however, and special legislation now bars antitrust damage actions against municipalities or against actions directed by them; injunctive relief is still available. Local Government Antitrust Immunities Act of 1984, 98 Stat. 2750 (Oct. 24, 1984).

More recent cases have shown a greater reluctance to use antitrust as a check on state and local activity. Continuing its insulation of lawyer regulation, the Court next held that state bar examiners were immune from antitrust suit, in Hoover v. Ronwin, 466 U.S. 558 (1984). The challenged grad-

---

5. The Court distinguished the contrary result in City of Lafayette v. Louisiana Power & Light Co., supra, on the ground that the city's action in *Boulder* was not "proprietary" but "governmental" in character. For a close analysis demonstrating the inadequacies of this approach, see Robinson, *The Sherman Act as a Home Rule Charter: Community Communications Co. v. City of Boulder,* 2 Sup.Ct.Econ.Rev. 131 (1983).

ing formulation applied by the bar examiners had been approved by the state court.

Two cases decided in 1985 seem to signal a full retreat from post-Goldfarb cases. The first is Town of Hallie v. Eau Claire, 471 U.S. 34 (1985), where one municipality, Hallie, asserted that another, Eau Claire, was abusing its sewage treatment monopoly to force neighboring towns to accept annexation and to use its sewage collection and transportation services. The Supreme Court rejected the antitrust claim. Wisconsin statutes gave municipalities the power to establish sewage treatment facilities as well as the right to refuse service to areas outside their domains. Thus, the anticompetitive effects alleged were contemplated by the state and this was enough to constitute a "clearly articulated" state policy as required under the state action rule. Distinguishing its position of two years earlier in *Boulder* (and reading the "compulsion" requirement in *Goldfarb* loosely), the Court ruled that neither state compulsion nor actual state supervision was required when municipal conduct was involved. "We may presume, absent a showing to the contrary, that the municipality acts in the public interest."

This renewed confidence in local authorities—and the view that "there is little or no danger that [the municipality] is involved in a private price-fixing arrangement"—also controlled the Court's decision in Southern Motor Carriers Rate Conference v. United States, 471 U.S. 48 (1985). There trucking rate bureaus had established joint trucking rates for both intrastate and interstate carriers. The interstate carriers' rates were fixed by the Interstate Commerce Commission and therefore were exempt from antitrust requirements. But that federal regulation did not apply to intrastate ratemaking, which also was not compelled by state law. The Court noted, however, that the states encouraged collective ratemaking under a general grant of legislative authority and the governing state public service commissions had approved rates as submitted by each carrier. Relying upon this permissive state policy toward private regulation, the Court ruled that the state action doctrine was satisfied. It also extended the exemption for the first time to private parties.

The Court revisited the state action doctrine again in 1988 and 1992. In both cases, the Court gave increased significance to the active supervision element of the *Midcal* test. In Patrick v. Burget, 486 U.S. 94 (1988), the Court held that a state had failed to exercise sufficient oversight of a peer review mechanism through which a group of physicians had determined that a rival doctor was not entitled to hospital privileges. For state oversight to constitute active supervision, state officials must "have and exercise power to review particular anticompetitive acts of private parties and disapprove those that fail to accord with state policy." In FTC v. Ticor Title Ins. Co., 504 U.S. 621 (1992), the Court withheld antitrust immunity from groups of title insurance companies on similar grounds. Several states had authorized title insurance companies to set their rates jointly, subject to potential state veto of the resulting rates. The Court concluded that the states did not actually regulate the joint rates, however. The states either failed to engage in any meaningful substantive review of rate submissions or failed to require firms to provide the data necessary to engage in effective rate regulation.

This rise and fall of the state action doctrine between 1975 and 1992 illustrates the difficulty of integrating antitrust with regulation, especially regulation at the state and local level. Often regulation appears to be a cover for private cartels or exclusionary practices; but many state and local regulations can also be justified by the need to control monopoly power or externalities. Issues of federalism make the integration even more difficult.[6] At least for now, it seems unlikely that the Court will allow federal antitrust laws to be applied where substantial state or local regulation is imposed.

B. ANTITRUST IMMUNITY

The state action doctrine seeks to resolve potential conflicts between state economic regulation and the federal antitrust laws. A similar conflict often arises between federal regulation and the Sherman Act, and the cases seeking to reconcile the two are in many situations indistinguishable. Thus the case law finding that federal regulation has immunized

6. See Elhauge, *The Scope of Antitrust Process,* 104 Harv. L.Rev. 668 (1991); Pierce, *Regulation, Deregulation, Federalism and Administrative Law: Agency Power to Preempt State Regulation,* 46 U.Pitt.L.Rev. 607 (1985); Easterbrook, *Antitrust and the Economics of Federalism,* 26 J.L. & Econ. 23 (1983).

the regulated activity from antitrust scrutiny frequently borrows from concepts developed under the state action doctrine—and vice versa. There are differences, however, in that federal regulatory schemes rely far less on private delegations and generally involve full-time staffs with considerable expertise. Still, the ultimate question is identical, namely whether Congress intended for the regulatory scheme to oust antitrust review of the challenged action.

The role of antitrust in an industry subject to federal regulation varies widely. Where the industry is explicitly exempted from antitrust jurisdiction or is so "pervasively" regulated that government oversight has replaced market forces in controlling critical management decisions, the role of antitrust is usually minimal. In most situations, however, the regulatory scheme is less complete, yet little direct attention has been given by Congress to whether administrative regulation should replace antitrust rules. Faced with a potential conflict between antitrust and administrative regulation, the usual judicial approach has been to follow the national commitment to competition policy as expressed in the Sherman Act and allow antitrust challenges. Only where the two are considered to be wholly incompatible is prominence given to regulatory programs. Within this framework, direct conflicts are seldom found. When pressed, agency policy can usually be reconciled (or forced to fit) with antitrust principles.

Stated in terms of legal rules, industry immunity from antitrust is not lightly inferred and "repeal of the antitrust laws by implication is not favored." It is "only when there is a 'plain repugnancy between the antitrust and regulatory provisions' "[7]that Congress will be found to have superceded antitrust with administrative regulation. The role of the courts in determining the application of the antitrust laws to regulated industries, then, is twofold: first, to determine whether (and where) the antitrust laws apply to regulated industries; and second, to decide how antitrust policy should be applied in regulatory decisions. The first is addressed in this section; the latter is discussed in the next.[8]

The touchstone of analysis for deciding whether administrative regulation immunizes regulated activity from antitrust scrutiny is congressional intent. The simplest case, of course, is where Congress has already addressed the issue directly. Express immunity has occasionally been granted to particular industries subject to federal regulation, including agriculture, insurance, shipping and transportation. In each instance Congress has directed that the antitrust laws shall not apply to particular specified businesses or activities. See, e.g., 7 U.S.C.A. §§ 291–292 (Capper–Volstead Act of 1922 exemption of agricultural cooperatives

7.   Gordon v. New York Stock Exchange, 422 U.S. 659 (1975), quoting United States v. Philadelphia Nat'l Bank, 374 U.S. 321 (1963). Accord, National Gerimedical Hospital v. Blue Cross of Kansas City, 452 U.S. 378 (1981), quoting United States v. National Ass'n of Securities Dealers, Inc., 422 U.S. 694 (1975).

8.   Chapter 14 discusses a related third question, namely whether courts should defer to agencies and allow them a first opportunity to consider the antitrust issue.

from the antitrust laws); see National Broiler
Marketing Ass'n v. United States, 436 U.S. 816
(1978) (whether producers of broiler chickens
were "farmers"); cf. Folsom, *Antitrust Enforcement Under the Secretaries of Agriculture and
Commerce*, 80 Colum.L.Rev. 1623 (1980). In these
situations the regulatory agencies are relied upon
to protect consumers from monopoly prices and
output restrictions. In addition to such express
statutory immunities, Congress has also delegated
to the regulatory commissions and others the authority to shield particular transactions from antitrust attack. These include ocean shipping
agreements approved by the Federal Maritime
Commission, activities of defense contractors and
small businesses found by the President to be in
the national interest, and joint operating arrangements by newspapers upheld by the Attorney
General. Finally, in some instances Congress has
rewritten the antitrust standard to be applied to
certain industries or special practices. Bank mergers, for example, are unlawful only if their anticompetitive effects are "clearly outweighed" by
beneficial effects on the convenience and needs of
bank customers. 15 U.S.C.A. § 1828(c) (Bank
Merger Act of 1966). Similarly, associations engaged in "export trade" are exempted from the
Sherman Act provided that the association's activities do not affect prices charged in the United
States. 15 U.S.C.A. §§ 61–65 (Webb–Pomerene
Act).[9]

    9. Although sometimes overlooked, in point of fact the most
important express exemption from antitrust is not for industry

Several questions, nonetheless, may arise regarding the application of antitrust to such industries and practices. The most immediate is whether the specific exemption covers the challenged activity. In *Georgia v. Pennsylvania R. R.*, 324 U.S. 439 (1945), several railroads had agreed upon tariffs they would file before the Interstate Commerce Commission for approval of general rate levels as well as specific rates. Georgia now sought to bring an antitrust action asserting that these "prevailing agreements" constituted an illegal combination that would harm economic activity in the state. Denying the railroads' argument that the statutory scheme coupled with the ICC's approval provided antitrust immunity, the Supreme Court held that the Commission was not empowered either to control or prevent an illegal conspiracy. ICC approval of the rates was merely a determination that they were within a zone of reasonableness and were themselves lawful. However, in upholding Georgia's claim that the railroads' actions were not wholly exempt from antitrust review, the Court did not decide whether the rates set were in fact the product of an illegal conspiracy; it only determined that the agreement to file particular tariffs was subject to antitrust review.[10]

but for labor. Section 6 of the Clayton Act specifically protects union activity, including collective bargaining, from antitrust attack. 15 U.S.C.A. § 17. Without this immunity, such agreements would constitute per se price fixing violations. Section 20 of the Clayton Act also forbids injunctions against labor strikes and boycotts, a policy that was reasserted and expanded in the 1932 Norris–LaGuardia Act. 29 U.S.C.A. §§ 101–115.

10. Congress responded to *Georgia v. Pennsylvania R. R.* by passing the Reed–Bulwinkle Act which formally sanctions and

A second illustration is the legislative exemption from antitrust regulation for the insurance industry under the McCarran–Ferguson Act. 15 U.S.C.A. §§ 1011–1015. This exemption is expressly limited to "the business of insurance" and applies only insofar as it is regulated by state law and not excepted by the proviso that the conduct not involve a "boycott," "coercion" or "intimidation." The meaning of each of these terms has been vigorously controverted. See Union Labor Life Insur. Co. v. Pireno, 458 U.S. 119 (1982) (peer review not the "business of insurance"); Group Life & Health Insur. Co. v. Royal Drug Co., 440 U.S. 205 (1979) (contracts between insurance company and drug stores fixing fees for filling prescriptions are not the "business of insurance"); St. Paul Fire & Marine Insur. Co. v. Barry, 438 U.S. 531 (1978) (defining boycott so as not to cover challenged conduct).

Another question that arises when someone seeks to apply the antitrust laws to regulated conduct is whether the regulatory commission with authority to immunize a transaction has in fact approved it. If so, this raises the further question of whether that approval is in accordance with the agency's legislatively approved authority and meets the usual standards of review (i.e., is not arbitrary and capricious). Not surprisingly, these questions can lead to lengthy and complex litigation. See, e.g., Hughes Tool Co. v. TWA, 409 U.S. 363 (1973). While there

authorizes "rate bureaus" designed to create rate agreements among railroads as long as they also obtain the ICC's approval. 49 U.S.C.A. § 5b.

are relatively few cases on point, courts have generally deferred to agency judgments and relied on the administrator's continuing supervision to protect antitrust interests.

Even where the agency has not approved the arrangement, if it has the authority to do so and the plaintiff is seeking only an injunction or declaratory relief, courts will generally dismiss an antitrust suit and instead refer the matter to the agency for initial consideration. Thus in Far East Conference v. United States, 342 U.S. 570 (1952), the Court ruled that an antitrust challenge to an unfiled, unapproved cartel agreement involving dual rates charging higher prices to shippers not using cartel-controlled vessels exclusively had to be considered by the FMC first. That agency could punish the failure to file and it had the authority to decide the reasonableness of the anticompetitive conduct. See Chapter 14 (primary jurisdiction). Any other approach could lead to inconsistent results depending on whether the matter was pursued before the agency or an antitrust court. Accord, Pan American World Airways v. United States, 371 U.S. 296 (1963).

On the other hand, where the antitrust plaintiff seeks damages in a similar situation, the Supreme Court has held that the FMC's authority to approve ratemaking agreements does not either oust the antitrust laws or require first consideration by the FMC. Carnation Co. v. Pacific Westbound Conference, 383 U.S. 213 (1966). In that case no direct conflict between the court and agency could arise as to future conduct, although the Court did not discuss the fact that the plaintiff's treble damage claim was in addition to possible administrative fines. But see Keogh v. Chicago & N. W. Ry., 260 U.S. 156 (1922). See also Square D Co. v. Niagara Frontier Tariff Bureau, Inc., 476 U.S. 409 (1986).

Even more difficult to decide is whether to imply immunity where Congress has neither granted an express immunity nor specifically authorized an agency to regulate the challenged conduct. The general principles are clearly set forth in the cases and readily summarized; it is their application that has proved perplexing. The first rule is that the antitrust laws represent a "fundamental national economic policy" which is not lightly abandoned. For this reason, implied antitrust immunity is not favored. Congressional intent governs, of course, "but this intent must be clear." National Gerimedical Hospital v. Blue Cross of Kansas City, 452 U.S. 378 (1981). On the other hand, where there is a clear contradiction between the antitrust laws and the regulatory system, repeal may be implied. That intent to repeal is more likely to be found when the regulatory agency has power to authorize or require the type of conduct in question. Finally, substantial regulation of an industry is not itself viewed as sufficient evidence of an intent to repeal all antitrust enforcement within the industry. The critical factor is whether repeal is "necessary to make the [regulatory scheme] work, and even then [it will be implied] only to the minimum extent necessary." Id. quoting Silver v. New York Stock Exchange, 373

U.S. 341 (1963). See generally, Balter & Day, *Implied Antitrust Repeals: Principles for Analysis,* 86 Dickinson L.Rev. 447, 472 (1982).

Illustrating these principles in action is the recent case of National Gerimedical Hospital v. Blue Cross of Kansas City, supra. There a health insurer refused to accept a new hospital as a "participating member" entitled to full cost direct reimbursement because the hospital was not approved by the local health system agency—a private, nonprofit, federally-funded corporation responsible under the National Health Planning and Resources Development Act of 1974, 42 U.S.C.A. § 300k et seq., to coordinate the planning and construction of health facilities in Kansas City. The defendant claimed a blanket antitrust immunity asserting that its actions were not subject to antitrust review because the 1974 Act represented an overriding policy. Under its view, an insurer could not be held liable in treble damages merely for complying with the judgment of a local planning agency established under the Act to prevent overinvestment in and maldistribution of health facilities. To do so, it said, would punish the insurer for acting consistent with the Act's policy and mandate.

Despite the obvious appeal of this argument, the Court rejected it as too sweeping a claim for blanket antitrust immunity. First, the 1974 Act relied only upon persuasion and cooperation. Second, the local planning agency was not a governmental entity but only a federally supported firm without governmental power. Third, as a result, the action being challenged was neither compelled nor approved by any regulatory body. The Court also noted that in 1979 (after the conduct in question here) Congress had amended the Act to direct that the planning process give special consideration "to the importance of maintaining and improving competition in the health industry." Its holding, however, was limited and only denied that Congress had approved a pervasive repeal of the antitrust laws over every action in the health care planning process. The Court went to special lengths to observe that the challenged conduct did not involve cooperation among providers (which apparently might be exempt since that was the primary focus of the Act) but only an insurer's failure to deal with a provider who refused to heed the advice of a planning agency.

Further illustrating the particularized nature of the inquiry as well as how difficult it is to reconcile case results are three cases involving the jurisdiction of the Securities and Exchange Commission. In the first, Silver v. New York Stock Exchange, supra, the Court ruled that the SEC's authority to oversee stock exchange rules did not immunize private conduct from antitrust review where that conduct was not necessary to realize regulatory goals. Thus, an exchange decision to disconnect direct telephone links with a broker was held to be subject to antitrust review. On the other hand, in Gordon v. New York Stock Exchange, 422 U.S. 659 (1975), the Court ruled unanimously that price fixing by members of a stock exchange is not subject to antitrust scrutiny. The SEC not only had authority to modify exchange rules but it had in fact exercised that jurisdiction vigorously. Thus, without immunity it was possible that antitrust and regulatory policy would collide. Finally, in United States v. National Ass'n of Securities Dealers, Inc., 422 U.S. 694 (1975), the Court held that price fixing in secondary market transactions by mutual funds, underwriters, dealers and the NASD was immune because Congress had given final authority over minimum prices to the SEC. The difficulty with this analysis is that the Commission had never exercised that authority. Why three decades of agency silence and inaction constitute approval was not explained. Nor is this tension between antitrust principles and regulatory policy, and its reflection in seemingly irreconcilable judicial decisions, confined to securities cases. See also United States v. American Telephone & Telegraph Co., 461 F.Supp. 1314 (D.D.C. 1978); MCI Communications Corp. v. American Telephone & Telegraph Co., 708 F.2d 1081 (7th Cir.1983).

C. APPLICATION OF ANTITRUST PRINCIPLES

Even when the regulatory scheme immunizes conduct from antitrust review, the regulatory agency may be required to consider competition policy under the "public interest" or other standard governing agency regulation. One early case illustrating this requirement is McLean Trucking Co. v. United States, 321 U.S. 67 (1944). There the Supreme Court held that the ICC's assessment of the truckers' probable impact of a merger should include a consideration of the effect of the mergers on competition in the industry. However, the ICC was not bound by antitrust standards and the Supreme Court has frequently upheld ICC approval of mergers that it would not have upheld in other contexts. Compare Penn–Central Merger & N & W Inclusion Cases, 389 U.S. 486 (1968) and United States v. ICC (Northern Lines), 396 U.S. 491 (1970), with United States v. Pabst Brewing Co., 384 U.S. 546 (1966) and United States v. Von's Grocery Co., 384 U.S. 270 (1966). Congress had delegated to the ICC responsibility for determining how the industry should be structured in order to achieve a sound transportation system. Thus, as long as the Commission gave serious consideration to competition concerns, its conclusions would be approved if supported by an adequately developed record and a reasoned judgment.

While this approach is not unusual, it is also true that whether or not a federal agency is required to consider the competitive consequences of its decision depends on the legislative history of each particular statute. See, e.g., Gulf States Util. Co. v. FPC, 411 U.S. 747 (1973). As a consequence, few principles—other than a vague but oft-cited general presumption favoring competition—can be stated. Recent remarkable developments, first in airline deregulation and then in motor carrier and communications deregulation, demonstrate the flexibility of the public interest standard as applied by agencies and courts and thus the broad discretion given agency administrators to regulate or, alternatively, to rely on market forces under most organic acts. See also FCC v. WNCN Listeners Guild, 450 U.S. 582 (1981) (upholding FCC policy not to supervise changes in radio station format under the "public interest" standard).[11]

Over the past decade, the difference between antitrust and federal regulation of the electricity and natural gas industries has become increasingly subtle. FERC has used traditional antitrust remedies— mandating equal access to essential facilities and prohibiting firms from tying monopoly services to goods that otherwise would be sold in competitive markets—in order to maximize the role of competition in governing the gas and electricity markets. See section 15C. Courts increasingly defer to FERC's superior industry-specific expertise and ability to implement systematic remedies by declining to provide separate judicially-imposed antitrust remedies such as treble damages. See, e.g., City of Chanute v. Williams Natural Gas Co., 955 F.2d 641 (10th Cir.1992). See also Town of Concord v. Boston Edison Co., 915 F.2d 17 (1st Cir.1990) (courts

11. The effect of contemporary views of the appropriateness of competition as a standard for regulation and of the flexibility of the public interest standard is reflected in judicial review of FCC decisions. In Hawaiian Tel. Co. v. FCC, 498 F.2d 771 (D.C.Cir.1974), the commission was rebuked for presuming that competition in telephone services were in the public interest, whereas just a few years later the FCC was rebuked by the same court for not indulging the very same presumption. MCI Telecommunications Corp. v. FCC (Execunet I), 561 F.2d 365 (D.C.Cir.1977).

should not adjudicate cases involving alleged anti-competitive conduct of regulated firms because FERC is in a better position to adjudicate such disputes).

D. APPEALS TO GOVERNMENT[12]

Related to the question of the immunity of government action from antitrust prosecution is whether businesses or others seeking the protection of government regulation are subject to the antitrust laws. Certainly once the regulatory scheme is in place, their actions—if within the boundaries of the state action or antitrust immunity doctrines—are protected.[13] In addition, the first amendment clearly applies to individual petitions to government, a coverage extended in recent years to commercial speech and other overt corporate political speech.[14] To be sure, manipulation of government for corrupt ends ought to be prohibited and is not constitutionally protected, but criminal law rules against bribery of public officers provide substantial

12. See generally, Fischel, *Antitrust Liability for Attempts to Influence Government Action: The Basis and Limits of the Noerr–Pennington Doctrine*, 45 U.Chi.L.Rev. 80 (1977).

13. Similarly, the federal antitrust laws do not apply to actions of the federal government or even to cooperation between federal officials acting within their authority and private firms. See United States v. Rock Royal Co-op., Inc., 307 U.S. 533 (1939).

14. See note 2 supra; First National Bank v. Bellotti, 435 U.S. 765 (1978) (state cannot prohibit corporations from spending money to express their views on referendum questions even if such issues are not directly related to their business interests); p. 141 supra.

protection against such misuse of private power. Likewise, public discussion and publicity tend to insure that official actions reflect the public interest.

On the other hand, a broad exemption of all business activity related to government regulation may invite predation by abuse of government procedures and present an increasingly dangerous threat to competition. See generally, R. Bork, *The Antitrust Paradox* ch. 18 (1978). In deciding where to draw the line between what constitutes permissible petitioning of government and impermissible individual or joint action obstructing legitimate competition, it is important to note that vexatious litigation or other harassing techniques may fully serve their purpose even though competitive entry is not in fact prevented. That is, merely delaying new competition can protect an occupant of a lucrative market, and successful predation in this form does not necessarily require any particular advantage or deep pocket, or even entail high antitrust visibility.

There are relatively few cases outlining the types of business conduct that are protected, and they generally fall into two categories. One group suggests an area of complete immunity from antitrust liability. It is illustrated by the leading case of Eastern R. R. Presidents Conference v. Noerr Motor Freight, Inc., 365 U.S. 127 (1961), where joint efforts by businesses—24 railroads and an association of railroad presidents—to obtain legislative and executive action unfavorable to competing trucking firms was held not to violate the Sherman

Act. The desirability of public participation in governmental processes, even though that participation is for selfish rather than "public" reasons, was ruled to outweigh antitrust considerations. Ignoring the tautology, the Court contended that the adoption of legislation reflected a determination that the result served the public interest, which a court should not overturn for private purposes. Central to the holding of *Noerr* is that the decision to pass a law or adopt a policy is the responsibility of the legislature and executive and depends upon an open and robust discussion. Business and individuals are to be allowed group as well as independent presentations; examination of their motives is irrelevant for it is a central assumption of the democratic process that participants will often act out of self-interest.

On the other hand, the *Noerr* decision did not rule that every attempt to affect governmental action is beyond the reach of the Sherman Act:

> There may be situations in which a publicity campaign, ostensibly directed toward influencing governmental action, is a mere sham to cover what is actually nothing more than an attempt to interfere directly with the business relationships of a competitor and the application of the Sherman Act would be justified.

The Court, in other words, suggested in dictum a qualification on the immunity it recognized. While constitutional and policy protections require that those presenting their views to government be given broad latitude, it seems equally important that government agencies not be misused. The principle is easy to state. Like the state action doctrine of Parker v. Brown or the rules for antitrust immunity, however, its application can be difficult and a review of the cases is not always instructive. Nonetheless, they are a starting point for analysis and suggest some of the broader outlines of what is permitted or denied.

In *Noerr* the railroads had allegedly propagandized the general public and lobbied the legislature solely for the purpose of injuring truckers and destroying them as competitors for long-distance freight business. The conduct was immune from antitrust prosecution even though the railroads employed deceptive tactics such as publicity that the prorailroad views were from independent groups and civic persons, and even if its purpose or effect was directly aimed at injuring competing truckers. To involve the courts in determining the limits of "fair argument" would be asking them to draw an impossible line. Justice Black, himself a former legislator, while not enthusiastic about the conduct, recognized that such a " 'no-holds-barred fight' between two industries both of which are seeking control of a profitable source of income ... commonplace in the halls of legislative bodies."

Similarly, in United Mine Workers v. Pennington, 381 U.S. 657 (1965), the Court held that those persuading the Secretary of Labor to establish a minimum wage for employees of contractors selling coal to the Tennessee Valley Authority and to curtail spot market purchases (exempt from the minimum wage order) were not subject to antitrust liability. This was, instead, lawful persuasion of an executive officer to take action within his lawful discretion: "The conduct of the union and the operators did not violate the ... [antitrust laws, because] the action taken to set a minimum wage for government purchases of coals was the act of a public official who is not claimed to be a coconspirator."

Illustrative on the other side are two cases in which the Supreme Court has found antitrust liability for misuse of administrative and judicial processes. In Walker Process Equip., Inc. v. Food Mach. & Chem. Corp., 382 U.S. 172 (1965), the Court ruled that "the enforcement of a patent procured by fraud on the Patent Office may be violative of Section 2 of the Sherman Act." As Judge Bork has pointed out, the Court was not saying that fraud itself on the patent office violated the antitrust laws—since that might suggest that anyone litigating a patent ultimately found invalid could be subject to antitrust sanction—but rather that "pressing claims known to be without foundation for the purpose of stifling competition" is prohibited by them. R. Bork, supra at 353.

This limitation on the *Noerr-Pennington* doctrine was confirmed in California Motor Transport Co. v. Trucking Unlimited, 404 U.S. 508 (1972), where the Court sustained a complaint that a combination of the 19 largest trucking firms in California violated the antitrust laws when they opposed *all* applications, regardless of their merits, by smaller truckers before federal and state agencies as well as in all available courts. Relying on allegations that the defendants had warned the small truckers that they could avoid the costs being inflicted on them only by not asking for new operating rights, the Court distinguished *Noerr-Pennington* and ruled that conduct which amounted to a sham is not protected by the first amendment. Implicit in this holding is the suggestion that misrepresentation or other unethical conduct is more readily reached by the antitrust laws when used to subvert adjudicative processes which are less able to protect themselves and where other societal interests (e.g., in preserving fair processes) are implicated. Mere vexatiousness does not seem sufficient to warrant antitrust intervention. Accord, Otter Tail Power Co. v. United States, 410 U.S. 366 (1973); United States v. Otter Tail Power Co., 360 F.Supp. 451 (D.Minn.1973).

The Court indicated its unwillingness to use antitrust law to deter public corruption in the context of zoning ordinances, however, in City of Columbia v. Omni Outdoor Advertising, Inc., 499 U.S. 365 (1991). The Court rejected, on state action grounds, the plaintiff's claim that its competitor had conspired with corrupt public officials to exclude the plaintiff from the market by enacting a zoning ordinance that had that effect.

In other recent cases, the Court has focused on identifying the permissible targets of petitioning activity and describing the contours of the sham exception. In Allied Tube & Conduit Corp. v. Indian

Head, Inc., 486 U.S. 492 (1988), the Court held that an effort to restrain competition by influencing the standard-setting activities of a private association is not immune under *Noerr* because the association is not an institution of government. In FTC v. Superior Court Trial Lawyers Ass'n, 493 U.S. 411 (1990), the Court held that a group boycott undertaken by lawyers to induce a local government to increase the fees it paid to lawyers who represent indigent criminal defendants was not immune because the lawyers used an illegal means to obtain the desired government action. In Professional Real Estate Investors, Inc. v. Columbia Pictures Indus., Inc., 508 U.S. 49 (1993), the Court held that litigation with a potential anticompetitive effect is a non-immune "sham" if: (1) no reasonable litigant could expect to succeed on the merits; and, (2) the litigation is an attempt to interfere with a rival's business through the process of government deliberation rather than through the outcome of that process.

CHAPTER XIV

PRIMARY JURISDICTION

When an action is brought against a person or firm challenging conduct also subject to control by a regulatory agency, one question that is frequently raised by the defendant is whether the court should refrain from deciding the case until the agency has had an opportunity to review the controversy. The doctrine of primary jurisdiction describes the allocation of decision-making power and seeks to define those situations in which courts will refer matters to the agency for initial determination. Where the court also concludes that its consideration is not merely stayed but terminated (at least until the administrative action is appealed—and usually to a different court), the agency is said to have exclusive as well as primary jurisdiction. However, dismissal may also be the remedy where the agency has only primary jurisdiction, and these terms are often used interchangeably and tend to be confusing insofar as the agency action can ultimately be reviewed; hence this text avoids this distinction and refers only to primary jurisdiction in its broader sense. Primary jurisdiction, then, is a method for avoiding immediate judicial review and is most frequently applied in connection with antitrust challenges to conduct by regulated firms.[1]

A. BASIC DOCTRINE

There are two principal reasons for requiring that a litigant resort to the administrative process before pursuing his damage claim: first, the litigation may involve issues of fact which are beyond the conventional experience and expertise of judges, or the decision may require the exercise of administrative discretion under broad statutory standards; and, second, the requirement of preliminary decision by the agency also serves the goal of national uniformity in regulatory programs.

The objective of uniformity was the justification given in the first case establishing the doctrine, Texas & Pacific Ry. v. Abilene Cotton Oil Co., 204 U.S. 426 (1907). There, claiming that the defendant railroad's published rate was unreasonable, a shipper brought a common law action for the overcharge. The Court, however, ruled that a shipper seeking reparations based upon the unreasonableness of an ICC approved rate must "primarily invoke redress" through the ICC. This result in the

1. Primary jurisdiction is distinguishable from the administrative law doctrine of exhaustion of administrative remedies to which it is closely aligned. The exhaustion doctrine is applied by courts where *premature judicial review* of agency action is being sought and the agency defends on the ground that it should be allowed to complete its action. Although primary jurisdiction rests on the some premise—that the agency has the authority to make the basic decision at issue—it comes into play when the original (rather than review) jurisdiction of the court is invoked to decide the merits.

face of a clear statutory grant of concurrent jurisdiction in reparation cases to both the courts and
the ICC was justified on the ground that any other
result "would render enforcement of the [ICC] act
impossible." The contrary provisions of the ICC Act
were explained away by concluding that the Act
"cannot be held to destroy itself."

Agency expertise is the more commonly used
ground for applying the doctrine. For example, in
United States v. Western Pac. Ry., 352 U.S. 59
(1956), the question was whether a railroad's incen-
diary bomb or lower gasoline-in-steel-drum rate
should be applied to a shipment of bomb casings
filled with napalm but without the triggering fuses
necessary to make them explosive. Even though
neither counsel nor the lower court had suggested
that this was anything other than a question of law
involving construction of the railroad's tariff, the
Supreme Court ruled that a decision would require
the ICC's expert understanding of railroads and
whether special handling was necessary—and therefore that the ICC had primary jurisdiction. The
difficulty with this analysis is that the issue of tariff
interpretation can also be characterized as a question of law within a court's special province, as the
ICC did in fact on remand in holding that a tariff
covering an article by its usual name applies even
though shipped without all its parts.

On the other hand, if the issues raised in an
action fall outside the ambit of the regulatory agency's special expertise or primary authority, the
claim will generally not be barred by the doctrine of

primary jurisdiction. Thus in Nader v. Allegheny Airlines, Inc., 426 U.S. 290 (1976), the Court held that the CAB's statutory power to abate deceptive practices was not synonymous with common law fraud and misrepresentation. Since the Board could not immunize carriers from this kind of liability, the Court allowed Ralph Nader to sue the airline for fraudulent misrepresentation in his claim that the airline had deceptively failed to disclose that it might overbook flights and deny boarding to passengers with confirmed reservations. The Court's analysis is important reaffirmation of the doctrinal foundations of primary jurisdiction. In particular it noted that the issue was not one on which an accurate decision "could be facilitated by an informed evaluation of the economics or technology of the regulated industry"; rather, the common law fraud standards "are within the conventional competence of the courts and the judgment of a technically expert body is not likely to be helpful in the application of these standards to the facts of this case."

These cases illustrate several facets of the doctrine worth noting. First, it is most likely to be applied in intensively regulated industries where entry, price, and the nature and quality of service are closely controlled. Even then, however, not all questions which arise will fall within the doctrine: primary jurisdiction is most likely to apply when the issues are factual rather than legal, or when they are discretionary rather than governed by detailed rules. In these situations the need for administrative expertise seems most pressing.

Second, primary jurisdiction is a one-way doctrine protecting only the agency's jurisdiction. It is applied by a court to stay or dismiss a proceeding before it until the agency can act upon the matter; it is not applied to defer or dismiss agency action until a court has decided a question—even if the doctrine ordinarily would not be invoked if the case had been presented first to a court. There are, however, less substantial alternatives occasionally used by courts, such as inviting agencies to file an amicus brief or even appear as a party in the litigation.

Third, the doctrine only allocates jurisdictional priority. Once the agency renders its decision, recourse to the courts—that is, judicial review of agency action—is still available. Primary jurisdiction, in brief, does not assign final jurisdiction between courts and agencies; it is only one of several techniques used to set an appropriate time for judicial review.

Fourth, the principal justification for the doctrine is to coordinate the work of agencies and courts. Their activities are most likely to come into conflict where the agency's regulation is pervasive and coordinated, and uniform interpretations are necessary to assure effective regulation. However, application of the doctrine does not assure uniformity or prevent agency inconsistency. Reviewing courts do not always interpret legal questions or identify fact questions identically. Nor does the Supreme Court resolve every conflict among the circuits. Primary jurisdiction serves merely to avoid major conflicts, not to eliminate every possible disagreement or inconsistency. The doctrine is designed to take advantage of whatever contribution the agency can make within its area of specialization. In point of fact, of course, allowing an agency the first opportunity to decide an issue or case will also probably give it the final voice in most cases.

B. THE RELATIONSHIP OF ANTI-TRUST LAW AND PRIMARY JURISDICTION

The relationship between antitrust and administrative regulation has spawned important primary jurisdiction cases and allocated specific responsibilities to courts and agencies. For example, as explained in *Far East Conference*, discussed in section 13 B, where the Supreme Court held that the lawfulness of a "dual rate" system favoring cartel ships was within the primary jurisdiction of the maritime agency, the antitrust court has the initial obligation to decide whether the particular conduct being challenged is immune from antitrust attack under the regulatory statute. Only after this threshold immunity question is answered negatively does the issue of primary jurisdiction arise where an antitrust court must decide whether the case is to be referred to an agency. As a result, there are two hurdles—antitrust immunity and primary jurisdiction—that must be surmounted by an antitrust plaintiff before a court will consider its claim.

While this analytical framework is literally correct, it is not applied rigidly; the issues of immunity and primary jurisdiction are technically separate, but not all cases follow this analysis. For example, the general rule is that legal issues are within the special province of a court to decide. Yet a reading of the cases suggests that even on these questions referrals to the regulatory agency can be justified on the ground that its views may enlighten the court about the scope of the antitrust immunity, the importance of uniformity and agency expertise—and therefore the applicability of primary jurisdiction.

Moreover, these and similar pressures (such as economy of court time) tend to work differently in damage cases as compared to those involving injunctive relief. As *Far East Conference* illustrates, where the regulatory agency has authority to deal with the problem (of dual rates favoring carriers participating in the cartel), questions of injunctive relief should be left to the regulators. Accord, Pan American World Airways v. United States, 371 U.S. 296 (1963). Otherwise the agency could undercut the antitrust court's verdict by authorizing or approving continuation of the challenged conduct.

On the other hand, the regulatory commission does not have the same ability to in effect overturn an antitrust judgment for treble damages or even criminal sanctions. Thus damage actions in the same circumstance may be upheld. See, e.g., Carnation Co. v. Pacific Westbound Conference, 383 U.S. 213 (1966). Even here, however, regard for uniformity and agency expertise as well as double punishment of the same conduct (for example, if the agency also decides to penalize the actions under its authority) may caution against too independent a judicial course.

That at least seems to be the message of the Supreme Court in Ricci v. Chicago Mercantile Exchange, 409 U.S. 289 (1973), where the denial of an Exchange seat to the plaintiff was being challenged as a violation of the Sherman Act as well as of the Exchange's rules and the Commodity Exchange Act. The Court held that the antitrust complaint should be stayed pending a decision of the Commodity Exchange Commission to determine whether the defendant's conduct violated either the Exchange's rules or the Act. Both were the exclusive domain of the regulatory commission. However, if the Exchange had violated a rule, the antitrust case could proceed. An examination of the opinion further suggests that the doctrine of primary jurisdiction was used by the Court to avoid having to answer the difficult question of implied immunity or of having to decide factual issues that the agency seemed better equipped to evaluate. See also United States v. American Telephone & Telegraph Co., 461 F.Supp. 1314 (D.D.C.1978).

CHAPTER XV

REGULATORY FAILURE, DEREGULATION AND REGULATORY REFORM

The primary justification for government regulation of business is, at bottom, that intervention is required to correct market failures or to assure business actions not prompted by market forces. Economic market failure such as that caused by natural monopoly is the classic basis for regulation. Over time other justifications have been offered, including scarcity of resources, ruinous competition, and more recently the need to control externalities such as environmental pollution and occupational hazards. The latter have also been the foundation of much of the social regulation that was adopted in the 1970's.

Increasingly, analysis of government regulation has shown not only that natural monopoly or other bases of regulation do not justify most regulation—at least to the degree originally supposed—but also that even where some intervention in the market place is defensible, the scope, degree or direction of that regulation cannot be defended. Symbolized by campaign promises to "return government to the people" or to get "government off the people's back," several distinctive approaches have been developed in recent years. They include: identifying regulatory mismatches;[1] deregulating where regulation is no longer (if ever) justified, especially in economic regulation;[2] adopting market-type incentives in regulation, such as performance standards rather than design requirements or other command-and-control type regulations;[3] coordinating and overseeing agency regulation by other branches of government;[4] and continuing efforts to improve and simplify administrative procedures.[5]

A. REGULATORY PERFORMANCE

Economists have long debated the effects of economic regulation. Until recently, however, the debates were usually inconclusive. It was relatively

1. For helpful analyses and summaries, see Breyer, *Analyzing Regulatory Failure: Mismatches, Less Restrictive Alternatives, and Reforms*, 92 Harv.L.Rev. 547 (1979); ABA Commission on Law and the Economy, *Federal Regulation: Roads to Reform* chs. 3 & 4 (1979).

2. See, e.g., Airline Deregulation Act of 1978, 49 U.S.C.A. §§ 1301–1551.

3. See, e.g., *Promoting Competition in Regulated Industries* (A. Phillips ed. 1975); C. Schultze, *The Public Use of Private Interest* (1977); R. Stavins & B. Whitehead, *The Greening of America's Taxes: Pollution Charges and Environmental Protection* (1992).

4. See Executive Order No. 12866, 29 Weekly Comp.Pres.Doc. 1925 (1993); Executive Order No. 12498, 50 Fed.Reg. 1036 (Jan. 8, 1985); Executive Order No. 12291, 46 Fed.Reg. 13193 (Feb. 19, 1981); S. 1080, 97th Cong., 1st Sess. (1981).

5. See J. Mashaw & D. Harfst, *The Struggle for Auto Safety* (1990); Verkuil, *The Emerging Concept of Administrative Procedure, 77 Colum.L.Rev. 258 (1978).*

easy to make the theoretical case in support of the potential beneficial effects of price controls imposed on a natural monopolist. See section 2B1. Conversely, it was easy to make the theoretical case that traditional cost-of-service regulation greatly attenuates regulated firms' incentives to operate efficiently and often introduces incentives to operate inefficiently. It was impossible, however, to demonstrate the net effects of economic regulation either in theory or through empirical analysis.

This situation changed in the wake of the deregulation of transportation and financial services in the late 1970s and the wholesale market for natural gas in the 1980s. Each of the initial experiments with deregulation produced enormous efficiency gains, usually accompanied by significant price reductions. Within a few years, numerous studies documented the dramatic improvements spawned by elimination of traditional cost-of-service regulation in each of the newly deregulated industries. See, e.g., Pierce, *Reconstituting the Natural Gas Industry from Wellhead to Burnertip,* 9 En.L.J. 1 (1988). See generally Hahn & Hird, *The Costs and Benefits of Regulation: Review and Synthesis,* 8 Yale J.Reg. 233 (1991). Those studies have convinced many analysts, legislators, and administrators that traditional methods of economic regulation create massive efficiencies. The studies of recently deregulated industries also have encouraged the development of more reliable methods of predicting the effects of a potential future change in methods of government intervention in a regulated market. Using two such methods, an experienced analyst has estimated that a transition to greater reliance on competition in the electricity industry would produce consumer savings of $24 to $31 billion per year. See Studness, Estimating the Financial Cost of Utility Regulation, Fortnightly 48 (Nov. 1, 1993).

The many new studies demonstrating the poor performance of industries subject to traditional cost-of-service regulation have motivated scholars, legislators, and regulators to search for alternatives. Deregulation, discussed in the next section, has been the result in some industries. In other industries, however, the structure of the market and the cost characteristics of some critical functions seem inconsistent with complete deregulation. Yet, changing the nature of government intervention to reduce the scope of cost-of-service regulation and to allow greater opportunities for competitive market forces to determine outcomes offers the prospect of improved performance in these industries as well. In the network industries—telecommunications, natural gas, and electricity—regulators have replaced pervasive cost-of-service regulation with a combination of three new mechanisms—unbundling of products and services, mandatory equal access to natural monopoly facilities, and unregulated competition for non-monopoly products and services. We describe these related forms of government intervention in section 15C. In markets that are subject both to economic regulation and to significant environmental regulation, e.g., generation of electricity, regulators are attempting to devise methods of integrating the two forms of regulation. We discuss that effort in section 15D. With respect to the remaining natural monopoly markets, e.g., local distribution of electricity, natural gas, and water, regulators are searching for methods of "incentive regulation" to replace traditional cost-of-service regulation. We discuss incentive regulation in section 15E. In Section 15F, we discuss the movement to subject the nation's largest industry, healthcare, to a new form of regulation, managed competition. Finally, in section 15G, we discuss a problem that arises in any transition from one form of government intervention to another, how to allocate the frequently large transition costs among market participants.

B. DEREGULATION

The most direct response to increasingly persuasive information that government regulation is often either ineffective or undesirable has been the movement for deregulation, especially where both theoretical and practical evidence show that existing price and entry regulation is unsound.

The movement has generally occurred in four stages. First, there is a questioning, usually in academic literature, of the appropriateness of regulation. For example, the natural monopoly or infant industry arguments for transportation regulation were challenged in a series of provocative articles written mainly by economists. Next, empirical studies show that instead of keeping prices and services at competitive levels, regulation frequently protects established firms from market discipline, fosters inefficient service and mistakenly approves prices that are too high, leaving consumers unprotected, or denies producers competitive returns, making investment capital difficult to attract. Third, this message begins to be heard increasingly in Congress and frequently even persuades the regulators who may initiate some deregulatory steps on their own. Depending on the industry's leverage and political astuteness, this effort may be challenged or slowed by Congress. Finally, as the practical evidence of the costs of overregulation mounts, legislation may be proposed and adopted which codifies and extends administratively initiated deregulation.

This somewhat idealized scenario is best illustrated in practice by the deregulation in 1977 of air cargo transport and in 1978 of air passenger traffic. Both were spurred by numerous studies a decade or two earlier (primarily by economists), thoughtful Congressional hearings under the persistent guidance of a powerful Senator (Edward Kennedy), and courageous agency leadership by a charismatic and knowledgeable economist (Alfred Kahn). Demonstrating the flexibility of the "public interest" standard, the Civil Aeronautics Board experimented with rules opening routes to new entry and allowing airlines limited discretion on pricing. At first reluctantly and then with considerable enthusiasm, Congress followed suit and mandated the elimination of administrative controls on entry and pricing. 49 U.S.C.A. § 1374.

Preliminary results have been sufficiently favorable despite a subsequent recession and large-scale fuel cost increase that deregulation in other industries has been encouraged. This is not to say, however, that deregulation has not imposed some dislocation costs. Several airlines, especially long-protected scheduled firms and charter companies, were unable to survive the new competitive challenge and the industry has been restructured as a consequence.[6] Competition has resulted in complex discount fares as airlines have sought to increase traffic by filling off-peak capacity. Deregulation provided protection against service interruption for small communities, but not in intermediate size markets and some have lost substantial service. In addition, some consumers are now served by nonjet commuter airlines whose service is viewed as inferior by consumers. On the other hand, regional and commuter airlines have expanded greatly and innovative pricing and services are increasingly the mark of competition in the industry. Retrospective studies have found that airline regulation cost consumers approximately $19.4 billion in 1977. Morrison & Winston, *Enhancing the Performance of the Deregulated Air Transportation System,* Brookings Papers on Economic Activity: Microeconomics (1989).

Regulatory reform in terms of deregulation has proceeded more cautiously elsewhere. For example,

6. For a critical assessment of this aspect of deregulation, see Phillips, *Airline Mergers in the New Regulatory Environment,* 129 U.Pa.L.Rev. 856 (1981).

the Railroad Revitalization and Regulatory Reform Act of 1975, 49 U.S.C.A. § 10101 et seq. (the 4R Act), authorized deregulation only in those markets where railroads did not dominate "transportation services," and the ICC interpreted "dominance" so broadly that rate decontrol was limited to a very few markets. It was only in 1979 that the Commission moved to deregulate more than half of all freight tonnage. Similarly, despite sweeping reforms proposed by the Carter Administration, the Staggers Rail Act of 1980, 49 U.S.C.A. § 10101 et seq., modified the ICC's authority only slightly, permitting greater liberality for rail line abandonments and loosening some price controls. The ICC (under its new name, the Surface Transportation Board) is still required to enforce rate ceilings and service requirements on standard carload shipments. Despite this authority, ICC regulation of the railroads has declined dramatically as both railroads and shippers have realized significant benefits from their new-found competition with other modes of transportation. Regulation of rail rates cost the nation between $9.7 and $16.2 billion per year. C. Barnekov & A. Kleit, *The Costs of Railroad Regulation* (1988).

Similarly, under the Motor Carrier Deregulation Act of 1980, 94 Stat. 793 (codified in scattered sections of title 18 & 49 U.S.C.A.) the ICC largely jettisoned the most restrictive regulations on trucking prices and service, although a substantial regulatory residue remained. The law still required that motor carriers obtain operating permits (certificates of public convenience and necessity), and that they must file and abide by their published rates. These requirements forced truckers to file about a million tariffs annually, although they were in fact unexamined by an ICC that had neither the staff nor the inclination to investigate the propriety of these rates. They were not without impact, however, as the ICC enforcement staff regularly sought fines for truckers caught charging less than the rates filed as well as for motor carriers providing extra services to shippers. Moreover, the Supreme Court surprised all participants in the trucking market by holding that courts must enforce the high rates in filed tariffs even when a shipper and a trucker have agreed on much lower rates. Maislin Industries v. Primary Steel, 497 U.S. 116 (1990). That holding produced a great deal of complicated litigation, as trustees for bankrupt trucking firms attempt to collect billions of dollars from shippers that paid contract rates well below the rates in the filed tariffs of trucking firms. This situation illustrates the danger of deregulating a market incompletely or with insufficient attention to statutory details. Congress finally eliminated the rate filing requirement in the Trucking Industry Regulatory Reform Act of 1994.

Trucking is unregulated today and the transition from 50 years of regulation has been remarkably successful. Most rates, after adjusting for inflation, have fallen since deregulation. Service to small communities has improved and competition has intensified. Although still challenged by the Teamsters

Union and trade association spokesmen—concerned about nonunion competition or their jobs—most analysts consider trucking deregulation a major improvement. One study estimates the costs of trucking regulation at $11 billion per year. Felton, *The Costs and Benefits of Motortruck Regulation,* Q.Rev. Econ. & Bus. 7 (1978).

C. UNBUNDLING, EQUAL ACCESS, AND COMPETITION

Complete deregulation is not an attractive option for application to an industry in which some important functions remain natural monopolies. In the telecommunications industry, for instance, some analysts believe that the "local loop" through which most small consumers have access to each other and to long distance markets remains a natural monopoly. Similarly, local distribution of natural gas remains a natural monopoly, as do transmission and distribution of electricity.

In each of these network industries, however, other important functions either never were, or no longer are, characterized by natural monopoly conditions. Economies of scale and barriers to entry are sufficiently low with respect to these activities that an unregulated market can support robust competition among multiple firms. This is true of provision of telecommunications equipment (e.g., telephones), long distance telecommunications service, production and sale of natural gas, and generation and sale of electricity.

In each of these industries, the U.S. is in the process of replacing pervasive cost-of-service regulation with a combination of three functionally related policies–unbundling, equal access, and unregulated competition. Similar restructuring is taking place simultaneously in scores of other countries. The best overview of the U.S. restructuring process is contained in Kearney & Merrill, *The Great Transformation of Regulated Industries Law*, 98 Colum. L. Rev. 1323 (1998). Unbundling refers to a regulatory rule that requires a firm that previously provided a single comprehensive service, e.g., phone service, electric service, or natural gas service, to unbundle and make separately available each of several constituent products and services. Thus, for instance, local phone service was unbundled from long distance service through the terms of the 1982 antitrust consent decree that required divestiture of AT & T's local phone service assets and division of those assets among seven regional phone companies. See United States v. AT & T, 552 F.Supp. 131 (D.D.C.1982). In orders issued in 1985 and 1992, FERC required natural gas pipelines to provide service on an unbundled basis; henceforth, pipelines were required to sell natural gas, transportation service, and storage service as separate products and services. See FERC Orders 436 and 636. Similarly, Congress' 1992 authorization of electricity sales by exempt wholesale generators (EWGs) and its mandate that FERC require owners of transmission lines to provide equal access to their facilities have created a legal environment in which electric service is virtually certain to be unbundled into several discrete products and services, e.g., electricity itself, transmission service, and distribution service. See Energy Policy Act of 1992, Pub.L. No. 102–486, §§ 711–726.

1. NATURAL GAS

Unbundling enables regulators to use different methods to govern provision of the now discrete products and services that previously were available only on a bundled basis. This is advantageous where some of the unbundled services involve economies of scale so large that they constitute natural monopolies, while other unbundled products and services can be traded in a competitive market. In the natural gas industry, for instance, production and sale of gas is not a natural monopoly function. The U.S. has thousands of gas producers that will compete aggressively to sell to millions of consumers, assuming that each producer has access to markets. Access to markets is dependent on pipelines, however, and pipeline transportation of gas remains a natural monopoly function in some markets. By unbundling gas sales from gas transportation, regulators can regulate the monopolistic transportation market and allow competition to govern the gas sales market. Competition in the gas sales market is effective because of the combination of unbundling and one of the main features of the new regulatory regime applicable to pipelines—they are required to provide all participants in the gas sales market equal access to pipeline transportation.

Mandatory equal access to natural monopoly facilities is a necessary prerequisite to the competition made possible by unbundling. This is the basic system of regulation FERC established in the sequence of orders it issued between 1985 and 1992. Congress ratified FERC's major changes in regulatory policy by enacting the Natural Gas Wellhead Decontrol Act of 1989, Pub.L. No. 101–60, 103 Stat. 157.

Eventually, even the pipeline transportation market may become susceptible to governance primarily by unregulated market forces. FERC has authorized holders of transportation capacity rights to resell those rights in a secondary market. Some analysts refer to this approach as the many straws model of pipeline transportation. A pipeline can be viewed not as a single facility but as a bundle of transportation capacity rights that can be subdivided and traded in a competitive market. As the secondary market in pipeline transportation capacity evolves and matures, the price charged for a unit of capacity inevitably will vary with changes in supply and demand for each segment. If excess capacity exists on a particular route segment, the price of capacity on that segment will be low, thereby inducing maximum utilization of the excess capacity. If capacity on a particular route segment is severely constrained, the price of capacity on that segment will be high. That high price will simultaneously ration scarce capacity among competing users and provide a market signal indicating the need to expand capacity over that route segment. FERC has significantly relaxed its regulatory barriers to entry in the pipeline transportation market to allow market participants to respond to such price signals by building new capacity.

Unbundling has also been adopted to a lesser extent at the local distribution level of the gas market. Many state PUCs have followed FERC's lead in authorizing, or compelling, local distribution companies to make sales and transportation service available separately to at least some classes of consumers. Unbundling has its limits as an effective policy option, however. One limit becomes particularly apparent at the local distribution level of the gas market. Contracting separately for purchase of gas, pipeline transportation of gas, storage of gas, and local distribution of gas requires a consumer to incur much higher transactions costs. The benefits of being able to purchase at least some of the unbundled components of gas service on a competitive market are likely to exceed the increased transactions costs for most large volume consumers. For small residential and commercial consumers, however, the higher transactions costs of acquiring unbundled service from multiple suppliers may exceed the benefits attributable to the ability to buy some components of gas service in a competitive market. Unbundling can produce net benefits even for small consumers, however. Once the natural monopoly functions are separated from the many functions that can be subjected to competitive markets, independent marketing companies are able to acquire a bundle of related goods and services and to rebundle them for sale to consumers. Through the actions of these new market intermediaries, small consumers obtain access to the benefits of a competitive market without having to incur the high transaction costs attendant to direct purchase of a complicated package of unbundled goods and services. See Pierce, *Intrastate Natural Gas Regulation,* 9 Yale J.Reg. 407 (1992).

The second limit on the desirability of unbundling exists to some extent in all contexts. Unbundling can reduce efficiency by making it more difficult and more costly to coordinate the components of unbundled service. At least arguably, for instance, a gas pipeline can coordinate the related functions of gas acquisition, transportation, storage, and delivery more efficiently and effectively than can hundreds of separate firms linked to each other and to the pipeline only by necessarily imperfect contracts. The extent of the sacrifice of economies of coordination attributable to unbundling is an empirical question that is difficult to resolve. In some contexts, that reduction in efficiency may exceed the efficiency gains available from unbundling. Again, however, independent marketers can create an efficient market environment. This new class of market intermediaries acquires gas supplies, pipeline capacity, distribution capacity, and storage services from hundreds of sources and performs the important functions of coordinating and rebundling each of those related components of gas service.

2. TELECOMMUNICATIONS

The general principles that underlie the decision to unbundle gas service also apply to telecommunications and to electricity. During the 1970's and 1980's, FCC and a court enforcing the antitrust laws began unbundling telecommunications service. FCC began by unbundling part of the equipment market. It compelled AT & T to allow customers to purchase and use their own non-AT & T phones. See, e.g., North Carolina Utilities Commission v. FCC, 552 F.2d 1036 (4th Cir.1977). During the same period, FCC began to unbundle local service from long distance service by compelling AT & T to allow its competitors in the long distance market access to AT & T's local loop facilities. See, e.g., MCI Telecommunications Corp. v. FCC, 580 F.2d 590 (D.C.Cir.1978). The 1982 antitrust divestiture order then carried unbundling a step further by creating seven regional Local Exchange Carriers (LECs) that were prohibited from providing long distance service but that were required to provide equal access to AT & T and its competitors in the long distance market. That corporate level unbundling of local and long distance service also had the effect of limiting the ability of regulators to require consumers of long distance service to cross-subsidize consumers of local service. Unbundling usually reduces the opportunities for regulators to require cross-subsidization.

By 1996, telecommunications unbundling was saving consumers an estimated three billion dollars per year in reduced long distance fees. Hahn & Hird, *The Costs and Benefits of Regulation: Review and Synthesis*, 8 Yale J. Reg. 233 (1991). Congress perceived opportunities for additional savings in two areas, however.

First, Congress believed that greater savings could be achieved in the long distance market if more firms with sophisticated expertise were allowed to enter that market. Three firms–AT & T, MCI, and Sprint–dominate the long distance market. The LECs argued that they could increase the intensity and efficacy of competition in the long distance market if they were allowed to enter that market. Thus, the LECs lobbied Congress to enact a statute that would vacate the portion of the 1982 divestiture order that prohibited them from entering the long distance market. Second, Congress believed that consumers could obtain additional benefits if competition was introduced in local telephone markets. The long distance companies argued that they could create effective competition in local service markets if Congress enacted a statute that authorized them to enter those markets and that required the LECs to take the steps necessary to allow the long distance carriers to enter the local markets.

Congress enacted the Telecommunications Act of 1996 in an attempt to further the dual goals of increasing competition in the long distance market and introducing competition in the local service market. The basic mechanism Congress relied on to further these goals was a quid pro quo. The Act authorizes an LEC to enter the long distance market if, but only if, it has first created conditions that allow effective competition in its local service market. In other words, Congress relied on the LECs' strong desire to enter the long distance market to provide a powerful incentive for the LECs to take the actions necessary to open their local service markets to effective competition.

The Act also changed the relationships between the FCC and state regulators in many ways, and it instructed both the FCC and state regulators to take a variety of actions that were intended to create competitive local service markets. Congress hoped thereby to create robustly competitive local and long distance markets within a year or two. So far, however, the Act has created far more litigation than competition. The basic problems lie within the Act. It is long and complicated. It is also laced with ambiguities and internal inconsistencies.

The 1996 Act anticipated that competition for local service would come from either or both of two sources—facilities-based competition and non facilities-based competition. Facilities-based competition would come from new local service providers who would construct and operate their own new facilities to provide local service through use of promising new technologies. Those new technologies include fiber optic cables, changes to the wires through which most people already receive electricity service and cable television service, and various wireless technologies. So far, none of those new technologies have proven to be inexpensive enough to penetrate the local service market in competition with the twisted copper wires that the LECs have long used to provide local service. In other words, facilities-based local service remains a natural monopoly function at present. Of course, the rapid pace of technological innovation in this field could produce viable facilities-based competition for local service at any time.

In the absence of viable facilities-based competition, the FCC and state regulators have focused most of their attention on efforts to create effective non facilities-based competition for local service. Non facilities-based competition is viable only if the LECs are compelled to allow third parties access to at least some of their facilities. The Act authorizes the FCC to require the LECs to provide "access to such network elements as are ... necessary" for a third party to provide local service and to provide access to "network elements" the absence of which would "impair" a third party's ability to provide local service.

Providing a right of access to natural monopoly facilities is not sufficient alone to create a competitive local service market, however. If the terms on which access is made available are too onerous, no third party will seek and obtain access, and there will be no resulting competition. Thus, much of the debate about implementation of the 1996 Act has focused on the terms on which the LECs must provide third parties access to their facilities.

Congress hoped that the LECs and the third parties who sought access to the LECs' facilities would be able to rely primarily on negotiation and arbitration to reach agreement with respect to the terms on which access is made available. Thus, the Act authorized and encouraged negotiation and arbitration of access disputes. Congress recognized, however, that the LECs and the potential competitors who sought access to the LECs' facilities had sharply conflicting interests that made it inadvisable to rely solely on negotiation and arbitration to determine terms of access. Congress conferred authority on both the FCC and state regulators to act in ways that would assure that the LECs provided access to third parties on fair and efficient terms.

Unfortunately, Congress was not at all clear in allocating jurisdictional authority between the FCC and state regulators. The Act confers general rulemaking power of uncertain scope on the FCC. It also provides that state regulators are to conduct the arbitrations through which Congress anticipated that most access disputes would be resolved. The Act provides substantive standards that state regulators are required to apply in arbitrating access disputes and in accepting or rejecting proposed terms of access. The Act also provides, however, that the FCC can displace a state regulator in performing these roles if the FCC concludes that a state regulator is not acting in ways that will create viable non facilities-based competition in the local service market.

Six months after the Act was passed, the FCC issued a comprehensive set of rules to implement the access provisions of the Act. The FCC interpreted its jurisdictional authority broadly. It purported to prescribe in detail all of the major terms and conditions for third party access to LEC facilities, including detailed prescription of the permissible method of calculating the rates the LECs could charge for access. Substantively, the FCC resolved all of the major issues in favor of third parties and against the LECs. Thus, for instance, the FCC rules required the LECs to provide third parties access to any and all of the "network elements" of the facilities the LECs used to provide local service. The rules also required the LECs to make all of their facilities available to third parties at rates based on "total element long run incremental cost" (TELRIC). Under this methodology, the LEC's rates for third party access are based on the cost of a hypothetical, state-of-the-art local service network. Since the actual networks owned by the LECs were installed piecemeal over many decades, they are considerably more costly than the hypothetical systems that are the basis for the TELRIC rates.

State regulators appealed the FCC rules on the basis that the FCC had exceeded its jurisdictional authority and usurped power that Congress conferred on state regulators. LECs appealed the FCC rules both on jurisdictional grounds and on the basis that the rules also violated other provisions of the Act. The LECs noted that the FCC rules would allow any third party to enter a local service market by relying exclusively on the use of an LEC's facilities and by paying the LEC access rates that are far below the LEC's actual costs. Under the FCC rules, the LECs would fall billions of dollars short of recovering the actual cost of their investments in the assets required to provide local service. Thus, the FCC rules had the effect of requiring the LECs to absorb large "stranded costs"—a topic that we will discuss in detail in section 15G.

The Eighth Circuit first stayed and then vacated the FCC rules. Iowa Utilities Board v. FCC, 120 F.3d 753 (8th Cir.1997). The circuit court held that the rules exceeded FCC's jurisdiction and usurped power Congress had granted to state regulators. In the meantime, the FCC rejected every petition by an LEC to enter the long distance market. The Act conferred on the FCC the power to determine whether a local service market is subject to effective competition. The Act permitted an LEC to enter the long distance market only after the FCC made a determination that the LEC's local service market was subject to effective competition. The FCC refused to make such a determination with respect to any local service market. The FCC orders declining to make those determinations suggested that the FCC was unlikely to determine that any local service market was subject to effective competition unless and until the LEC serving that market adopted the access conditions required by the FCC access rules. Yet, the Eighth Circuit had vacated those rules on the basis that they exceeded FCC's jurisdiction. Thus, the jurisdictional dispute had the effect of making it impossible to further either of the goals that induced Congress to enact the 1996 Act.

The Supreme Court took a major step toward breaking this logjam in AT & T v. Iowa Utilities Board, 119 S.Ct. 721 (1999). A five-Justice majority reversed the Eighth Circuit and held that FCC had jurisdiction to issue the local service access rules. Even the majority recognized that the jurisdictional issue was close and difficult. At the end of its long and complicated opinion, the majority provided a candid description of the Act:

> It would be gross understatement to say that the Telecommunications Act of 1996 is not a model of clarity. It is in many important respects a model of ambiguity and even self-contradiction. That is most unfortunate for a piece of legislation that profoundly affects a crucial segment of the economy worth tens of billions of dollars.

The Justices then addressed some of the substantive issues raised by the LECs. The Justices raised serious questions about the validity of many important parts of the FCC access rules. They were also critical of the quality of the reasoning process that led the FCC to adopt many of the most important parts of the rules.

A seven-Justice majority held that the access rules were overly broad. The rules required the LECs to provide third party access to any and all of the "network elements" that LECs use to provide local service. The Court noted that the Act requires the LECs to provide access only to those elements that are "necessary" to provide local service and to which lack of access would "impair" a third party's ability to provide local service. The Court suggested that the "necessary" and "impair" standards required the FCC to distinguish between network elements that have natural monopoly characteristics and those that do not. The Court criticized the FCC for failing to give "some substance" to the "necessary" and "impair" standards. It suggested strongly that the FCC would have to reduce the scope of the access rules to natural monopoly facilities and functions in order to obtain a judicial decision upholding the rules.

Justice Breyer—a highly respected expert on government regulation—wrote a separate opinion that includes a detailed critique of the reasoning the FCC used to support the access rates contained in its rule. He criticized the FCC's TELRIC methodology as difficult to apply, speculative, and questionable in its effects. He noted that TELRIC is an application of the principle that assets should be valued at their replacement cost—a principle that the Court embraced in its 1898 opinion in Smyth v. Ames but then rejected as unworkable in its 1944 opinion in FPC v. Hope Natural Gas. Justice Breyer criticized the FCC for failing to consider seriously three alternatives to TELRIC that are easier to implement and that have the potential to yield better results on both equitable and efficiency grounds.

The three alternatives that Justice Breyer urged the FCC to consider are: (1) depreciated original cost; (2) Ramsey pricing; and (3) the efficient component pricing rule. We discuss the debate between depreciated original cost and present cost of replacement in sections 5A and B. We discuss Ramsey pricing in section 6C2. The efficient component pricing rule combines depreciated original cost with Ramsey pricing. It permits a firm to charge a price based on the element's market price if the element is sold in a market or the element's depreciated original cost if the element is not sold in a market. Some respected economists argue that the efficient component pricing rule maximizes social welfare. See W. Baumol and J. Sidak, *Toward Competition in Local Telephony* (1994); Kahn & Taylor, *The Pricing of Inputs Sold to Competitors: A Comment*, 11 Yale J. on Reg. 225 (1994).

Justice Breyer concluded his opinion with a broad criticism of the FCC access rules:

> Rules that force firms to share *every* resource or element of a business would create not competition, but pervasive regulation, for the regulators, not the marketplace, would set the relevant terms . . . A totally unbundled world—a world in which competitors share every part of an incumbent's existing system . . .—is a world in which competitors would have little, if anything, to compete about.

It is apparent that the FCC will have to make major changes in its access rules to satisfy the courts.

Regulatory reform in the telecommunications industry is far from complete. The eventual outcome will depend partly on political forces, partly on agency and court decisions, and partly on the constantly evolving changes in telecommunications technology. If a technology with large economies of scale becomes dominant, e.g., digital fiberoptics, the telecommunications market may become a classic natural monopoly that requires some form of economic regulation. If a competing technology with low economies of scale becomes dominant, e.g., a wireless system, economic regulation is unlikely to serve any socially beneficial function. Similarly, if multiple technologies become approximately equivalent in cost and quality, regulation will become both unnecessary and counterproductive.

3. ELECTRICITY

The electricity industry is also partly through the unbundling process. Until 1978, virtually all electricity service was provided on a fully bundled basis by one of hundreds of integrated firms. The integrated utility generated its own electricity, transmitted that electricity across its high voltage lines, and distributed the electricity to all customers in its service territory. Since it had a legally conferred monopoly in its service area, its rates to consumers were regulated.

This traditional industry structure and regulatory approach broke down completely during the period from 1978 through 1990, for several reasons. First,

Congress enacted the Public Utility Regulatory Policies Act of 1978. Section 210 of that Act, 16 U.S.C.A. § 824a–3, required utilities to purchase power generated by cogenerators and small power producers. As originally implemented, PURPA section 210 performed poorly. State regulators determined the price a utility must pay a third party generator by estimating the full amount of the costs the utility would avoid by making such a purchase. Many states greatly overestimated utilities' avoided costs, thereby burdening utilities and their customers with contractual obligations to buy bulk power at inflated prices. The PURPA section 210 mechanism demonstrated, however, that electricity could be provided through use of an industry structure in which generation is separate from transmission and distribution.

Second, the massive regulatory disallowances of utility investments in generating plants during the 1980s, discussed in section 5B2b, changed utilities' incentives. The high risk of regulatory disallowance of utility investments induced most utilities to prefer to buy power from non-utility generators rather than to invest in their own generating plants.

Third, analysts and regulators became aware that changes in technology had eliminated the natural monopoly rationale for regulating generation of electricity. See section 2B1. This revelation induced state PUCs to change their method of implementing PURPA section 210. Instead of administratively determining the price a utility must pay a non-utility generator, PUCs began to rely on competitive contracting to determine which non-utility generators were permitted to sell to utilities and at what prices. Competitive contracting is a several step process: (1) a utility issues a request for proposals (RFP) to meet its expected need for new generating capacity; (2) it receives bids from competing prospective suppliers in the form of proposals to enter into complicated long term contracts to purchase power; (3) it evaluates the competing proposals using criteria approved by the PUC; and, (4) it negotiates final contracts with the winning bidders. Competitive contracting for wholesale power produced excellent results. The average RFP elicited proposals that exceeded the utility's needs by a factor of ten, and the winning bids invariably were on terms far more favorable to utilities and to consumers than were the contracts produced by the initial method of implementing PURPA section 210. See Joskow, *Regulatory Failure, Regulatory Reform, and Structural Change in the Electrical Power Industry,* Brookings Papers on Economic Activity: Microeconomics 125 (1989).

Fourth, the Energy Policy Act of 1992 provided further impetus to the movement to unbundle electric service. The Act created a new category of exempt wholesale generators (EWGs) that are authorized to sell electricity to utilities without being burdened by federal regulatory rules. Almost anyone can enter the generating market by becoming an EWG. Many utility RFPs elicited bids from large U.S. and foreign manufacturing firms and from EWG subsidiaries of other utilities. The Energy

Policy Act also requires FERC to assure that owners of transmission lines provide equal access to all other utilities and all EWGs. This provision broadened the geographic scope of the wholesale electricity market by allowing non-contiguous utilities and EWGs to bid on equal terms in response to a utility RFP.

Fifth, FERC issued Order 888 in 1996. That order requires all transmission-owning utilities to provide third parties equal access to their transmission lines. Order 888 has allowed competitive wholesale markets to evolve throughout the country. A substantial amount of electricity is now sold on spot markets, rather than pursuant to the terms of long term contracts.

Significant unbundling of electric service now seems inevitable. Transmission and distribution will continue to be subject to some form of economic regulation because they are natural monopoly functions. Generation and wholesale of electricity will be governed by a competitive market. It is not yet clear whether retail sales of electricity will be governed primarily by regulation or primarily by a competitive market. The Energy Policy Act specifically prohibits FERC from authorizing retail wheeling, i.e., use of a transmission line to transmit electricity owned by a third party to a consumer, and many utilities are adamantly opposed to competition in the retail electricity market. States have the discretion to allow retail competition, however, and nineteen states had already adopted some version of retail competition by 1999.

Implementing regulatory reform of this type presents many difficult problems in any industry. Implementing equal access to high voltage transmission lines presents unusually difficult problems. North America is served by an integrated transmission grid that consists of interconnected high voltage lines owned by hundreds of separate utilities. Electricity does not flow across the grid in accordance with the provisions of contracts. Instead, it flows in accordance with the laws of physics. Depending on myriad variables, a transaction putatively requiring use of a single transmission line between Pittsburgh and Philadelphia, for instance, may reduce the capacity available on scores of other transmission lines as far south as Georgia and as far north as Canada. Many industry analysts believe that unbundling and equal access to transmission lines ultimately will require further major restructuring of the electricity industry, new computer-controlled operating protocols, and new forms of contracts between owners of particular transmission lines and the necessarily centralized operator of the integrated transmission grid. See Hogan, *Electric Transmission: A New Model for Old Principles,* Elec.J. 18 (March 1993).

In order to understand the difficult issues that arise in the process of creating a competitive electricity market, it is first necessary to understand the physical operation of an integrated electricity transmission grid. North America has an integrated grid in each region. Each grid covers several U.S. states, and some grids include Canadian provinces and/or Mexican states. Generally, the transmission links within a regional grid are sufficient to allow large quantities of electricity to traverse a grid between input and output points (referred to as nodes) on a grid at most times. Each regional grid is interconnected with neighboring grids, but the connecting links usually have limited capacity.

Electricity flows across a grid in accordance with Kirchoff's law: flows are in inverse proportion to the impedance on each line within the grid. Electricity cannot be economically stored, and the demand for electricity fluctuates rapidly and within a very wide range. As a result, levels and patterns of flows on a regional grid vary every second, as demand fluctuates at each node and as generators are added and subtracted from the grid at various nodes.

Every grid experiences congestion at some times and locations—that is, the grid is physically unable to accommodate all of the transactions that parties desire to make. Congestion has the effect of forcing someone, or some institution, to choose among competing transactions. This is a familiar problem of allocation of scarce resources. It is susceptible to a simple, market-based solution. If the parties that are competing to use the scarce capacity are confronted with the full marginal cost of their use, the market will allocate the scarce capacity to the user who places the highest value on that capacity.

In this context, as in many others, the primary cost of engaging in a transaction is the opportunity cost of foregone transactions. Thus, for instance, if two generators seek access to the grid at a time when the grid can accommodate only one, the cost of allowing access to one is the opportunity cost of denying access to the other. Generators vary significantly with respect to their marginal costs, and hence with respect to the prices at which they are willing to sell electricity. From a social welfare perspective, a generator that costs two cents per kilowatt hour is better than a generator that costs three cents per kilowatt hour. Assume that generator one costs two cents, and generator two costs three cents. On these facts, a decision to give generator two access, and to deny access to generator one, has an opportunity cost of one cent. We will obtain the least cost combination of generation and transmission only if firms that want to use the grid at a time and place where it is affected by congestion confront a transmission price that reflects the opportunity cost of displacing low cost generation with high cost generation. In the electricity industry, injecting power from a generator into a grid is called "dispatch," and dispatching a higher cost unit in place of a lower cost unit is called "out of merit dispatch."

Finding a good solution to this problem is complicated by the operating characteristics of integrated grids. Three characteristics of a grid are particularly important. First, the relevant time frame is very short—a matter of minutes. Grid conditions can change significantly and rapidly. Second, the integrated nature of the grid has the effect of producing congestion in many locations that are remote from the source of the congestion. Thus, for instance, dispatch of a generator at one node can produce congestion that adversely affects numerous nodes hundreds of miles away. Third, the displacement effects of out-of-merit dispatch are complicated and non linear. Thus, for instance, the decision to dispatch 200 megawatts from a generating unit at one node can foreclose the ability to dispatch 600 megawatts from a generating unit at another node. In that situation, the opportunity cost of dispatching the first unit can be very high.

Before the computer revolution, this problem would have been nearly impossible to resolve in an efficient manner. Today, however, it is relatively easy to resolve. Each of the regional grids in North America has long been subject to reliability-based control by a quasi-governmental body—the National Electric Reliability Council (NERC). Each of the regional units of NERC and each transmission owning utility maintains computer software that includes an algorithm that describes mathematically all of the important characteristics and interrelationships that characterize a regional grid. It is relatively easy to modify this software in ways that permit instantaneous and simultaneous calculation of the opportunity costs of any conceivable combination of dispatch and load conditions.

Once the software is modified in this manner, it can be used to implement a competitive bidding system. Every owner of generating capacity submits a schedule of bids to supply electricity to the grid during the next day. The bid schedule is broken down into small time periods, e.g., five minute intervals. The bids are entered into the computer along with the expected load profile for the next day. The output of the program is a complete dispatch schedule for the next day. The program automatically determines the price to be paid each generator based on the lowest price bid that will satisfy all of the expected demand on the grid. The program also calculates the price of electricity at each of hundreds of nodes on the grid. If the grid is unaffected by congestion throughout that day, the prices at each node will be virtually identical. If the grid is affected by congestion during that day, the price of electricity will vary among the nodes. The existence of a difference between the price at one node and the price at another node reflects the existence of congestion on the grid between those nodes. That difference in nodal prices is the opportunity cost of dispatching a unit in circumstances in which that dispatch decision will preclude dispatch of a lower cost unit.

We will next try to make this exercise in applied physics, mathematics, and economics more accessible by providing a less-detailed economic overview of grid operations and transmission pricing. We begin with the basic principle that prices should be based on marginal cost whenever possible. See sections 2A2a and 7A and B. In the absence of congestion, the marginal cost of transmitting electricity over a grid is small. It consists only of the value of the typically small amount of electricity that is lost in the transmission process. The cost of the investments in the capital assets that comprise the grid is irrelevant in calculating the marginal cost of a transmission transaction. They are sunk costs that are unaffected by the number or nature of the transactions that take place on the grid. In the presence of congestion, however, the marginal cost of a transmission transaction is much higher. It includes the opportunity cost of foregone transactions: that is, the cost of out-of-merit dispatch of generating units. It is important that participants in the transmission market confront prices that reflect the high cost of transmission in conditions of congestion. The resulting price signals will enhance social welfare both in the short-term and in the long-term. In the short-term, those price signals will induce market participants to choose the lowest cost combination of generation and transmission that will satisfy demand on the grid. In the long-term, those price signals will induce market participants to make the optimum combination of investments in generating and transmission assets. Thus, for instance, a firm that is considering construction of a new generating unit to attach to a grid will know the locations at which grid congestion often causes the cost of transmission to be very high. It will then have a natural incentive either to construct the generating plant at a location that is not adversely affected by grid congestion or to invest in an upgrade in the capacity of the grid in order to reduce the adverse effects of congestion at its preferred location for the plant.

As is often the case when regulating a natural monopoly, however, prices based on marginal cost will not be sufficient alone to allow firms to recover all of their fixed or sunk costs. See section 7B3. Yet, both equity and efficiency require adoption of some mechanism through which grid owners can recover those costs. In the absence of such a mechanism, no one would be willing to make socially-beneficial investments in expansions of the capacity of a grid. That sunk cost recovery mechanism must be chosen with care, however, to minimize its potential distortive effect on participants in the transmission market. The best mechanism that has been identified to date is a regional postage stamp rate; that is, a rate that is assessed per unit of electricity provided to the grid independent of its source or putative destination. This is simply a variant of the two-part rates that have long been used to good effect in regulating many natural monopolies. See section 7D for a discussion of two-part rates. See Pierce, *FERC Must Adopt an Efficient Transmission Pricing System*, The Electricity Journal, Oct. 1997, at 79, for a more detailed discussion of transmission pricing.

It should be obvious from the foregoing discussion that an integrated regional grid can only be operated and regulated efficiently on a regional basis. Yet, the pattern of ownership of each regional grid in the U.S. makes it difficult to implement that crucial principle. Each grid consists of scores of interconnected transmission lines. Those lines are owned by anywhere between fifteen and fifty different electric utilities.

There is an obvious solution to this problem. The owners of the lines that comprise an integrated grid can cede operational control over the lines to a separate entity called an Independent System Operator (ISO). The ISO can then operate the grid on an integrated basis and implement the computerized auction system we previously described. The ISO also can collect the revenues attributable to use of the grid and distribute those revenues among the grid owners. This new institutional mechanism has been adopted and implemented in two regions as of 1999—New England and the middle Atlantic states. In addition, two states—California and New York— have created statewide ISOs.

So far, FERC has encouraged, but not required, the formation of regional ISOs. As a result, ISOs have not yet been formed in most regions. There is continuing debate as to whether FERC has the statutory authority to require transmission-owning utilities to form regional ISOs. That debate focuses primarily on the meaning and effect of section 202(a) of the Federal Power Act. That provision states in pertinent part:

"For the purpose of assuring an abundant supply of electric energy ... with the greatest possible economy ..., the Commission is empowered and directed to divide the country into regional districts for the voluntary ... coordination of facilities for the generation, transmission, and sale of electric energy.... It shall be the duty of the Commission to promote and encourage such coordination within each such district and between such districts."

As of 1999, a majority of the FERC Commissioners had not (yet) concluded that FERC has the power to require creation of a regional ISO in each region.

In the absence of a regional ISO, electricity markets perform poorly. Each owner of transmission lines charges a per-transaction rate based on the average embedded cost of its investment in its transmission assets. Because of the pattern of ownership of the lines that comprise an integrated grid, parties that want to buy electricity from a generating unit at one node on the grid and to obtain an equivalent amount of electricity at another node on the grid usually must pay transmission charges to two or more owners of transmission lines.

This method of governing and pricing the operation of an integrated regional grid produces at least two severe adverse effects. First, it produces small, highly concentrated electricity markets that perform poorly. In the absence of a regional ISO, the cost of transmission is far above marginal cost, both because rates based on average embedded cost are far above marginal cost and because of "rate pancaking:" that is, the need to pay separate transmission fees to each of several owners of transmission lines. Those high transmission rates artificially limit the geographic scope of an electricity market to a size that is too small to support effective competition.

Second, in the absence of a regional ISO, transmission prices do not reflect the existence of congestion at some times and places on an integrated regional grid. In the absence of a market mechanism to allocate scarce transmission capacity, regulators must implement much less efficient methods of administrative allocation of scarce transmission capacity. See chapter 11. Moreover, in the absence of price signals that reflect the existence of congestion on parts of the grid, investors have a perverse incentive to locate new generating plants on the wrong side of a transmission capacity constraint, and they have no incentive to invest in expansions of transmission capacity that would reduce the incidence and effects of capacity constraints. Thus, the viability and efficacy of the competitive wholesale electricity markets that FERC is trying to create depend critically on FERC's willingness to require owners of transmission lines to join regional ISOs— a step FERC has so far been unwilling to take. See Pierce, *Why FERC Must Mandate Efficiently–Structured Regional ISOs,* The Electricity Journal, Jan./ Feb. 1999, at 49.

As of 1999, nineteen states had adopted retail electricity competition regimes, with mixed results. Efforts to extend competition to small consumers of electricity are plagued by the same basic problem that has rendered it difficult to extend competition to small consumers of natural gas. Providing service to small customers involves relatively high costs per transaction and relatively low benefits per transaction. See section 15C1.

In the electricity industry, like the telecommunications industry, it is too early to predict reliably the ultimate structure of the industry or the methods of government intervention that will apply to that structure. It is easy to predict, however, that neither industry will resemble the pervasively regulated legal monopoly structure that existed before unbundling began.

D. INTEGRATING ECONOMIC REGULATION AND ENVIRONMENTAL REGULATION

Traditionally, economic regulatory agencies focused narrowly on protection of consumers from potential exploitation by monopoly service providers. As societal concern about the environment increased, however, economic regulatory agencies began to incorporate environmental costs into their decisionmaking. Congressional enactment of the National Environmental Policy Act of 1969 (NEPA), 42 U.S.C.A. §§ 4321–4347, was a major milestone. NEPA requires every federal agency to consider the environmental impact of a proposed action, and its alternatives, before the agency can take any action that significantly effects the environment. Most states have enacted similar legislation.

Traditionally, environmental regulatory agencies like EPA relied primarily on command and control techniques to further their missions of improving air and water quality. EPA relied heavily on specific, technology-based standards applicable to each of the many types of major sources of pollution. The standards were promulgated with little regard to their costs. EPA was able to improve air and water quality significantly through use of command and control methods during the 1970s and 1980s, but only at very high costs. Moreover, command and control methods of regulation invariably permit some level of emissions of pollutants. It is simply impossible to perform many socially beneficial functions, e.g., generation of electricity, without some adverse environmental consequences. Traditional methods of environmental regulation created no incentive for firms to reduce their levels of emissions below the levels permitted by applicable technology-based standards.

Beginning in the late 1980s, economic regulators increased their efforts to incorporate environmental factors in their decisionmaking processes in systematic ways, and environmental regulators increased their efforts to incorporate economic factors in their regulatory systems in systematic ways. These trends have the potential to create large social gains by improving the performance of both economic regulation and environmental regulation, if they are implemented with care.

The major change in environmental regulation involves increasing substitution of market-based regulatory systems for command and control systems. As discussed in section 2B4, pollution creates an externality problem. Society bears the costs of pollution caused by an activity, but the firm that is engaged in the activity does not bear that cost. As a result, absent government intervention of some type, firms have no incentive to reduce their levels of pollution. Moreover, consumers engage in excess consumption of goods and services that cause pollution because consumers confront prices that do not reflect the full marginal social cost of the goods and services they consume.

Scholars have long urged legislators and regulators to address environmental problems more directly by using forms of intervention that require firms to internalize in their costs the otherwise external social costs of pollution. This can be accomplished through use of either of two mechanisms— environmental taxes or marketable emissions permits. An environmental tax is a tax on an activity set at a level equal to the best available estimates of the environmental harm caused by that activity. Thus, for instance, if emission of SO_2 from a coal-burning generating plant causes environmental harm approximately equal to \$250 per ton of SO_2, emissions of SO_2 should be taxed at that level. The tax will increase the cost of electricity generated through use of high sulfur coal to the point at which consumers are paying the full marginal social cost of that electricity, including its environmental costs. Consumers will reduce their consumption of the good subject to the tax accordingly, substituting therefor electricity generated through use of lower polluting fuels and technologies, increased home insulation, or more efficient electrical appliances. Generating firms are affected by the tax in two ways. First, the reduced consumer demand for electricity generated through use of high sulfur coal induces the firm to reduce its use of high sulfur coal to generate electricity. Second, the tax induces the firm to identify and to implement new methods of reducing the amount of SO_2 emitted in the process of using coal to generate electricity. The net results of the tax include reduction of environmental harm attributable to SO_2 emissions and enhancement of allocative efficiency by requiring producers and consumers to modify their behavior to reflect the full social costs of their behavior.

Marketable emissions permits have the same effects as environmental taxes. They differ only with respect to the method used to force internalization of environmental costs. The critical variable in a marketable permits system is the total number of permits issued. Sometimes it is easier to estimate the total quantity of emissions that will yield a socially optimal level of environmental harm than it is to estimate the marginal environmental cost of each unit of emissions. Once the decision has been made to limit emissions of a pollutant to a particular level and to reflect that decision in the form of a ceiling on total emissions, a marketable emissions permit system induces beneficial changes in behavior in the same ways as an emissions tax. In order to emit a given level of pollutant, a firm must either incur the out-of-pocket cost of buying emissions permits or the functionally equivalent opportunity cost of foregoing the opportunity to sell emissions permits. Those costs induce firms both to search for ways of reducing their emissions and to increase the prices they charge for products and services made available by engaging in the polluting activity. Those price increases, in turn, induce consumers to reduce their level of consumption of goods and services made available by engaging in environmentally costly activities.

Many academic studies demonstrate that use of these two market-based methods of environmental regulation can reduce the costs of achieving a given level of environmental quality by 50 to 90 per cent. It follows that use of these methods enable society to improve the quality of the environment significantly without increasing the cost of environmental regulation. See R. Stavins & B. Whitehead, *The Greening of America's Taxes: Pollution Charges and Environmental Protection* (1992).

In the late 1980s, market-based methods of environmental regulation moved from the corridors of academia to the corridors of legislatures and agencies. The marketable permits system applicable to SO_2 emissions contained in the 1990 Clean Air Act Amendments, 42 U.S.C.A. §§ 7701–7716, is representative of the trend. SO_2 emissions cause a variety of environmental injuries, including damage attributable to acid rain. Most SO_2 emissions are from coal-burning generating plants. Between 1970 and 1990, EPA relied on command and control regulation to achieve a 30 per cent reduction in SO_2 emissions, at enormous cost. The marketable permits system will achieve a 50 per cent additional reduction in SO_2 emissions by 2000 at less than half the cost required to achieve the same results through use of command and control regulation.

Just as environmental regulators have increased their reliance on economics to achieve their goals, many economic regulatory agencies have increased their incorporation of environmental factors into their decisionmaking. Many state PUCs have begun to incorporate "environmental adders" in the criteria they apply to the process of competitive contracting for generating capacity described in the prior section. Environmental adders are premised on the same general reasoning that underlies the use of market-based methods of environmental regulation. The mechanism, and its underlying reasoning, can be illustrated by a simple example. Assume that a utility has a choice between contracting to purchase electricity from A, a high polluting generator, or B, a low polluting generator. A offers to provide electricity at 4 cents per kwh, while B offers to provide electricity at 5 cents per kwh. Absent government intervention, the utility will choose to buy from A rather than B. Yet, if the additional pollution created by A produces uninternalized environmental costs greater than 1 cent per kwh, society will suffer a net loss as a result of the utility's decision. Environmental adders are intended to avoid this result by requiring each utility to add to the contract price each competing generator proposes to charge an "adder" based on the state PUC's estimate of the environmental cost of generating electricity through use of particular fuels and technologies.

Environmental adders seem conceptually appealing. Their actual effects on both air quality and economic efficiency are unfortunate, however, for a variety of reasons. First, they do not reflect the fact that market-based methods of environmental regulation already produce internalization of environmental harm attributable to electricity generation. Superimposing adders on market-based methods of environmental regulation involves a double counting of environmental harm. Second, the actual adder systems adopted by state PUCs are based on grossly inaccurate estimates of environmental harm, reflecting PUC's lack of expertise in environmental economics. Third, a state PUC's jurisdiction is so limited, both geographically and with respect to the sources of air pollution, that adders imposed by state PUCs yield a variety of unintended adverse effects on the environment. Massachusetts' high adder applicable to SO_2 emissions illustrates those unintended effects. That adder has the effect of increasing acid rain in Massachusetts by reducing the cost of SO_2 emission permits to Illinois utilities, thereby inducing them to increase their SO_2 emissions. Those emissions, in turn, arrive downwind in Massachusetts in the form of acid rain. For detailed analysis of this topic, see Black & Pierce, *The Choice Between Markets and Central Planning in Regulating the U.S. Electricity Industry,* 93 Colum.L.Rev. 1339 (1993).

State PUCs are attempting to integrate economic regulation and environmental regulation in another way as well. Most PUCs are requiring, or strongly encouraging, electric utilities to purchase "nega-watts"; in the form of a subsidy provided to a consumer that agrees to buy more efficient electricity consuming equipment that will reduce the quantity of electricity the consumer buys from the utility. Negawatt acquisition programs are based on a three-step reasoning process: (1) negawatts are functionally equivalent to megawatts; (2) conservation should compete with consumption on a "level playing field"; and, (3) a negawatt purchase that costs a utility 4 cents per kwh saved should be preferred to purchase of additional generating capacity at a cost of 5 cents per kwh. Most PUCs have adopted this reasoning in support of aggressive negawatt acquisition programs.

The reasoning is flawed, and the programs are destructive for four reasons. First, negawatts are no more the functional equivalent of megawatts than books are the functional equivalent of negabooks. Both books and megawatts are socially useful goods. Both negawatts and negabooks are literally nothing. Second, negawatt acquisition programs are premised on the assumption that markets do not encourage sufficient conservation. That assumption is false both generally and with specific reference to the electricity market. Prices provide a signal to consumers that their purchase of a good or service comes at a particular cost in the form of consumption of scarce resources. If price is equal to marginal social cost, as is increasingly true in the electricity market, the price of the good provides an appropriate incentive to conserve. Third, the programs waste scarce resources by encouraging excessive production of high efficiency electric motors and appliances. The resulting artificial increase in the price of electricity constitutes an unjustified transfer of wealth from consumers to subsidy recipients. Fourth, negawatt acquisition programs are totally incompatible with a competitive electricity market. Utilities cannot recover the costs of investments in negawatts in a competitive market. Regulators must choose between encouraging negawatt subsidies and creating a competitive market in electricity. That choice should be easy. A competitive market in electricity will increase social welfare, while negawatt subsidies will waste scarce resources. See Black & Pierce, supra.

E. INCENTIVE REGULATION

Even after unbundling and deregulation have been carried to their logical limits, some important markets will continue to have characteristics that require use of economic regulation to protect at least some consumers from exploitation by firms with monopoly power. Good candidates for continued economic regulation of some type include at least transmission and distribution of electricity, distribution of natural gas and water, and perhaps provision of local telecommunications service and pipeline transportation of gas. There is broad consensus, however, that alternatives must be found to traditional cost-of-service regulation even for application to monopoly markets. Regulators throughout the world are searching for methods of incentive regulation. The term refers to forms of economic regulation that rely less on detailed prescriptive rules of conduct and more on rules that are designed to channel and to influence the conduct of regulated firms.

The search for methods of incentive regulation is being driven primarily by two factors—widespread dissatisfaction with the results of application of traditional cost-of-service regulation and recognition that few regulated firms possess strong monopoly power with respect to all the customers they serve. We describe the basis for the first motive in section 15A. The second requires some explanation.

Even in markets where a regulated firm retains significant market power with respect to some customers, it often has little or no market power with respect to other customers. A gas distribution company, for instance, is in a position to exercise significant market power with respect to most small volume residential consumers. Those consumers have extremely limited alternatives to purchase of gas service from the local distribution company, at least in the short term. For that reason, they need to be protected from potential monopolistic exploitation by the distributor. Consumers in this position are often referred to as captive customers. Many large volume customers have economical access to multiple alternatives, however, often including use of a fuel other than gas and purchase of gas directly from a pipeline. Traditional cost-of-service regulation is designed to apply to a firm that has strong monopoly power throughout a market. It works poorly when it is applied instead to a firm that provides products and services in a competitive market.

To illustrate the problems that arise in this now common situation, consider a gas distributor with a market that includes a large industrial consumer that can use either gas or oil. If traditional cost-of-service regulation were applied to the distributor, it would be required to charge the industrial consumer a specified rate based on the variable costs of providing service, e.g., $2.00 per MMBtu, plus some administratively determined portion of the distributor's fixed costs, e.g., $0.80 per MMBtu. This approach would produce bad results for the distributor, the industrial consumer, and the captive customers. The industrial consumer will switch between gas and oil depending on the relative price of the two fuels. Oil is sold in a competitive market with considerable price volatility. If the price of oil falls below $2.80 per MMBtu, the industrial consumer will cease buying any gas from the distributor. That will hurt the distributor and its captive customers by depriving them of any contribution to the distributor's fixed costs from the industrial customer. At any price above $2.00 per MMBtu, the distributor and its captive customers are better off providing service to the industrial customer. In the real world, the situation is more complicated because most regulated firms have numerous customers with access to a wide variety of alternatives to regulated service.

The generic solution to the problem illustrated in the prior paragraph is to allow the distributor discretion to provide service to its customers with access to alternatives at any price above $2.00 per MMBtu. The agency then must adopt rules governing the total revenues the firm is allowed to earn and the rates it is allowed to charge its captive customers that give the distributor an incentive to extract from its customers with access to alternatives the maximum available contribution to the firm's fixed costs. The agency might, for instance, adopt formulas that have the effect of allocating the revenues in excess of variable costs attributable to service to customers with access to alternatives between the firm's shareholders and its captive customers. See R. Pierce, *Regulation and Competition in Natural Gas Distribution* (1990). Many agencies are moving in that direction, but appropriate formulas are difficult to devise and difficult to explain to the satisfaction of captive customers of regulated firms.

In the railroad industry, incentive regulation has taken the form of a band of permissible rates that a railroad can charge a customer. The rate floor is the short-term marginal cost of providing the service, while the rate ceiling is the cost the customer would incur to obtain rail service on a stand alone basis, i.e., if it were the railroad's only customer. See Burlington Northern R. Co. v. ICC, 985 F.2d 589 (D.C.Cir.1993).

A 1986 study of incentive ratemaking in the electricity industry produced disappointing results. See

Joskow & Schmalensee, *Incentive Regulation for Electric Utilities,* 4 Yale J.Reg. 1 (1986). The vast majority of incentive systems focussed on a single narrow goal, e.g., providing a financial incentive for a utility to maximize the availability or thermal efficiency of its generating units. The incentives were effective in furthering those goals, but invariably with adverse effects on other goals. Utilities subject to these incentive systems had fewer days of forced outage and higher thermal efficiencies, but they also had much higher maintenance costs. The net effect of the incentive on the utility's overall efficiency was either negative or uncertain.

Since that study was completed, one form of incentive regulation has attracted the attention of many regulators. When Britain privatized its telecommunications industry in 1984, it rejected U.S. style cost-of-service regulation because of the inefficiencies spawned by that system. Britain adopted instead a system called CPI–X. Under this system, the prices charged by a regulated firm are determined not with reference to the firm's actual costs but by adjusting its prices each year by adding a percentage equal to the change in the consumer price index (CPI) and subtracting X, e.g., 3 per cent, to reflect the expected annual improvement in the firm's productivity. The CPI–X formula is designed to restore a regulated firm's incentive to operate efficiently by eliminating the linkage between the firm's actual costs and the prices it is allowed to charge. The firm earns additional profits to the extent that it is able to keep its costs below the revenues generated by application of the formula, and it suffers losses to the extent that its costs exceed those revenues. See J. Hillman & R. Braeutigam, *Price Level Regulation for Diversified Public Utilities* (1989). The FCC has adopted versions of the CPI–X system for application to several segments of the telecommunications market. See, e.g., Policy and Rules for Rates for Dominant Carriers, 54 Fed.Reg. 19,836 (1989). Many other state and federal agencies are considering adoption of the formula for application to a variety of regulated markets.

There are reasons for concern about the efficacy of the CPI–X formula. The formula is supposed to serve as a proxy for changes in the uncontrollable costs of operating an efficiently managed firm. There is little basis to believe, however, that those costs will vary in accordance with a formula that reflects only a measure of the general level of inflation in the economy and a necessarily arbitrary estimate of the future annual increase in an industry's productivity. Instead, the formula is likely to produce seriously inadequate revenues during some periods and grossly excessive revenues in others. See Pierce, *Price Level Regulation Based on Inflation Is Not an Attractive Alternative to Profit Level Regulation,* 84 Northwestern U.L.Rev. 665 (1990). In either case, the agency will be under intense pressure to address the problem by changing the X factor. In fact, that is precisely what has happened in Britain. The agency has changed the X factor several times because of perceptions that the formula was producing inadequate or excessive revenues. See *OFTEL Statements on British Telecom's Prices and Interconnection,* Utilities L.Rev. 65 (Summer 1992). As applied in this manner, the CPI–X formula seems to offer few, if any, advantages over traditional cost-of-service regulation.

Despite the difficulty of the task, the search for effective methods of incentive regulation will continue simply because it must. The evidence is overwhelming that traditional cost-of-service regulation has produced poor results in the past and is likely to produce even worse results in the future.

F. MANAGED COMPETITION IN HEALTHCARE

The cost of healthcare in the U.S. increased at an unusually rapid rate during the 1970s and 1980s. The reasons are many and various, e.g., people are living longer, many beneficial new technologies are expensive, and increases in violent crime and drug abuse are adding costs to the system. Many analysts believe, however, that the high cost of healthcare is attributable in part to a serious flaw in the healthcare market. Consumers of healthcare have little incentive to consider cost in deciding to purchase a service, and in deciding how much to pay for a service, because third parties (government agencies and insurance companies) pay most of the cost of the service. See section 2B7.

In the early 1990s, a group of analysts known as the Jackson Hole Group proposed a new method of structuring the financing and delivery of healthcare that was designed to correct for this flaw—managed competition. The details of managed competition are complicated, but the basic structure is relatively simple. See Enthoven, *The History and Principles of Managed Competition,* Health Affairs, 1993 Supplement. Each consumer would purchase a basic health care benefits package through a regional Health Insurance Purchasing Cooperative (HIPC). Each HIPC would make available a choice of providers of healthcare benefits, e.g., several health maintenance organizations (HMOs), one or more preferred provider organizations (PPOs), and one or more conventional fee-for-service insurance plans. Each provider would be prohibited from excluding pre-existing conditions from its scope of coverage and from excluding individuals with greater than average health risks from its membership roles. This would eliminate the now common practice of providers competing with each other by excluding high cost or high risk individuals from coverage. Each provider would be required to make available to all consumers the same basic benefit package. Uniformity in the basic benefit package would force providers to focus on price and quality competition. Consumers would be free to choose among providers, but the identity of the basic benefits package would encourage consumers to choose the lowest cost provider of the highest quality service. That, in turn, would encourage each provider to maximize the efficiency of its delivery system, in order to maximize its profits by selling its benefit package to a large number of consumers.

Many analysts considered universal health coverage an essential corollary to managed competition. Universal coverage would further independent humanitarian and distributional goals, of course, but it also was linked with managed competition in two ways. First, managed competition may not be politically viable unless it is coupled with universal coverage. Second, managed competition is not likely to be fully effective in limiting health care costs in the absence of universal coverage. The existence of millions of people with no health insurance produces significant cost-shifting from uninsured people to insured people. Hospitals and other providers treat uninsured and impecunious people and shift those treatment costs to the insured population.

Coupling universal coverage with managed competition would create a healthcare system that is more expensive initially than the present system, particularly if basic benefits package is generous. That, in turn, created a major political obstacle to adoption of managed competition. It is difficult to sell any program to the public if that program requires additional taxes of perhaps $50 billion per year. The difficulty of that task, in turn, induced many politicians to propose to include various forms of price controls in a managed competition framework. Most proponents of managed competition oppose price controls, however, both because of the adverse effects they have created in numerous other contexts and because they are likely to interfere with the workings of the competitive market managed competition is designed to create.

In 1993, the Clinton Administration proposed a comprehensive plan to reform the healthcare market. Putatively, the Clinton plan was a method of implementing the combination of managed competition and universal coverage. In fact, however, it was an extraordinarily complicated plan that relied primarily on pervasive regulation of the healthcare market by a dozen or more new agencies. Congress declined to enact any version of the Clinton plan.

Ironically, the movement toward managed competition progressed rapidly in the wake of congressional rejection of the Clinton plan. The movement was driven by market forces. Employers—the primary source of healthcare coverage in the United States—recognized that HMOs and other managed care organizations provided healthcare coverage at significantly lower cost than the traditional system of fee-for-service subject to insurance reimbursement that had long-dominated the U.S. health care system. Managed care providers charge a fixed per capita annual fee that has the effect of eliminating the adverse effects of the third party payment systems that we describe in section 2B7. Large employers began to provide their employees a menu of healthcare benefit options from which to choose. The typical menu includes one or more traditional insurance plans and one or more managed care plans. Employers began to offer these options at costs to employees that correlated with the differences in the cost of the options. This allowed employees to choose between expensive traditional insurance and less expensive managed care. During the 1990s, a constantly increasing proportion of the population switched from traditional health insurance to a managed care service provider. By the end of the decade, the vast majority of consumers who obtain healthcare from private sector providers were covered by a managed care organization rather than a traditional fee-for-service subject to insurance reimbursement plan—a complete reversal of the situation that existed at the beginning of the decade.

The movement to managed care had powerful efficiency-enhancing and cost-reducing effects. For most of the 1990s, the annual rate of increase in the per capita cost of private healthcare in the U.S. was a small fraction of the rate of increase that characterized the prior two decades. Government-provided healthcare costs—Medicaid and Medicare—continued to increase rapidly, however, largely because the government was unable or unwilling to make a similar large-scale transition to primary reliance on managed care organizations. There is continuing debate about appropriate responses to that problem.

By the end of the 1990s, however, three other problems in the performance of the healthcare market began to create new controversies and proposals for reform. The first was a return to relatively high annual rates of increase in private sector healthcare costs at the end of the decade. This phenomenon may be inevitable, given our affluence and strong desire for access to high quality healthcare services.

The initial transition to managed care organizations eliminated many billions of dollars per year in unnecessary healthcare costs during the 1990s, but the primary factors that caused the earlier cost increases—an aging population and increased availability of expensive new procedures—will continue to produce large annual cost increases even in an efficiently-functioning healthcare market.

The second problem is the large number of coverage disputes between managed care providers and their customers. Even though 80 per cent of managed care customers report that they are satisfied with the services they receive, there are thousands of coverage disputes between customers and providers every year. This problem can be usefully conceptualized as a problem created by incomplete contracts. In theory, the problem would disappear if a provider and its customers entered into a contract that specified all of the diagnostic and treatment procedures the provider is required to make available and the circumstances in which it will make each available. That, of course, is a practical impossibility. The resulting contract would be thousands of pages long, and it would have to be amended constantly to reflect advances in the field. Thus, the managed care providers use shorter contracts that describe excluded and included procedures only in general terms that leave ample opportunity for differing interpretations.

In 1999, Congress and many state legislatures are considering ways of addressing this problem. The result probably will be some variation of a statutory

Patient's Bill of Rights. Depending on the version that is enacted, some outside body—an agency, an independent arbitrator, or a tort court—will have the power to tell a managed care organization that it is required to provide a procedure that it did not believe it was required to provide. This new form of regulation of managed care organizations will increase healthcare costs by some uncertain amount.

Third, the proportion of the population that lacks any health insurance or coverage by a managed care organization has increased during the 1990s. This problem exists primarily among employees of small firms and their families. Elderly people are covered by Medicare. Poor people are covered by Medicaid. Virtually all employees of large firms and their families are covered by private plans obtained through their employers. Less than half of employees of small firms have healthcare coverage, however. This phenomenon is attributable primarily to two factors. First, small employers lack the economies of scale that would allow them to obtain healthcare for their employees on terms as favorable as the terms large firms are able to obtain. Second, most employees of small firms receive lower salaries than employees of large firms. As a result, many are unable or unwilling to purchase healthcare benefits at the higher price at which those benefits are available through small firms. Ironically, the increased cost of healthcare produced by enactment of a Patient's Bill of Rights will increase this affordability problem and increase still further the proportion of the population that has no healthcare coverage. No one has as yet identified a viable solution to this problem.

G. STRANDED COSTS

Any major change in regulatory policy, e.g., deregulation or unbundling, requires some market participants to incur stranded costs, i.e., one-time changes in wealth attributable to the change in regulatory policy. Stranded costs are inevitable when a change in regulatory policy increases the efficiency of a previously regulated market. The prior regulatory system invariably induced firms to hire too many employees, to employ the wrong mix of employees, to pay excessive wages, to make excessive investments in capital assets, to invest in the wrong mix of capital assets, and to enter into long-term contracts at excessive prices. Elimination or relaxation of regulatory constraints and introduction of competition forces many market participants to restructure their operations to eliminate excessive costs.

Stranded costs can take the form of: (1) layoffs and salary reductions (the primary consequences of deregulation of air transportation and financial services); (2) the bankruptcy of many firms (one of the primary consequences of deregulation of trucking); (3) contractual disputes between previously regulated firms that committed to pay excess prices and their contractual suppliers (one of the primary consequences of deregulation of the wholesale natural gas market); and, (4) significant reductions in the value of many assets owned by previously regulated firms (one of the expected consequences of deregulation of generation and sale of electricity).

The expectation of large one-time stranded costs should not deter legislatures and agencies from making changes in regulatory policy that will yield much larger permanent increases in social welfare. To give just two examples, the transition to a deregulated wholesale gas market required pipelines and producers to absorb one-time wealth reductions of approximately $20 billion, but that transition has produced social welfare gains of approximately $5 billion per year. The transition to a deregulated electricity market is expected to require utilities to absorb a one-time reduction in wealth of approximately $100 billion, but it is also expected to save consumers between $24 and $30 billion each year for the indefinite future. Of course, it is important to recognize that costs that are stranded by a regulatory reform are sunk costs in any event. They cannot be avoided or reduced. They can only be allocated among market participants.

No market participant willingly bears large stranded costs. Participants in a regulated market that expect to absorb large stranded costs as a result of a proposed regulatory reform engage in a series of actions designed to avoid incurrence of those costs or to reduce the magnitude of the costs each must absorb. These actions include: attempts to block regulatory reform, attempts to delay regulatory reform, and attempts to convince legislatures, agencies, and courts to reallocate stranded costs to other market participants. Proponents of regulatory reform often must devote more time and energy to disputes concerning allocation of stranded costs than to all other aspects of the process of regulatory reform. See, e.g., Pierce, *Transition Costs in the Natural Gas Industry* (1993), in working papers of Harvard Electricity Policy Group.

FERC was the first agency to confront the stranded cost issue directly. It did so initially in the context of the reforms of the natural gas market it began to implement in the 1980s. FERC allocated stranded costs fifty-fifty between regulated pipelines and their customers. As might have been predicted, the regulated pipelines resisted proposed changes in regulation that would have the effect of requiring them to absorb billions of dollars in stranded costs. They responded by refusing to cooperate with FERC's attempts to implement regulatory reform and by engaging in a great deal of litigation that was designed to thwart FERC's reform initiatives, to delay their implementation, and/or to force FERC to reduce the amount of stranded costs the pipelines were required to absorb. While FERC ultimately was successful in implementing its first round of reforms, the vigorous resistance of the regulated pipelines greatly complicated and delayed its efforts to do so.

When FERC decided to implement a second round of regulatory reform of the gas industry in 1992, it announced a change in its position with respect to stranded costs. FERC announced that it would allow regulated pipelines to allocate 100 per cent of their stranded costs to their customers. About the same time, FERC announced its first proposed set of major reforms of regulation of the electricity industry. Implementation of that set of reforms was expected to have the effect of stranding at least $100 billion worth of assets owned by electric utilities. FERC announced that it would apply its new 100 per cent of stranded cost recovery policy to the electricity industry as well.

FERC stated two bases for its change in position with respect to recovery of costs stranded by a change to greater reliance on competitive markets. First, FERC stated its belief that it would be able to implement regulatory reform more effectively and expeditiously if it assured regulated firms in advance that they could recover their stranded costs. Second, it stated its belief that its new 100 per cent stranded cost recovery policy was required by both equity and efficiency.

FERC's first stated reason for its policy might be sufficient alone to justify its position. FERC experienced much greater cooperation with its regulatory reform efforts, and much less active resistance to those efforts, once it announced its new position. More broadly, any regulatory agency that attempts to implement a major initiative that requires regulated firms to absorb billions of dollars in stranded costs confronts active resistance and scorched-earth litigation tactics that greatly complicate and delay its efforts to implement a reform.

Two other examples illustrate this point. First, in section 15C2, we described the FCC's attempts to implement the Telecommunications Act of 1996. Those attempts have been successfully thwarted by the Local Exchange Carriers (LECs) for three years so far. The LEC's thus-far successful strategy to litigate every issue to the fullest extent possible was a product of the FCC's decision to adopt an access pricing system that would require the LECs to absorb billions of dollars in stranded costs. Second, in 1996 the state of New Hampshire adopted a retail electricity competition plan that required utilities to absorb 50 per cent of their stranded costs. Three years later, that plan has not yet been implemented. It is still enmeshed in litigation. Massachusetts also adopted such a plan in 1996, except that the Massachusetts plan allowed utilities to recover 100 per cent of their stranded costs. The Massachusetts plan was implemented immediately.

In addition to those purely pragmatic arguments, proponents of 100 per cent recovery of stranded costs have supported their position with both legal arguments and policy-based arguments. The legal arguments have focused primarily on the Takings Clause of the Fifth and Fourteenth Amendments. See J.G. Sidak & D. Spulber, *Deregulatory Takings and the Regulatory Contract: The Competitive Transformation of Network Industries in the United States* (1997); Sidak & Spulber, *Deregulatory Takings and the Breach of the Regulatory Contract*, 71 N.Y.U.L. Rev. 851 (1996). The legal argument has several steps. First, the courts have long held that a firm is entitled to be compensated for any costs it incurs in reliance on a contract with the government. Second, regulated firms made billions of dollars of investments in capital assets in reliance on the "regulatory contract." That contract is implicit in regulatory statutes, agency decisions, and court opinions. Third, the regulatory contract has clear terms that include a promise by the government to allow a regulated firm to recover all of its prudently-incurred costs free of the adverse effects of competition. Fourth, the government is in the process of "taking" a large proportion of the value of the regulated firms' investments in capital assets by subjecting the value of those assets to competition, in breach of the terms of the regulatory contract. Fifth, it follows that the firms are entitled to compensation for the costs stranded by the government's breach of the regulatory contract.

Numerous commentators have raised questions about each element of that argument. See, e.g., Hovenkamp, *The Takings Clause and Improvident Regulatory Bargains*, 108 Yale L.J. 801 (1999); Rossi, *The Irony of Deregulatory Takings*, 77 Tex. L. Rev. 297 (1998); Williamson, *Deregulatory Takings and Breach of the Regulatory Contract: Some Precautions*, 71 N.Y.U.L. Rev. 1007 (1996); Williams, *Deregulatory Takings and Breach of the Regulatory Contract: A Comment*, 71 N.Y.U.L. Rev. 1000 (1996). The criticism begins with the case law under the Takings Clause. The Court has often held that a firm is entitled to compensation when the government violates an explicit formal contract with the firm, but it has never held that a firm is entitled to compensation for damage caused by a change in regulatory rules in the absence of such a formal, explicit contract. See, e.g., United States v. Winstar, 518 U.S. 839 (1996); Munn v. Illinois, 94 U.S. 113 (1876); Proprietors of Charles River Bridge v. Proprietors of Warren Bridge, 36 U.S. 420 (1837). Moreover, the terms of the "implied regulatory contract" are far from clear. Thus, for instance, the regulatory contract arguably includes the doctrine that authorizes a regulatory agency to disallow recovery of an investment in an asset that is no longer "used and useful." See section 5B2b for discussion of the used and useful doctrine. It follows that, if there is a "regulatory contract," the government has not violated that contract. Finally, it is at least arguable that the value of a regulated firm's assets has declined primarily because they have become technologically and economically obsolete; the government has merely allowed the market to reflect the effects of the obsolescence of the firm's assets.

The argument that the Constitution compels the government to allow regulated firms to recover 100 per cent of their stranded costs is dubious in most contexts. In a typical illustrative case, an electric utility made a one billion dollar investment in a generating plant in 1985. That plant still had a book value of $600 million in 1998. A legislature or regulatory agency then allowed owners of more efficient generating plants to compete with the owner of the plant. Competitive market forces then reduced the value of the plant from $600 million to $300 million, leaving the owner with $300 million in stranded costs. No court has yet accepted the validity of the Takings Clause argument in that typical context.

The Takings Clause argument is stronger in another context, however. As we described in section 5B2b, there were numerous rate disputes involving newly-constructed generating plants during the 1980s. Some of those disputes were resolved in settlement agreements in which the regulated firm agreed to absorb a portion of the cost of the plant in return for the agency's agreement to allow the firm to recover the rest of the cost of the plant in its rates. Those settlement agreements may well qualify as contracts the breach of which constitutes a violation of the Takings Clause. The First Circuit has relied on that argument as part of its basis for issuing a preliminary injunction that prohibits New Hampshire from implementing a retail electricity market plan that would have the effect of precluding a utility from recovering all of the costs covered by a prior settlement of a rate case. See Public Service Co. of New Hampshire v. Patch, 136 F.3d 197 (1st Cir.1998).

Three distinguished economists wrote a monograph in which they argue that utilities should be allowed to recover 100 per cent of their stranded costs as a matter of sound public policy. W. Baumol, P. Joskow & A. Kahn, *The Challenge for Federal and State Regulators: Transition to Efficient Competition in Electric Power* (1994). Their policy-based argument has the same starting point as the legal argument. They argue that regulated firms agreed to make massive investments in capital assets based on the government's implicit promise that the firms would be allowed to recover their investments in their regulated rates. The economists then argue that other firms will be reluctant to make similar investments in other contexts in the future if the government reneges on its implied promise to allow regulated firms to recover the cost of their investments.

Like the legal arguments, the policy-based arguments in support of 100 per cent recovery of stranded costs have elicited numerous critical responses. See, e.g., McArthur, *Cost Responsibility or Regulatory Indulgence for Electricity's Stranded Costs*, 47 Am. U. L. Rev. 775 (1998); Michaels, *Stranded Investment Surcharges: Inequitable and Inefficient*, Pub. Util. Fort., May 15, 1995, at 21. Many of the policy-based arguments are similar to the legal arguments. In addition, critics of the policy-based argument in support of 100 per cent stranded cost recovery assert that regulated firms voluntarily invested in capital assets in the hope (sometimes-realized) that they would be able to earn an excessive rate of return on those investments through operation of the Averch–Johnson effect. See sections 5C and 8C for discussion of the Averch–Johnson effect. Like the legal arguments, the policy-based arguments for 100 per cent recovery of stranded costs are more compelling in some contexts than in others. They are particularly powerful in the context of the high-priced contracts to purchase power that electric utilities were required to enter into by section 210 of the Public Utility Regulatory Policies Act of 1978. See discussion in section 15C3.

Once a regulatory agency authorizes a regulated firm to recover some portion of its costs that will be stranded by a change to a competitive market, the agency must estimate the magnitude of the stranded costs and provide an appropriate mechanism to allow the firm to recover those costs. In choosing a stranded cost recovery mechanism, the agency's goal should be to minimize the potential distortive effect of the mechanism on the decisions of participants in the newly-competitive market. A non-by passable charge for access to distribution or transmission lines furthers that goal well. See Joskow, *Does Stranded Cost Recovery Distort Competition?* The Electricity Journal, April 1996, at 31.

So far, most agencies have allowed regulated firms to recover 100 per cent of their stranded costs. This policy has an obvious disadvantage from the perspective of consumers; they will not see the full price-reduction effects of a regulatory reform initiative until all stranded costs have been recovered. That effect has produced a populist backlash against 100 per cent stranded cost recovery in some jurisdictions. Thus, for instance, voters in California and Massachusetts had the opportunity to enact referenda in November 1998 that would have prohibited 100 per cent recovery of stranded costs. Both referenda failed after electric utilities sponsored an advertising campaign critical of the referenda.

INDEX

References are to pages